D1206340

NABOKOV: THE CRITICAL HERITAGE

THE CRITICAL HERITAGE SERIES

GENERAL EDITOR: B. C. SOUTHAM, M.A., B.LITT. (OXON.)

Formerly Department of English, Westfield College, University of London

For a list of books in the series see the back end paper

NABOKOV

THE CRITICAL HERITAGE

Edited by
NORMAN PAGE
Professor of English, University of Alberta

ROUTLEDGE & KEGAN PAUL
LONDON, BOSTON, MELBOURNE AND HENLEY

First published in 1982
by Routledge & Kegan Paul Ltd
39 Store Street, London WC1E 7DD,
9 Park Street, Boston, Mass. 02108, USA,
296 Beaconsfield Parade, Middle Park,
Melbourne, 3206, Australia, and
Broadway House, Newtown Road,
Henley-on-Thames, Oxon RG9 1EN
Printed in Great Britain by
The Thetford Press Ltd
Thetford, Norfolk

Library of Congress Cataloging in Publication Data

Nabokov, the critical heritage.

(Critical heritage series)
Bibliography: p.
Includes index.
1. Nabokov, Vladimir Vladimirovich, 1899–
1977 – Criticism and interpretation – Addresses,
essays, lectures. I. Page, Norman. II. Series.
PG3476.N3Z787   813'.54   82–3716

ISBN 0–7100–9223–7   AACR2

General Editor's Preface

The reception given to a writer by his contemporaries and near-contemporaries is evidence of considerable value to the student of literature. On one side we learn a great deal about the state of criticism at large and in particular about the development of critical attitudes towards a single writer; at the same time, through private comments in letters, journals or marginalia, we gain an insight upon the tastes and literary thought of individual readers of the period. Evidence of this kind helps us to understand the writer's historical situation, the nature of his immediate reading-public, and his response to these pressures.

The separate volumes in the *Critical Heritage Series* present a record of this early criticism. Clearly, for many of the highly productive and lengthily reviewed nineteenth- and twentieth-century writers, there exists an enormous body of material; and in these cases the volume editors have made a selection of the most important views, significant for their intrinsic critical worth or for their representative quality—perhaps even registering incomprehension!

For earlier writers, notably pre-eighteenth century, the materials are much scarcer and the historical period has been extended, sometimes far beyond the writer's lifetime, in order to show the inception and growth of critical views which were initially slow to appear.

In each volume the documents are headed by an Introduction, discussing the material assembled and relating the early stages of the author's reception to what we have come to identify as the critical tradition. The volumes will make available much material which would otherwise be difficult of access and it is hoped that the modern reader will be thereby helped towards an informed understanding of the ways in which literature has been read and judged.

B.C.S.

To Edward and Marian Griew

Contents

'Look at the Harlequins!' (1974)

Acknowledgments

Every effort has been made to locate copyright holders, but
the editor and publishers regret that it has proved impossible to trace some of them. We wish to thank the following for permission to reprint copyright material: Ardis
Publishers for No. 2; 'Art International' for No. 61;
Georges Borchardt, Inc., for No. 31, from 'The Reporter'
(© 1962); Brigid Brophy for No. 68 (© Brigid Brophy
1972); the 'Daily Telegraph' for Nos 27 and 32; Denis
Donoghue for No. 58; 'Encounter' for Nos 25, 43 and 70;
the 'Guardian' for No. 36; Harcourt Brace Jovanovich, Inc.,
for No. 16, from 'Speaking of Literature and Society' by
Lionel Trilling (Copyright © 1980 by Diana Trilling and
James Trilling); 'The Hudson Review' for No. 55, reprinted
by permission from 'The Hudson Review', Vol. XIX, No. 3
(Autumn, 1966) (Copyright © 1966 by The Hudson Review,
Inc.); 'The Kenyon Review' for Nos 15 and 19 (Copyright
1957 by Kenyon College); Frank Kermode for No. 12; 'The
Nation' (New York) for No. 50; 'The New Republic' for Nos
8, 23, 29, 38 and 56 (© 1947, 1959, 1962, 1964, 1966 The
New Republic, Inc.); the 'New Statesman' for Nos 10, 18,
20, 34, 40, 44, 49, 57, 73 and 75; 'The New York Review
of Books' for No. 47 (reprinted with permission from 'The
New York Review of Books'. Copyright © 1965 Nyrev, Inc.);
'The New York Review of Books' for No. 62 (reprinted with
permission from 'The New York Review of Books'. Copyright
© 1969 Nyrev, Inc.); 'The New York Times' for Nos 5, 35,
39 and 72 (© 1942, 1963, 1964, 1974 by The New York Times
Company. Reprinted by permission); 'The New Yorker' for
No. 37 (Reprinted by permission; © 1964 The New Yorker Magazine, Inc.); 'Partisan Review' and John Hollander for No.
13 (© 1956 by Partisan Review, Inc.); 'Partisan Review'
and Dwight Macdonald for No. 30 (© 1962 by Partisan
Review, Inc.); Paul Pickrel for No. 22, from 'Harper's
Magazine' (© Paul Pickrel 1959); 'Poetry' for No. 46
(Copyright 1965 by The Modern Poetry Association); 'Punch'
xi

for No. 11; 'Saturday Review' for Nos 9, 59 and 69 (Copyright © 1947, 1969, 1973 by Saturday Review. All rights reserved. Reprinted by permission); 'Slavonic and East European Review' for No. 1; the 'Spectator' for Nos 7, 17, 21, 41, 45 and 53; Times Newspapers Ltd for Nos 24, 28, 48, 52, 64 and 67 from the 'Times Literary Supplement' and No. 74 from 'The Times'; Stephen Wall for No. 42; Weidenfeld & Nicolson Ltd, William Morrow & Co., Inc., and Robert Alter for No. 63, from 'Nabokov: A Tribute', ed. Peter Quennell (Copyright © 1979 by George Weidenfeld & Nicolson Ltd); 'The Yale Review' for Nos 60 and 66 (Copyright 1969, 1971 by Yale University); the 'Yorkshire Post' for Nos 26 and 33.

Introduction

I

Nabokov's biography of Gogol, the Russian writer with whom
he has been most often compared, begins with the subject's
death and ends with his birth; and the critical reception
of Nabokov's work is infected by something of the same
topsy-turvy quality. This is partly because, although his
literary activity covered some sixty years, fame came to
him very late. But in order fully to explain how it came
about that reviewers in the English-speaking world were
confronted by some of his early novels only *after* some of
the later novels had been widely read and discussed, it
will be necessary to sketch the highly unusual pattern of
his career.

At home in both Russian and English from his earliest
years, Nabokov began writing in Russian very young; and a
volume of his poems was privately printed when he was
seventeen. This elicited his first review: a journalist
'who had reason to be grateful to my father' wrote 'an im-
possibly enthusiastic piece about me'. The review was
never published but, according to the account in Nabokov's
autobiography, it had a far-reaching effect upon his attitude to his critics:

> The whole business cured me permanently of all interest
> in literary fame and was probably the cause of that al-
> most pathological and not always justified indifference
> to reviews which in later years deprived me of the emo-
> tions most authors are said to experience. ('Speak,
> Memory' 1967, 238-9)

After the Nabokov family left Russia for exile in 1919, he
continued, like other émigré authors, to write in Russian
for a small émigré readership. He wrote, as Gleb Struve

1

notes, 'at first prolifically, but, as time went on, more discriminately' (Notes on Nabokov as a Russian Writer, 'Wisconsin Studies in Contemporary Literature', 8 (1967), 153); and during the 1920s and 1930s nine novels were published, as well as short stories, plays and poems. Nabokov's translation of two of his novels into English in the late thirties forms a link with the next major phase of his career, a phase inaugurated symbolically by his departure for America in 1940. From that date, after which he wrote little in Russian, his work consists of two main strands: one comprises novels originally written in English, from 'The Real Life of Sebastian Knight' (1941) to 'Look at the Harlequins!' (1974); the other comprises translations of his Russian novels, the latter undertaking being completed with the publication of 'Glory' in 1972. Most of the translations were carried out with the aid of one or more collaborators, of whom the most prominent was his son Dmitri. (For the moment it will be convenient to leave out of account Nabokov's short stories, as well as his multifarious other publications from poems to chess problems.)

There are thus three main branches of novelistic activity to reckon with, covering altogether a period of half a century: novels in Russian, novels in English, and self-translations from Russian to English. The symmetry of the *oeuvre* is satisfyingly completed by Nabokov's publication in 1954 of a Russian version of his autobiography, and by his translation of the English-language novel 'Lolita' into Russian (published in New York in 1967).

Most of the Russian novels were reviewed on their appearance by the émigré journals that flourished in Paris and other European cities between the wars. A full account of this phase of Nabokov's critical reception is beyond the scope of the present volume; but it will be briefly discussed in the second section of this Introduction, and three sample reviews from this period stand as the first items in the selection that follows. The English novels of the forties — or, from another point of view, American novels, for Nabokov became a US citizen in 1945 — were reviewed in the USA but received little attention in Britain. When Walter Allen reviewed 'The Real Life of Sebastian Knight' in the 'Spectator' in 1946, he found it necessary to acquaint his readers with the novelist's personal background; for although Nabokov was by now in his late forties and had been publishing novels for twenty years, he was still virtually unknown to British readers. It was not, indeed, until the late fifties — by which time Nabokov, one year older than the century, was in *his* late fifties — that the sensation over 'Lolita' made his name widely familiar and stimulated a demand for, and critical discussion of, the earlier work.

Nabokov had sought in vain for an American publisher who would accept 'Lolita', and it was eventually published in Paris. But there was no reluctance in America or Britain to handle the books that followed: as an obituarist in 'The Times' was primly to observe, with the appearance of 'Lolita' he had 'emerged in middle age to a notorious fame' (5 July 1977, 16). No fewer than ten novels, newly written or newly translated, appeared between 1962 and 1972, in addition to the monumental edition of 'Eugene Onegin' and a revised version of the autobiography; and this substantial body of work generated wide critical discussion of a high quality, most of the leading British and American critics of the generation having their say on Nabokov at some time or other. In the process, a *succès de scandale* was transformed into a *succès d'estime*, though it must be added that Nabokov never lost the capacity to excite critical controversy and to provoke widely disparate judgments of his achievement. To quote 'The Times' obituarist again:

His reputation as a daring and titillating newcomer faded in the 1960s — and with it much of his casual popularity. In its place came recognition of an original literary artist of long apprenticeship and unusual perceptions. A flourishing critical industry now sprang up around his work, which was subjected to the kind of meticulous academic scrutiny that probably amused him and certainly aggravated critics who thought his novels self-indulgent, wilfully teasing and obscure, and who were unable to regard him as a serious practitioner of the art of fiction.

It remains one of the paradoxes of Nabokov's career that a man in many respects so precocious should have had to wait so long for recognition, and one of the ironies of that career that the door to fame and wealth should at last have been opened accidentally, as it were, by the largely extra-literary success of 'Lolita', which effectively restored the fortune that Nabokov had lost as a result of the Russian Revolution forty years earlier and enabled him to return to Europe.

The publication of that novel in Paris in 1955 marks the beginning of a period in which Nabokov's work was widely reviewed on its appearance; and most of the selections in this volume are subsequent to that date. Before 1955, reviews had been relatively few and usually short; now they suddenly became numerous, since critics found themselves called upon to deal with the productions of a prolific and newly famous writer who had a backlog created

by thirty years of largely unrecognized dedication to the
art of literature. Both new novels and old ones in translation appeared on the publishers' lists, the old ones
seemingly in no particular order; and critics faced the
task of coming to terms with a large and varied body of
writing from several decades. In the late fifties, it was
the new work, 'Lolita' and 'Pnin', which claimed attention; but 'Bend Sinister', hardly noticed when it appeared in 1947, was widely reviewed on its reissue in
1960. Meanwhile, 'Invitation to a Beheading', 'Laughter
in the Dark', and other Russian novels newly 'Englished'
(as Nabokov liked to say) demanded their share of attention; and for the next dozen years Nabokov's list of publications continued to contain a mixture of old and new.
A brand new novel, 'Ada' (1969), for instance, was followed by 'Mary', a translation of his very first novel
forty-five years after its original appearance.

As the translator of Lewis Carroll and an addict of
all kinds of puzzles and practical jokes, Nabokov must
have relished the problems created for reviewers by the
curiously convoluted pattern formed by the publication of
his work in the English-speaking world. Under the rubric
of 'new novels', reviewers were liable to find themselves
discussing books written, perhaps, before they were born,
and doing so with prior knowledge of books by the same
author written much later but published earlier. It is
as if Henry James had confronted his critics and his
public with 'The American' only after he had given them
'The Golden Bowl'. But before we look in detail at the
critical reactions to the novels in English (both 'American' and 'Englished'), it is worth glancing at the earliest
response to Nabokov's writings: the reception of his Russian novels during the period when he lived in Berlin.

II

After leaving Cambridge in 1922, Nabokov settled in Berlin
and remained there until 1937. During these years he con-
tributed extensively to Russian émigré journals under the
pseudonym of V. Sirin, presumably adopted to avoid con-
fusion with his father, another Vladimir Nabokov, who had
published on political topics. As early as 1920 he published poems in a Paris-based journal. His novel 'Zashchita Luzhina', which much later became 'The Defence', was
serialized in 'Sovremennye Zapiski' ('Contemporary Annals',
Paris) in 1929-30, and was the first of seven novels to
appear serially in that journal, which flourished from
1920 to 1940 and has been described by Andrew Field as

'the foremost publication of the Russian emigration'
('Nabokov: A Bibliography' (New York, 1973), 198; Field's
volume includes a section listing émigré reviews of Nabokov's work). A little earlier, two novels had been published in Berlin in volume form: 'Mashenka' (later 'Mary')
in 1926, and 'Korol, Dama, Valet' (King, Queen, Knave')
in 1928.

For the serialized novels in particular, their appearance in Russian was only the first step in what turned
out to be a multi-stage process of bilingual publication
extending over many years. Consider, for example, the
complex history of 'Otchayanie' (subsequently 'Despair').
Serialized in 'Sovremennye Zapiski' in 1934, it appeared
in volume form in Berlin in 1936, and an English translation by the author appeared in London in the following
year; nearly thirty years later, it was retranslated, with
many revisions and additions, and serialized in 'Playboy'
(of all places) before being issued in volume form in 1966.
The despair of bibliographers, indeed: no wonder George
Steiner has remarked that 'the Nabokov bibliography is
full of traps and obscurities' (in 'Nabokov', ed. A. Appel,
Jr and Charles Newman (Evanston, Ill., 1970), 122). Apart
from the two already mentioned, the novels originally
serialized in 'Sovremennye Zapiski' were 'Soglyadataj'
('The Eye', to give its subsequent title) in 1930; 'Podvig'
('Glory') in 1931-2; 'Kamera Obskura' ('Laughter in the
Dark') in 1932-3; 'Priglashenie na kazn' ('Invitation to a
Beheading') in 1935-6; and 'Dar' ('The Gift') in 1937-8.
In addition, Nabokov published short stories and plays in
émigré journals during his Berlin period.

All the novels so far mentioned made their bow at least
twice, in different languages, countries and generations.
Most of them were reviewed in the émigré journals, and
Andrew Field's bibliography lists 150 such reviews. When
Nabokov's first novel, 'Mashenka', appeared in 1926, it
was noticed by 'every major émigré journal', as Ludmila A.
Foster notes in her useful essay Nabokov in Russian Emigré
Criticism (in 'A Book of Things about Vladimir Nabokov',
ed. Carl R. Proffer (Ann Arbor, Mich., 1974), 42). But if
Nabokov did not suffer from the neglect of his fellow
exiles, the reception of his work was by no means uniformly
favourable. In Notes on Nabokov as a Russian Writer, mentioned earlier, Gleb Struve states that 'the reception of
Nabokov-Sirin by the Russian critics was mixed and recognition came slowly' (154), and Ludmila A. Foster notes the
existence during the Berlin period of 'a division between
Nabokov's "friends and foes", who were to some extent
aligned by journals'. She adds that 'it is curious to
note that the staid and traditional "Sovremennye Zapiski"

and "Will of Russia" remained steady supporters of Nabokov,
while the more explicitly literary and the literary avant-
garde journals remained predominantly hostile to him' (49).
    The reception of 'Zashchita Luzhina' was typical.
'Chisla' ('Numbers'), a literary journal published in
Paris, attacked Nabokov in a survey of his work up to that
date, describing him as 'not only an "imitator" of cheap
French and German bulk-literature, but also a "literary
impostor" and a pushy, banal journalist who was merely
technically deft' (Foster, 44). Other critics rushed to
his defence, and in 'Rossiia i slavianstvo' Nabokov was
described by Gleb Struve as 'the biggest gift of the emigration to Russian literature' (Foster, 45). Other novels
similarly found both attackers and defenders. Nabokov's
depreciators deplored his lack of 'Russianness' and of
'ties with Russian literature and its traditions' (Struve,
154), as well as (a complaint that was often to be echoed
later) his combination of external brilliance and inner
emptiness or absence of spiritual values. Foster suggests
that 'extraliterary criteria' were often used to judge
Nabokov's work — again, not for the last time — and
concludes that éemigé criticism provides no adequate
analysis or appreciation of it (52-3). On the positive
side, however, the important role of memory in Nabokov's
fiction was recognized very early; and three articles of
the 1930s, included in the present volume, deserve special mention. Struve's 1934 survey article (the second in
a series on 'Current Russian Literature') identified
Nabokov as 'the most original and accomplished' of a group
of young writers of promise (No. 1). In his discussion
of the Russian versions of the novels up to and including
'The Defence', Struve makes several points that recur in
later Nabokov criticism — among them, the voyeuristic
element in his work and his Gogolian lack of 'humaneness'.
P.M. Bitsilli's analysis of Nabokov's Russian style (No. 2)
draws attention to features of his prose that were later
to be paralleled in his English. (Bitsilli — the name
might provoke suspicions of a Nabokovian pun, were it not
fully authenticated — is also the author of a 1936
article, available in translation, which compares Nabokov to Gogol, Céline and other novelists: The Revival of
Allegory, reprinted in Appel and Newman, 102-18.) A
more comprehensive survey of Nabokov's Russian fiction to
date was made in 1937 by Vladislav Khodasevich, who has
been described as 'one of the most perceptive and constant
champions of Nabokov's ("Sirin's") work' (Appel and Newman, 96). Khodasevich's essay On Sirin (No. 3) detects a
central theme, amounting to an obsession, in the novels
up to and including 'The Defence'.

Nabokov's last Russian novel, 'Dar' ('The Gift'), was
never reviewed in a Russian journal, and by the time its
serialization was completed he had left Berlin for a brief
sojourn in Paris (1937-40). It was during this Parisian
period that there appeared the most notable of the early
reviews of Nabokov: Jean-Paul Sartre's review of a French
translation of 'Despair' (No. 4). (It will be convenient
henceforth to refer to the Russian novels by the titles
eventually bestowed upon their 'Englished' versions.)
Sartre compares Nabokov to Dostoevsky, a comparison that
pleased Nabokov so little that he included a disparaging
reference to the Russian writer when he revised his novel
in the sixties. Sartre also makes some perceptive comments
on Nabokov's self-consciousness; he judges 'Despair' un-
favourably, finding a hollowness at the core and linking
this emptiness with the experience of the exile.

III

From Paris Nabokov moved in 1940 to the USA, where he was
to spend some twenty years. In Europe he had eked out a
living as language-tutor and tennis-coach; in America
he became first a penurious free-lance writer, then a successful academic in two entirely different fields (literature and lepidoptery), and eventually a world-famous and
highly successful author. The move had far-reaching implications for Nabokov's work: crossing the Atlantic sym-
bolized his renunciation of Russian for English as a creative medium, and hence the abandonment of a very limited
émigré readership for a public potentially as wide as the
English-speaking world.
    During his time in Paris, Nabokov had produced the
first two of his self-translations into English, 'Despair' (1937) and 'Laughter in the Dark' (1938). The forties were not a very productive period, but they saw the
first of his English-language novels, 'The Real Life of
Sebastian Knight' (1941) and 'Bend Sinister' (1947). (The
dates given are those of American publication: the former
novel had to wait four years, and the latter thirteen,
before appearing in England.) At the time, these books
attracted relatively little critical attention: it was
not until their reissue after the success of 'Lolita'
that they were widely reviewed; and such attention as they
did receive in the forties was not markedly enthusiastic.
What may well be the first three significant American reviews of Nabokov's work appeared in January 1942, and
all were brief. In the 'Saturday Review' (17 January
1942, 6), Bess Jones suggested that 'The Real Life of

Sebastian Knight' had a dated quality and 'would have
seemed more sensational to the sophisticates of fifteen
years ago ... than it now seems to those who survived
that period intact'. She adds that Nabokov's 'private
little game' is 'amusing enough for a while, but restricted in its appeal.... The method is a kind of literary
chase.... That the thinness of the findings hardly justi-
fies the intensity of the hunt is of no importance. It is
part of Mr. Nabokov's joke'. She concedes, however, that
the book offers 'some wonderfully exciting literary
analysis, penetrating if precious observations on writing
and popular taste, digs at literary cults, and occasionally a nice little human touch'. A week later, however,
two reviews struck the note of approbation more firmly.
In 'New Republic' (26 January 1942, 124), Kay Boyle said
that the story was 'told with a brilliancy, a delicacy and
a grave and exquisitely venomous humour which make it a
delight to read', and speculated on its autobiographical
quality:

> To state that the facts of Sebastian Knight's life seem
> oddly similar to those of Vladimir Nabokov's, and that
> it might be possible to conceive of this book as a
> private individual's exposé of his public self, would
> be simplifying a matter which implies, but scarcely
> lends itself to, simplification. It is a far pro-
> founder and more symbolic issue which brings us to
> the startling and dramatic end.

The same reviewer noted, not quite accurately, that 'Nabokov has twenty volumes to his credit' and suggested that
the novel under discussion was 'an illuminating if restricted glimpse of a construction which has not yet been
revealed to us in its entirety'. The most enthusiastic
review came from Iris Barry in the books supplement of the
'New York Herald Tribune' (No. 6); she described the novel
as 'a little masterpiece of cerebration and execution' and
suggested, as many later critics were to do, that Nabokov
lies 'outside the main tradition of English story-telling'.
'The Real Life of Sebastian Knight' did not, then, go
altogether unappreciated. But other reviews were dismis-
sive: the 'New Yorker', in a brief note (27 December 1941,
60), described it as an 'oddish short novel.... Highly
individual stuff, with a surrealist tinge, but a trifle
tenuous', and a reviewer in 'Books Abroad' (October 1942,
444) complained that 'the only trouble with the book is
that one does not understand why it was written. A writer
of such extraordinary ability is expected to contribute more
permanent values than clever acrobatics in literary tech-

nique'. It was, it seems, a period when cleverness was
highly suspect in a novelist; and these accusations of
lack of high seriousness, of a discrepancy between Nabokov's evident gifts and the triviality of his effects,
were to be reiterated in the ensuing years. It is very
striking that, when the novel was reissued nearly twenty
years later, reviewers enjoying the benefit of hindsight
could judge it very differently. Virgilia Peterson, for
instance, writing in the 'New York Times Book Review',
found in it evidence of 'not only the mastery of image and
style he had already by then acquired in this second language but also how unmistakably *sui generis* Nabokov has been
from the start' (30 August 1959, 5); and in England Ronald
Bryden was able to praise the 'sheer performance' of the
novel and the brilliance of its narrative complexities,
finding it 'the most interesting of the early novels to
which the success of "Lolita" has brought exhumation'
('Spectator', 23 September 1960, 453-4). Earlier reviewers
were, of course, simply not in a position to make this kind
of comparative assessment, and we shall encounter other examples of a critical about-turn in a generation that had
been schooled by Nabokov's later work to respond more appre-
ciatively to his earlier books.

But this is to anticipate, and it is necessary to return
to the forties, a period for Nabokov of occasional appreciation but more general indifference and sometimes down-
right hostility or dismissiveness. The prize for the least
appreciative review of this novel should probably go to
P.M.J. in the 'New York Times Book Review' (11 January
1942, No. 5), who compares the novel to Somerset Maugham's
'Cakes and Ale' ('style and satire made [it] a good story')
and A.J.A. Symons's 'The Quest for Corvo' ('a classic
piece of detective biography'), very much to Nabokov's
disadvantage. The reviewer deemed Nabokov's style 'interesting in a Walt Disney sort of way' but clearly preferred
the less taxing prose of Maugham. In England, Walter
Allen and Henry Reed both reported unenthusiastically on
'The Real Life of Sebastian Knight'. Allen, in a vein now
becoming familiar, found 'technical virtuosity unaccompanied by adequate content' (No. 7). Reed's view was that
'neither Sebastian nor the other characters comes to life,
and the amount of incident in the book is extraordinarily
small'; he found, however, 'some good things in the book',
and added that 'one feels curiosity about Mr. Nabokov's
other novels, several of which apparently exist in Russian'
('New Statesman', 4 May 1946, 324).

The vicissitudes of 'Bend Sinister' were somewhat similar. In 1947 Diana Trilling gave it a notably hostile
reception; thirteen years later, reviewing the novel on

its publication in England, Frank Kermode was able to hail
Nabokov as 'a major novelist' and to discuss the style and
structure of the novel seriously and at length (No. 12).
The reception of this novel will be discussed more fully at
a later point in this Introduction.

Between these two novels there appeared Nabokov's short
study of Gogol (1944). Philip Rahv found this 'inadequate'
as a study of the Russian novelist: it exemplified 'the
radically one-sided approach of an extreme aesthete-
modernist who takes the literary act to be a phenomenon
solely "of language and not of ideas"', and failed to take
into account 'the dynamic plebeianism of Gogol's genius'
('Nation', 25 November 1944, 658). For this reviewer, a
whole dimension of Gogol's genius had been overlooked:

> Brilliantly appreciative as Nabokov is of the grotesque
> side of Gogol, and indeed, of all that side of him which
> relates to the poetry of the irrational and the spirit
> of incongruity and mystification, he has no eye what-
> ever for the social-historical and peculiarly national
> background of his subject. Thus he dismisses, with bad
> quips and worse logic, precisely those aspects of Gogol
> which situate him in the Russian milieu.

— a diagnosis of defects in Nabokov's field of vision
which recalls the émigré critics' accusations of his want
of 'Russianness'. But Edmund Wilson, writing in the 'New
Yorker' (9 September 1944, 72-3), was much more appreciative, though not without reservations:

> Himself a poet of complex imagery and a novelist of the
> non-realistic sort, he has written the kind of book
> which can only be written by one artist about another —
> an essay which takes its place with the very small body
> of first-rate criticism of Russian literature in English.
> Nabokov's 'Gogol' must be henceforth read by anybody who
> has any serious interest in finding out about Russian
> culture.

Like Rahv, Wilson deplored Nabokov's witticisms, especially
his 'particularly awful' puns; but he conceded handsomely
that 'aside from this, his mastery of English is in general
brilliant and amazing'.

A few years later, Nabokov published the autobiographical volume 'Conclusive Evidence' (1951), which covers the
years 1903-40. In England the work was titled 'Speak,
Memory', and this title was adopted for the 'revised and
expanded' version published in 1966 (1967 in England) as
'Speak, Memory: An Autobiography Revisited'. Maurice Hindus

found the book 'brilliant and moving', and added that 'not
since Joseph Conrad has a writer of Slav origin shown such
a brilliant mastery of the subtleties and beauties of the
English language' ('Saturday Review', 14 April 1951, 29).
Maurice Cranston praised the 'wit and gusto' of the book
and was grateful to find in it 'no old-fashioned Russian
soulfulness nor fashionable masochism' ('Spectator', 21
December 1951, 859). Margaret Lane, recognizing that
Nabokov was relating the story of a lost paradise, also
noted the absence of self-pity: 'the whine of the refugee
is never heard'; she adds that 'his recollections are those
of a man who has deliberately cultivated memory for the
sake of the polished fragments it can salvage from the
past', but raises the objection that 'with every point so
highly wrought, detail obscures the whole, and it is not
easy to carry away a coherent picture' ('New Statesman',
1 December 1951, 634, 636). Later D.J. Enright was to
express the view that if 'Pnin' was 'Nabokov's best book
to date', the autobiography was 'a close rival' ('New York
Review of Books', 3 November 1966, 3). Enright adds that
when, in the autobiography, Nabokov is 'writing about someone or something he loves, he is irresistible', and notes
the 'hallucinatory and almost suffocating density of minute
detail'.

IV

By 1955 Nabokov had been a US citizen for ten years, had
lived in that country for fifteen years, and had been publishing original works in English for almost as long and
English translations of his Russian novels for even longer.
But it could not be said that he was in America a highly
regarded writer, or even a very widely known one, while in
Britain his reputation stood even lower. As late as 1959,
indeed, V.S. Pritchett found it necessary to introduce him
to readers of the 'New Statesman' (10 January 1959, 38) as
'A Russian émigré writer ... who has lived a good time in
academic circles in America'. The controversy over 'Lolita'
changed all that. As one of Nabokov's obituarists, Richard
Boeth, was later to write: 'Nabokov, as he approached sixty,
was still better known as an erudite and didactic campus
eccentric than as a writer, and he might have died that way
but for the sensational intervention of "Lolita"' ('Newsweek', 18 July 1977, 44).
     The novel was completed at the beginning of 1954, and
in his essay On a Book Entitled 'Lolita', written to accompany selections published in the 'Anchor Review' in June
1957, Nabokov recalled that he 'began casting around for

a publisher' for his new book in the spring of that year.
It was turned down by four well-known publishing firms in
the USA, and F.W. Dupee subsequently argued that this
failure to embrace enthusiastically a work of literary merit
which also became a huge commercial success ought to cause
no surprise: the author's reputation was modest;   there
was a fear of censorship;   the cosmopolitan Nabokov had no
place in the currently fashionable native tradition in the
American novel ('the ancestral Anglo-American pattern');
and Nabokov the aesthete was not *persona grata* in a generation much preoccupied by morality in the novel (Lolita in
America, 'Encounter', February 1959, 30-3, 35).

Nabokov himself later confessed that his fruitless
attempts to find an American publisher were 'disheartening
and irritating' ('Strong Opinions', 1974, 270).   But in
1955 'Lolita' was published in Paris by the Olympia Press,
a publishing house well known for its association with
avant-garde writers and notorious for its list of pornographic titles.   The firm was run by Maurice Girodias, of
whom it has been said that 'his main fare was the infamous
Travellers Companion series, the green-backed books once so
familiar and dear to the eagle-eyed inspectors of the US
Customs' (Alfred Appel, Jr, Backgrounds of 'Lolita', in
Appel and Newman, 18).   But Nabokov, it seems, was unaware
of the reputation of the publisher under whose imprint
'Lolita' appeared, the matter having been arranged on his
behalf by a Paris literary agent.   Copies of the novel pur-
chased in Paris began to trickle back to the USA, and its
reputation began to spread, at any rate underground.   Inevitably, the book came to the attention of the American
customs officials;   but an inquiry by the publisher sent to
the Collector of Customs in New York City elicited the re-
assuring reply that 'certain copies of this book have been
before this Office and ... they have been released'.   The
French and British authorities were less enlightened, however: in December 1956 the Parisian police descended on
the offices of the Olympia Press, and the sale of twenty-
five of the firm's titles, 'Lolita' among them, was pro-
hibited in France.   The reason for this action against
Nabokov's novel emerged nearly three years later, when
'The Times' was able to report (21 September 1959, 9) that
the French Government had at last lifted the ban that had
been imposed in 1956 'after complaints from the British
Embassy that tourists were buying it and taking it home'.
At the time, the police action precipitated a literary
scandal in France, and the Olympia Press improved the
occasion by publishing a pamphlet, L'Affaire Lolita. The
story was picked up by the American magazine 'Time', which
reported it on 17 March 1957; and, as already noted, the

'Anchor Review' published selections from the novel a few
months later.

In August 1958, the entire novel was published in the
USA by Putnam's. It quickly went to the top of the best-
seller lists, and remained there for six months until displaced by Pasternak's 'Dr. Zhivago'; and the film rights
were acquired. (Nabokov went to Hollywood and wrote a
screenplay based on his novel, but the M.G.M. film issued
in 1962 was based on a different screenplay. Nabokov's
version was published in 1974.) There were some public
protests: a senator demanded, in vain, a ban on the book,
and two public libraries refused to stock it. But its
success, and Nabokov's late-found fame and wealth, were
assured, and it quickly gained an international celebrity
or notoriety. Publication in England followed in 1959,
and the tripping trisyllable of the heroine's name soon
underwent curious transformations in many tongues, becoming
(for instance) Laulitā in Hindi, Lo li t'ai in Formosa,
and Rorita in Japan; there were at least five unauthorized
translations into Arabic.

Given the circumstances of its appearance, the reception
of 'Lolita' could scarcely be confined to its literary
qualities as a work of fiction; indeed, this aspect sometimes seemed to be submerged by more urgent or more sensational issues. As F.W. Dupee noted,

> What is in question is obviously not only a novel but
> a phenomenon, and a many-sided one.... Besides figur-
> ing as a work of literature which excites a variety of
> serious responses, 'Lolita' represents a prodigy of the
> publishing business, a formidable addition to popular
> mythology, a major event in the career — already
> pretty fantastic — of its author.

The paradox and irony of the situation whereby Nabokov,
aesthete *par excellence*, achieved international fame for
largely non-aesthetic reasons, has been noted by Brigid
Brophy, who sees his career in the English-reading world as
'a paradigm of that world's mismanagement of literature':
'In 1958 and 1959, in the U.S. and Britain respectively,
artistic justice was suddenly accorded to Nabokov — for
the totally non-artistic reason that the theme of "Lolita"
coincided with a tiny thaw in Anglo-American puritanism'
('Listener', 27 April 1972, 552). In England, 'Lolita'
was the subject of heated debate long before it was at
last published there. Graham Greene recommended it to
readers of the 'Sunday Times' as one of the best books of
1955; and the 'Sunday Express' columnist John Gordon
thereupon attacked it as 'sheer unrestrained pornography'.

Greene's response to this attack took the form of an
ironical letter in the 'Spectator' (10 February 1956,
182). In America the exchange was reported briefly by
the 'New York Times Book Review' (26 February 1956, 8),
which two weeks later returned to the subject, noting that
the report had elicited 'a flurry of mail' from readers.
Evidently 'Lolita', though at that time still unpublished
in the USA, had already found an audience there. American publication renewed the debate in Britain, and a
letter in 'The Times' (23 January 1959, 11), signed by
twenty-one prominent men and women of letters, stated:

> We are disturbed by the suggestion that it may yet
> prove impossible to have an English edition of Vladimir
> Nabokov's 'Lolita'. Our opinions of the merit of the
> work differ widely, but we think it would be deplorable
> if a book of considerable literary interest, which has
> been favourably received by critics and widely praised
> in serious and respectable periodicals, were to be
> denied an appearance in this country.

This illustrates well the way in which, during the 'Lolita'
controversy, the novel's literary merits were apt to take
second place as a subject for debate to its significance as
a test-case for literary freedom. A. Alvarez, reporting
on the British cultural scene to American readers, noted
that the book had acquired an almost symbolic value in
the battle over censorship:

> I doubt if any book since the King James Bible has been
> more eagerly awaited and so avidly discussed.... It
> has been brought up by the M.P.s in the House of Commons
> and by the police in Bow Street Station; by critics,
> lawyers, *aficionados* of all banned books, defenders of
> public morality and by the usual letter-writing cranks.
> ...Even the gutter press has been on to it.... When [it
> is published], it will almost certainly be an anti-
> climax. It would take a work a good deal more sub-
> stantial than poor 'Lolita' to stand the strain.
> ('Partisan Review', Spring 1969, 288)

In the 'New Statesman', V.S. Pritchett urged that the still
unpublished 'Lolita' was 'a clever, sometimes a distinguished
book' but 'not a pornographic novel', for 'pornographers do
not laugh' (10 January 1959, 38). Pritchett went so far as
to add that he could 'imagine no book less likely to incite
the corruptible reader', and praised the style of Nabokov,
'a serious user of language'. Subsequent correspondence
showed, however, that not all readers of the journal were

swayed by his pleading. In the 'Spectator', Bernard Levin
noted that support for 'Lolita' had come from such distinguished literary figures as Graham Greene, E.M. Forster,
Lionel Trilling and Edmund Wilson; he concluded that 'in
so far as there is any significant "climate of opinion"
around the book, it is for unmolested publication, not
against' (9 January 1959, 32). Another writer in the same
journal demanded: 'If the law officers are not to be
guided by men like Lionel Trilling, Edmund Wilson, V.S.
Pritchett, and the distinguished signatories of "The
Times" letter ... who are they to be guided by?' (13 February 1959, 216).

Before the year ended, 'Lolita' was published in England
and an editorial in the 'Spectator' was able to suggest
that 'the fuss made about it for the past year seems very
curious and faded indeed ... the affair is encouraging in
that it shows that a spirited defence of freedom in literature, backed by sufficient people of reputation, can effectively spoil the yahoo's day out' (6 November 1959, 616).
The 'Lolita' controversy in Britain belongs to an important
phase of the struggle for literary freedom, for it was in
1958 that a Select Committee on Obscene Publications was
set up, and in 1959 an Obscene Publications Act was passed,
liberalizing the law with regard to works of literary merit.
It was the publication in 1960 of an unexpurgated version
of Lawrence's 'Lady Chatterley's Lover' that was seized on
as a test-case for the new Act; but the wide discussion
of 'Lolita' a little earlier had already made many of the
issues familiar and had probably served to modify the climate of opinion significantly. Within a dozen years of this
time, an annotated edition of 'Lolita' appeared (New York,
1970; London, 1971), designed 'particularly for use in
college literature courses'. Thus quickly had academic
respectability overtaken a work of alleged pornography:
probably never in the history of literature had a *succès
de scandale* so rapidly become a set book.

Not all of the debates concerning Nabokov's novel conducted on both sides of the Atlantic are strictly relevant
to the *critical* heritage, for clearly other matters were
at issue: the reception of this novel belongs to the history of intolerance and censorship as well as to the history of modern literature. But it has been necessary to
describe these events at some length because they had a
decisive effect on Nabokov's reputation and established
him as an author whose name was familiar to millions.
Before, however, we consider the effects of the novel's
success upon his career, the estimates made by some of its
critics and reviewers may be briefly summarized. (Some of
them have, inevitably, been mentioned already in passing.)

What follows is no more than a small selection from a prodigious quantity of material, for this work was reviewed in journals and newspapers which ranged from the 'Scotsman' to 'Sexology'.

'Lolita' is a complex work which presented different faces to different readers; and reviewers naturally varied considerably in the emphasis they placed on various elements — on the novel as a love story, a parody, a psychological study of obsessional behaviour, an evocation of certain aspects of American life, a book that makes for morality or immorality — as well as in their judgment of its success or failure, its pretensions and achievements. John Hollander (No. 13) stresses the comic and parodic elements ('just about the funniest book I remember having read') and sees it as 'the record of Mr. Nabokov's love affair with the romantic novel'. Donald Malcolm stressed the satirical element and declared that Nabokov had produced one of the finest examples of a 'small but select' class of satire: that in which 'vice or folly is regarded not so much with scorn as with profound dismay and a measure of tragic sympathy' ('New Yorker', 8 November 1958, 187, 190). Walter Allen (No. 18) also draws attention to 'the comic perception of American life' and applauds Nabokov's 'feat of impersonation' in creating his hero-narrator Humbert Humbert. Others were less amused. Rebecca West found it 'too full of puns, which are ... fatiguing in large quantities', and declared that 'the irony is universal, and thus defeats its own ends' ('Sunday Times', 8 November 1959, 16). The 'Times Literary Supplement' found in 'Lolita' 'a blended whimsicality and sentiment, quite destructive of the finest sort of seriousness, that belongs properly. not to Humbert Humbert but to Mr. Nabokov himself'; the same review noted that the argument over the novel's moral aspect resembled the similar argument conducted over Oscar Wilde's 'The Picture of Dorian Gray', and pursued the comparison between Nabokov and Wilde in respect of both their aesthetic attitudes and their style (13 November 1959, 657). The emphasis is placed elsewhere by such critics as Howard Nemerov (No. 15), who judges it 'a moral work', and by Lionel Trilling (No. 16) in what was probably the most substantial early discussion of this novel. Trilling's approach is moral and sociological in the main, though he also praises its 'remarkable ability to represent certain aspects of American life'; for him, it is a novel 'not about sex, but about love'. Robert Hatch raised the question 'why this clever book comes to the American market on a wave of such extravagant praise', and concluded:

Partly, I think, it is because the cleverness is of a
kind that particularly appeals to the literary professional. The mock trappings of scholarship make him
chuckle, the gay skating on the thinnest of 'good taste'
rouses his admiration, and I fear that Humbert Humbert
talks a prissy lingo that some professors would be
pleased to emulate. Also, the book looked like a lost
cause. It had been banned in Paris, of all places, and
one could assume that it would never be published here.
Since at the very least it is a literate curiosity,
this was clearly an outrage, and one tended to pitch the
adjectives to a high note in sounding a protest. Now
that it has been published, no one will be unduly embarrassed by this early praise. 'Lolita' is skilful
enough and outrageous enough to save faces all around —
though in the end it may prove to be more a japes than
a masterpiece. ('Nation', 30 August 1958, 97)

In a review which appeared in 'Esquire', Dorothy Parker
not only rejected the charge that it was pornographic and
greeted its comic quality, but drew attention to Nabokov
as a master of English style:

I do not think that 'Lolita' is a filthy book. I cannot
regard it as pornography, either sheer, unrestrained, or
any other kind.... An anguished book, but sometimes
wildly funny.... [Nabokov's] command of the language is
absolute, and his 'Lolita' is a fine book, a distinguished
book — all right, then — a great book.
    And how are *you*, John Gordon, Esq., of the London
'Sunday Express'? (October 1958, 103)

This may have been a calculated riposte not only to the
hapless John Gordon but to Orville Prescott's review a few
weeks earlier in the 'New York Times':

'Lolita', then, is undeniably news in the world of books.
Unfortunately, it is bad news. There are two equally
serious reasons why it isn't worth any adult reader's
attention. The first is that it is dull, dull, dull in
a pretentious, florid and archly fatuous fashion. The
second is that it is repulsive. (Quoted in Appel and
Newman, 20)

A similar attack, though in more sophisticated terms, was
later made by Kingsley Amis (No. 17), who found the novel
bad both aesthetically and morally, though 'certainly not
obscene or pornographic'. Perhaps it is not surprising
that Amis, himself a comic novelist with a style whose

best effects derive from a carefully calculated offhanded-
ness, should fird what he calls 'this *émigré*'s euphuism'
uncongenial. But one reviewer's euphuism is another's
stylistic brilliance, and Philip Toynbee took precisely
the opposite view of the same quality. He regarded
'Lolita' as marking 'a dizzying advance' on Nabokov's
previous novels: 'this writer is marvellously in command
of his medium.... It is here that we can read the most
agile, imaginative and beautiful English prose of our
time' ('Observer', 8 November 1959, 22). Toynbee adds
that 'Lolita' is, first and foremost, not a love story,
or a moral warning, or a satire on American life, but 'a
work of *poésie noire* written with a saving modern irony.
If there were no poetry it would be a monstrous act of
vulgarity'. Toynbee finds the only flaw to be Humbert's
'unconvincing remorse' at the conclusion. It was the
novel's stylistic brilliance that another novelist-
reviewer, Anthony Burgess, later drew attention to in his
obituary of Nabokov: 'Those who thought it pornographic
knew only the title. If the book was ever shocking, it
was stylistically so' ('Observer', 10 July 1977, 24).
Looking back, Burgess was also able to suggest that, for
Nabokov, 'Lolita' represents in a sense a beginning:
'Nabokov's career as the finest novelist of the post-
Joyce era began only when he was sixty, with the publication of "Lolita"'. In another sense, however, it represented an ending; for the success of this American novel
enabled him to leave the USA and return to Europe.
  Between the Paris and New York appearances of 'Lolita',
'Pnin' was published (1957). Howard Nemerov found this
short novel 'charmingly told, by turns funny and pathetic',
though so loosely constructed as to appear 'somewhat accidental' (No. 19); and this was a common verdict. Dorothy
Parker included it among her selection of the best fiction
of 1957, while noting that, although described as a novel,
'it is, and nothing against it either, a series of sketches,
touching and funny and perfectly written, all at once'
('Esquire', December 1957, 62). Walter Navighurst told the
readers of the 'Saturday Review' that 'no-one can read this
book without becoming a Pnin man' (9 March 1957, 15).
George P. Elliott found that the book, though lightweight,
bore the unmistakable stamp of Nabokov's intelligence:
reading it was 'like listening to a raconteur who is also
a great intellect' ('Hudson Review', Summer 1957, 289).
The same review urged that 'Lolita', 'a masterpiece of a
great comic writer', be published forthwith in the USA.
In England, Pamela Hansford Johnson praised its 'sweetness'
and found its hero's combination of absurdity and dignity
'a remarkable feat' (No. 20). The 'Times Literary Supple-

ment' also had high praise for Pnin ('a memorable character well within the orthodox tradition of European realism') and commented on Nabokov's narrative strategy: 'any
irritation we feel at the book's knowingness or air of
superiority is deflected towards the narrator, who is also
a character in his own right' (10 June 1960, 365). The
same reviewer found it necessary, however, to reassure
the hesitant reader that this was no 'Lolita': 'many a
reader whose stomach was turned by the cloying style of
Humbert Humbert should find "Pnin" wholly delightful'.
Victor Lange went so far as to describe Pnin as 'a saint
of the comic', comparing him to Goncharov's Oblomov and
Kafka's Gregor Samsa as 'the superb fictional embodiment
of a particular yet universal human situation' ('New
Republic', 6 May 1957, 16). A little later, John Wain
judged this novel 'perhaps the most perfect of all Nabokov's books' (No. 23). But Kingsley Amis, one of the most
consistent of Nabokov's detractors, would have none of
this: in a vigorous attack he expresses bafflement at
the praise the book has received, and describes it as
weak and derivative — a 'limp, tasteless salad' — and
a kind of literary confidence-trick (No. 21). The 'Times
Literary Supplement' in an earlier review had been not
much less severe: it found Nabokov's treatment of his
'Gogolesque' subject 'far from Russian — whimsy from the
"sophisticated" New York type of magazine with its self-
conscious and often long-winded funniness' (4 October
1957, 598).

V

In 1959 Nabokov moved to Montreux in Switzerland, where,
apart from occasional travels, he was to spend the rest of
his life. John Updike was later to deplore the move to
Switzerland:

> Alas, Nabokov doesn't want to be an American writer
> after all.... The pity is, his greatness waits here.
> To my taste his American novels are his best, with a
> fiercer frivolity and a cruelty more humane than in
> the fiction of his European decades.

'The loss', Updike added, 'is national, and sadder than
Sputnik' ('Life', 62 (13 January 1967), 11).
     At this stage, publishers began to reissue some of the
earlier novels, and reviewers to make amends for their
past neglect. After nearly twenty years, 'The Real Life
of Sebastian Knight' reappeared in America; republica-
tion in England quickly followed; and this time it

received a generous share of attention. The contrast between the coolness (with one or two exceptions) of its
earlier reception and the enthusiasm that greeted its
second coming has already been noted; further examples
will indicate that 'the author of "Lolita"' (as critics
now liked to dub him) was able to command a degree of
respectful attention that had been beyond his reach in
the 1940s. Burns Singer found the reissued novel 'the
best of Mr. Nabokov's books to date ... because it is the
most central to his own experience', and found its characters 'firmly rooted in the real world' ('Encounter',
January 1961, 78). R.C. Churchill described Nabokov as
'a Proteus among novelists, a many-varied talent who has
boxed his compass from sultriest "Lolita" to westernmost
"Pnin", and speculated how far the novel under discussion
might contain autobiographical elements ('Birmingham Post',
4 October 1960, 4). Norman Shrapnel found it 'an altogether charming piece of Anglo-Russian impressionism —
dreaming spires, so to speak, in a Slavonic mist', and
added, as if haunted by the 'Lolita' affair, that it 'is
also, for anybody who may have misgivings on this score,
as sexless as an albumful of old aunts' ('Manchester
Guardian', 30 September 1960, 8). The 'Times Literary
Supplement' reviewer (30 September 1960, 625) offered
some perceptive comments on Nabokov's self-consciousness
as a writer and noted the claustrophobic element that re-
curs in his fictional world:

> Mr. Nabokov writes as if he had someone looking over
> his shoulder — that someone being himself. In other
> words, he is a very self-conscious, self-critical
> writer. Owing to the vigilance of this reader over his
> shoulder, there is hardly a badly written line in the
> book...; the prose is always sparkling and alive ...
> and one senses throughout an artistic care for good
> writing and a feeling for literature as such that is
> all too rarely met with elsewhere. Yet at the same
> time this persistent critical presence means that Mr.
> Nabokov can never get away from himself, and one is
> conscious throughout of a feeling of intellectual op-
> pression as if one were shut, without hope or possi-
> bility of escape, in the prison of one's self.

At about the same time, 'Invitation to a Beheading'
appeared for the first time in English (New York, 1959;
London, 1960), and 'Bend Sinister' was published in England (1960) thirteen years after its American publication.
The shadow of 'Lolita' continued to fall across Nabokov's
earlier books: Paul Pickrel, for instance, found 'the

richness of invention' and 'the wonderful comedy' of that
novel absent from both 'Invitation to a Beheading' and 'The
Real Life of Sebastian Knight' (No. 22). Ronald Bryden,
like others, searched the former novel for signs of the
novelist that Nabokov had subsequently become:

> It's interesting to seek out in it traces of those
> Byzantine later qualities, both rich and dubious....
> Already there's the delighted excess which Trilling
> asks of genius: the triumphant sense of a subject
> being suffused and encompassed with inky intelligence,
> as by some playful academic cuttlefish....
>   Nabokov's wild parable doesn't quite add up as
> either fiction or farce, but it gives a clearer glimpse
> than the later novels of the core of the anarchic
> tragi-comedian behind them, grimly asserting that in
> all dependence lurks absurdity and shame. ('Spectator',
> 3 June 1960, 810)

Peter Green found himself obliged to ask: 'After "Lolita",
what? A prolonged rummaging, it seems, in the bottom
drawer' ('Daily Telegraph', 3 June 1960, 16). Green returns to the earlier charge of Nabokov's derivativeness,
but finds his sources less in literature than in the cinema,
suggesting that the author of 'Invitation to a Beheading'
'had clearly sat through no end of *avant garde* films....
The hand of Cocteau and the early Bunuel are in evidence;
Mr. Nabokov seems to have found some of his props in
Dr. Caligari's Cabinet, while the final scene recalls
[René Clair's] "A Nous la Liberté"'. The same critic also
compares him to Dali and sees the novel as 'a political
fantasy couched for good measure in surrealistic terms'.
He concludes that

> Quite a lot of dirty water has flowed under the bridges
> since 1935, and this particular brand of political fan-
> tasy has dated badly. What remains oddly impressive
> about Mr. Nabokov is not his box of psychological tricks
> and angled distorting mirrors, but the uncommon fidelity
> and power with which he can describe minuscule objects —
> a moth, an ordinary pencil, a child's drawing. This
> mescalin touch deserves a better vehicle.

An interesting implication here, not pursued by the reviewer, is that the novel may not have been the best vehicle
for Nabokov's distinctive talents; certainly the 'mescalin
touch' is more brilliantly in evidence in the autobiography
than anywhere else. An anonymous reviewer in the 'New
Yorker' praised the same quality of fastidiously precise
description:

The book is at once a horror story, a parable about the
mystery of being human, and a 'Jubilate Deo' for that
twentieth-century epic hero whom Cocteau once called
'the Singular pursued by the Plural'. It is also a
thoroughly engrossing thriller, and what brings it off
is the familiar Nabokov mixture of exactly visualized
everyday detail — every hair on the hare — filtered
through a nightmare fantasy that is in dead earnest
on every page. (28 November 1959, 241)

The same reviewer adds that the book is translated into
'an English that is an nimble and as eccentric ... as
anything he has begotten more directly upon his adopted
language'. Others joined in praise of Nabokov's style,
even when they were puzzled or bored by other aspects of
the novel. Maurice Richardson found it 'a rather maddening
book' and suggested that the baffling allegory might be
'personal and metaphysical' rather than political; he
added, however, that 'it is excellently written and there
is talent stamped all over it' ('New Statesman', 4 June
1960, 833). The 'Times Literary Supplement' commented
that, although 'something of the atmosphere ... remains
indissociably linked with Berlin of the 1930s ... the style
of writing is still extremely fresh and Mr. Nabokov shows
in his use of words an inventive mastery that keeps them
always alive'; however, it noted in the style 'a displeasing element of rather arrogant pretension' (10 January 1960, 365). R.G.G. Price judged it 'a fantastic
story that is redeemed from dullness because, unlike most
modern fables, it is written in prose that is exciting
and not merely exhibitionist' ('Punch', 15 June 1960, 854).
John Wain's review of 'Invitation to a Beheading' contains
a fuller discussion of Nabokov's style (No. 23). J.D.
Scott spoke of 'Mr. Nabokov's wonderful liberated English'
and said that 'the language has that sense of liberation
that is Mr. Nabokov's special gift to it' ('Sunday Times',
5 June 1960, 18). But, again, Kingsley Amis found little
to praise ('the spirit of a second-rate version of [Kafka]
hangs heavily about this political-prisoner tale'). (The
comparison had been made much earlier: reviewing 'Bend
Sinister' in 1947, for instance, Hamilton Basso had said
that Nabokov 'seems to have started out to give Kafka a
run for his money', but had suggested that Kafka's money
was safe ('New Yorker', 14 June 1947, 86).) Of Nabokov's
much praised style he says that 'the language is flowery,
but without falling into the macaronic gobbledegook admired
by readers of "Lolita"' ('Observer', 5 June 1960, 18).
Benjamin DeMott, noting that the novel 'centres mainly on
the tormented self', found it 'abstract in conception: it

asks to be read as an allegory, and although the method is what is called surrealistic, the aim throughout is to express an idea rather than a sensation' ('Hudson Review', Winter 1960, 620).

The contrast between Diana Trilling's harsh treatment of 'Bend Sinister' in 1947 and Frank Kermode's high claims for it in 1960 has been briefly noted above. Diana Trilling opened her review ('Nation', 14 June 1947, 722) by noting ironically that she had succeeded in discovering 'four successful moments' in the novel; otherwise, she had found

> little relief from tedium ... in a book whose way was prepared by the acclaim which its predecessor, Mr Nabokov's 'The Real Life of Sebastian Knight', received in certain critical quarters.... I suppose it is Mr Nabokov's elaborate prose method that persuades his publishers that 'Bend Sinister' is so distinguished a work of fiction; and I daresay there will be a considerable public to agree with them. This will be the public that has become so tired of the arid prose and method of contemporary naturalism that it welcomes any change as a change for the better. But in point of fact, what looks like a highly charged sensibility in Mr Nabokov's style is only fanciness, forced imagery, and deafness to the music of the English language, just as what looks like an innovation in method is already its own kind of sterile convention.

But thirteen years later Frank Kermode was not the only critic to regard 'Bend Sinister' as worthy of serious consideration. Malcolm Bradbury saw it as 'a comedy about totalitarianism ... a moral fable told in an amoral voice' (No. 11). V.S. Naipaul found it 'a work of distinction', but added that 'the effort is too cerebral to arouse immediate response' and that Nabokov's vocabulary 'calls too much attention to itself' (No. 10). (Diana Trilling had attacked the 'elaborate chicanery' of the style.) John Coleman was prompted to voice more profound doubts about Nabokovian style and narrative technique:

> ...apart from the achievements of his books themselves, by dragging 'style' back into the contemporary novel he has created opportunities for a debate which may yet prove as valuable and stimulating as anything he has written. For doesn't one, however hesitantly, sense that there are relative limits to the amount of intrusion a serious novelist can allow himself between the reader and the characters his stories work through — and doesn't 'style', as Mr. Nabokov characteristically

exhibits it, constitute a sort of running threat to
our imaginative engagement in their life? ('Spectator',
25 March 1960, 444)

For P.N. Furbank, 'Bend Sinister' suffered by comparison
with 'Lolita':

> The simple plot of this horror-story is elaborated with
> the nervous and extravagant clowning which sometimes
> got out of hand in 'Lolita' and here does so much
> more.... The whole tone and intention of the book
> seem to some extent miscalculated. Nabokov has tried to
> exploit a kind of refugee humour, a resort to hysteri-
> cal and self-lacerating comedy as the last revenge of
> political impotence; but the result is artistically
> perverse and unbalanced in a way that 'Lolita' was not.
> ('Listener', 14 April 1960, 678)

A reviewer in the 'Times Literary Supplement' touched on
the difficulties of judging a novel which was, from different points of view, both new and old: 'Bend Sinister'
had been overtaken by events, in the world of literature
and in the larger world, and might be seen with hindsight
as 'a pale shadow of reality — or, indeed, of other similar works, such as [Orwell's] "1984", which it preceded'
(6 May 1960, 293). The same reviewer suggested that 'what
it fails to confirm is that the author of "Lolita" is a
profound moralist; didactic — inevitably with such a
theme — but not primarily concerned to reveal the wages
of sin or to postulate a coherent moral position'.
  'Laughter in the Dark' had a long wait for critical
attention, almost thirty years intervening between the
serialization in Paris of its Russian version and the re-
publication of the author's own translation in New York
and London in 1960-1. Its reception was generally unfavourable. Anthony Burgess, normally one of Nabokov's
champions, found it 'rather a nasty little story' (No.
26). (Mr Burgess was to publish 'A Clockwork Orange' in
the following year.) In other reviews, its alleged nastiness was a recurring theme. Ronald Bryden sought to explain the 'monstrosity' of Nabokov's work in terms of his
'rage for uniqueness':

> its main point seems to be the achievement of a situa-
> tion which no author could have staged before....
> Faced with his rage for uniqueness in such stark imma-
> turity, you begin to see how impossible it is to dis-
> entangle the inventive brilliance of his later work's
> sick riches from the underlying monstrosity. He must

make monsters: what else is a new thing in nature?
('Spectator', 17 March 1961, 375)

Martin Seymour-Smith claimed that 'Nabokov is a genuinely
"cruel" writer, and the cruelty of this book is appalling,
repulsive, and powerful' ('Encounter', August 1961, 82).
Like so many others, Seymour-Smith plays the game of hunting for signs of what was to come, and concludes that
'Laughter in the Dark' is in many respects 'an embryonic
"Lolita"; and this comment echoes Cecil Day-Lewis's description of it as 'a dummy-run at "Lolita"' (No. 27). The
most notable British review of 'Laughter in the Dark'
appeared in the 'Times Literary Supplement'; while expressing some reservations about the novel, it took the
opportunity to state the conviction that 'there is no
writer in English today who in sheer literary talent is
Mr. Nabokov's superior' (No. 28). One recalls that little
more than two years had elapsed since V.S. Pritchett had
patiently explained to readers of the 'New Statesman'
just who Nabokov was. The decisive part played by 'Lolita'
in his leap from relative obscurity and neglect to fame
and critical esteem is vividly apparent.

The next of Nabokov's new novels — that is, those
written for the first time in English — appeared in 1962.
'Pale Fire' was widely reviewed, and its reception showed
that there was still very far from being a critical consensus over his work. In June 1962, under the title A
Bolt from the Blue, Mary McCarthy published in 'New Republic' a long essay (No. 29) devoted to a detailed interpretation of this novel: an interpretation whose ingenuity
rivals that of the novel itself, of which Miss McCarthy
wrote that 'each plane or level in its shadow box proves
to be a false bottom; there is an infinite perspective
regression, for the book is a book of mirrors'. She concluded by declaring that it was 'one of the very great
works of art of this century'. (Later in the year her
essay was reprinted in 'Encounter'.) A prompt contradiction came from another American reviewer, Dwight Macdonald.
He began his account of the novel (No. 30) with the uncom-
promising statement that 'this is the most unreadable
novel I've attempted this season' and that it was 'too
clever by half'; in a postscript, added after reading Miss
McCarthy's review, he describes it as, like the novel, 'an
exercise in misplaced ingenuity'. The verdict of the 'Time'
reviewer fell somewhere between these two extremes: stirred
at first to superlatives ('surely the most eccentric novel
published in this decade'; its author 'probably the clever-
est in English since James Joyce ... the greatest verbal
prestidigitator of his time'), he reached the conclusion

that 'Pale Fire' was, like 'Lolita', 'monstrous, witty,
intricately entertaining', but unlike that novel 'does
not really cohere as a satire' (1 June 1962, 84). A
franker confession of uncertainty came from Paul Pickrel,
who suggested that the novel was 'an enormous hoax' but
admitted that 'exactly where the joke is aimed is a little
hard to say'; his own preference was to read it as a joke,
but he could accept that it might be plausibly interpreted
as a study of the terrible effects of monomania ('Harper's
Magazine', June 1962, 94).

Saul Maloff saw 'Pale Fire' as reasserting more emphati-
cally the attitude to the novel already evident in 'Lolita':

> To the degree that the novel as a literary genre takes
> as its subject matter man in society, Nabokov will have
> none of it. That great tradition he in fact holds
> explicitly in contempt, as he makes clear in his re-
> marks on Balzac and Mann in the Afterword to 'Lolita'
> and in one of the Notes to 'Pale Fire'. For him the
> novel is an open form akin to the condition of poetry,
> and must in its structure and development, by means of
> its language and imagery, attain the intensity and evo-
> cativeness of poetry, while yet remaining a fiction
> that tells a tale. Using every resource at his dis-
> posal, he makes us aware, not of lived life, not of
> the congeries of events which is the source of experi-
> ence, but of an idiosyncratic response to experience, its
> quality as felt by his inordinate and original fancy.
> Such a conception of the novel disdains to conceal its
> means, to remove them to some distant place on the
> edges of perception, where they may work upon us mys-
> teriously. We are continuously aware of the *making* of
> the work, of the process by which it is shaped and
> colored. And such a conception, in love with its means,
> may work as an impediment, so conscious are we of the
> contrivance — however dazzling the writer's ingenuity.

For Maloff, the new novel was too much of a good thing:

> What was true of 'Lolita' is even more apparent in
> 'Pale Fire'. Here structure clamors for attention;
> indeed the structure is so witty, and so obtrusive,
> that it threatens constantly to become its own end;
> we are made to attend so closely to it that the novel
> itself seems wholly subordinate to its mode of enclosure.
> Correspondingly, the insistence on style, on sheer per-
> formance, is so unremitting as to be oppressive: what
> begins in delight ends in surfeit.

In 'Pale Fire' Nabokov plays an elaborate game upon the theme of illusion and reality, the essential theme of all comedy; the difference is that most comedy derives its effects from observing the tension between the two, while in this novel they cancel each other out quite entirely. At its base is not a mode of observation, but a trick; the method of the trick — the legerdemain — is all: plot, circumstance, character — all ('Nation', 16 June 1962, 541-2)

In England, Frank Kermode opened his review by referring to the McCarthy-Macdonald disagreement; his own view was that Mary McCarthy was 'largely right about detailed interpretation and largely wrong about the value of the whole work' (No. 34). Nor could Cyril Connolly accept her high valuation of 'Pale Fire'. Connolly suggested that 'Nabokov is not quite enough of a poet to sustain a thousand lines of heroic couplets.... As far as his poetry counts Shade lived not an hour too long'; he also objected that the commentator 'can grow extremely boring' ('Sunday Times', 11 November 1962, 31). The construction, on the other hand, he found 'masterly': 'At last, an original plot!' Simon Raven, noting the disagreements generated by 'Pale Fire', suggested that it 'might have been written solely in order to make fools of reviewers', but continued, undeterred, by offering his own interpretation of it as 'a study in the processes and powers of artistic creation' ('Spectator', 30 November 1962, 865). Anthony Burgess (No. 33), Nigel Dennis (No. 32), Terry Southern and Malcolm Bradbury all praised the comedy of the novel, and Burgess and Southern in particular greeted its style and satire enthusiastically. Southern found it 'uproariously funny' and 'surely one of Nabokov's finest novels'; he drew attention to its 'devastating ridicule of literary criticism, or any likely "objectivity" of it', though reminding us that this is 'but a single deceptive surface of this extraordinary novel' ('Nation', 17 November 1962, 331). Bradbury suggested that Nabokov was both 'one of the most remarkable of present-day novelists' and 'one of the funniest'; his novels remind us that they are works of fiction, and 'Pale Fire' 'takes the game one step further' than 'Lolita': 'the whole book becomes a fanciful world of invention ... an anti-novel, one of the most important since Joyce's "Ulysses"' ('Punch', 12 December 1962, 875-6). A similar point had been made a few weeks earlier by Leslie Fiedler, who stressed the element of self-parody: 'it is an anti-novel, a camouflaged weapon in Nabokov's continuing war against the most bourgeois of genres' ('Manchester Guardian', 9 November 1962, 14). Richard Church, in the unlikely context of a

'Country Life' book column (17 January 1963, 133), placed
Nabokov in a tradition of experimental fiction that runs
from Lyly and Sterne through Joyce and Woolf, and also compared his linguistic self-consciousness to the 'verbal
foppery' of Ronald Firbank. For Laurence Lerner, however,
though the book was 'just about as ingenious as a novel (is
it a novel?) can get', the final verdict was that 'he can
go and play his cryptographic games on someone else, not
on me' ('Listener', 29 November 1962, 931). Like Lerner,
Philip Toynbee aligned himself with Dwight Macdonald, finding the novel 'arch, whimsical, exhibitionist and fundamentally frivolous', and suggesting that it fails at the most
superficial level, that of holding the reader's interest
as a story ('Observer', 11 November 1962, 24). One of
'Pale Fire's' earliest reviewers, George Steiner, had anticipated Macdonald's strictures: for him it was 'a Chinese
box, an occult artifice, a game for scholars and scholiasts
in some new Byzantium', 'pedantically recondite' in structure and style, a 'cumbersome *jeu d'esprit*', 'a pedantic
witticism spun out at great length and solemnity' (No.
31). Gilbert Highet, on the other hand, regarded it as
'a little masterpiece of ingenuity'; and the 'Times Literary Supplement' reviewer described it as 'a virtuoso performance, in which the author manipulates words and ideas
with the nonchalant deftness of a supreme juggler' (16
November 1962, 869). Once again, what was tedious pedantry
to some was brilliant ingenuity to others. Highet also
traced resemblances between 'Pale Fire' and some of Nabokov's earlier books: like 'Lolita', it was 'a study in
obsessional insanity'; like 'Pnin', 'a satire on the
European intellectual in America'; like 'The Real Life of
Sebastian Knight', 'the reconstruction of a dead author's
life through a study of his work and milieu'; it was also,
into the bargain, 'a farcical caricature of scholarship'
('Horison', July 1962, 90).

Among the more hostile American reviewers, some detected
symptoms of perversity or even misanthropy. For Robert
Martin Adams, 'Pale Fire' provoked comparison with Swift
and with the 'dark' Shakespeare: Nabokov's 'vaudeville,
like Swift's, is predicated on distaste for those greasy
commonplaces, flesh and blood; and "Timon of Athens" presides over the novel, suggesting not only Nabokov's title,
but one of his premises' ('Hudson Review', Autumn 1962,
423). William Peden found the novel too esoteric, 'withdrawn from humanity, grotesque and definitely diseased,
as monstrous as a three-headed calf ... a long, involved,
intricate, and essentially dull joke' ('Saturday Review',
26 May 1962, 30). (Peden's review, incidentally, contains
the phrase 'all this and much more', a reviewer's cliché

that Nabokov was to deploy ironically at the end of 'Ada'.)
Alfred Chester in 'Commentary' found the book more disturbing than the jokes about Eichmann that were currently
going the rounds: although it can be described in terms
that make it sound fascinating, it is 'a total wreck, and
for only one reason: it isn't funny, and it's supposed to
be.... Nabokov hates like Swift, but unlike Swift he is
without innocence. His comedy is a lie. It is dead. It
is evil, like racial prejudice' (November 1962, 451). This
Lawrencian denunciation of a novelist who always insisted
that his work had nothing to do with morality stands at
the opposite end of the spectrum from Mary McCarthy's
fervent advocacy. Probably none of Nabokov's novels, not
even 'Lolita', excited more diverse critical reactions
than 'Pale Fire'.

A novel by Nabokov was now liable to receive considerable critical attention, and 'The Gift', the author's
favourite among his novels, was widely reviewed (Jackson
R. Bryer and Thomas J. Bergin, Jr, include one hundred
items in their checklist). What is striking in the later
reviews is that Nabokov's outstanding quality as a novelist
and his position among twentieth-century masters are now
becoming increasingly recognized;   in particular, comparisons with Joyce become notably frequent. This is not to
say, of course, that his detractors have withdrawn from
the arena, or that every one of the numerous works he
published in his later years receives an equal share of
praise;   but the claims for his greatness are now being
made more insistently. 'The Gift' elicited high praise.
Stephen Spender pronounced it to be 'immensely rewarding'
and stated his conviction that Nabokov was 'a writer of
genius' (No. 35), and John Updike opened his review of
Nabokov's next novel, 'The Defence', with the assertion
that 'Vladimir Nabokov distinctly seems to be the best
writer of English prose at present holding American
citizenship' (No. 38). Donald Davie praised 'The Gift' as
'not just brilliant (Nabokov is always that), but also
profound and persuasive' (No. 36), and the 'Times Literary
Supplement' said that it offered 'a wonderfully fragrant
evocation of youth; flashes of insight into life and
literature; rich comedy, more than enough, in fact, to make
up for the insolence and the swank' (7 November 1963, 901).
Paul Levine said that the novel 'reminds us that fantasy
and alienation are the dual artistic heritage in Russia',
and that 'the ironic parallel between the writer and his
subject is beautifully handled in this generally exquisite
novel' ('Hudson Review', Autumn 1963, 462). Hilary Corke's
review compared Nabokov — a comparison that was often to
be repeated — to Prospero, 'the conjuror, the literary

illusionist' ('New Republic', 6 July 1963, 25). Updike's
retort to this kind of praise, however, was to insist that
'it needs to be said — so much has been pointlessly said
about Nabokov's "virtuosity," as if he is a verbal magician
working with stuffed rabbits and hats nobody could wear —
that Nabokov's characters live' (No. 38). Granville Hicks
defended Nabokov's fondness for 'tricks and mystifications':
'his trickiness reflects the complexity of life and the de-
ceitfulness of appearances' ('Saturday Review', 1 June
1963, 48).

   Critical approval of 'The Defence' was not unreserved.
P.N. Furbank found it 'not quite a masterpiece' (No. 43).
Nigel Dennis suggested that it showed signs of immaturity:
he found the hero 'utterly numb and dumb except when he is
engaged in chess', and declared that Nabokov had failed to
solve the problem of preventing such a hero from becoming
'plain boring' (No. 39). But the 'Times Literary Supplement', while expressing reservations, felt that 'it bravely
survives the double test of time and translation.... If
'The Defence' is ultimately a little disappointing it is
so as a work of art worthy of independent judgment' (19
November 1964, 1033). For this reviewer, the novel suffered from two faults:

> Granted that the suicide is an ending, it seems like an
> ending imposed on the book in the interests of the ana-
> logy Mr. Nabokov draws between the mentally hunted
> Luzhin and a chess-player desperately defending himself
> against defeat.... A more serious fault is that Mr.
> Nabokov's allusive style will not allow us to under-
> stand plainly whether the insane Luzhin believes his
> wife to be part of the conspiracy against him; and, the
> book being as much the story of their relationship as
> it is that of a self-destroying mania, the reader re-
> mains dissatisfied; but only because his interest, his
> compassion and his sympathies have been so strangely
> aroused.

Roger Sale found the first half of the novel 'wonderful,
vintage, adoring, unchauvinistic prose', and the account
of the chess game between Luzhin and Turati 'the best thing
in the book'; thereafter, however,

> a potentially great novel about a chess player becomes
> a mere tricksy novel governed by the imagery of chess....
> It is all brought off with élan, but Nabokov seems not
> to have realized that he created a character great
> enough that he could only be ruined in a switch from

the life of chess to the chess of life. ('Hudson
Review', Winter 1964-5, 611-12)

Sale concluded, however, that 'The Defence' 'offers ample
testimony to Nabokov's genius, his provinceless freedom,
his ability to create worlds unreachable by other routes'.
Robert J. Clements also judged the book 'uneven' and
summed it up as 'a less interesting novel than the genial
idea that prompted it: that of portraying life as a
dramatized chess game' ('Saturday Review', 26 September
1964, 45). Clements also noted the influence of Joyce and
Proust. Probably the most favourable as well as the most
critically illuminating review came from Frank Kermode
('New York Herald Tribune Book Week', 27 September 1964,
3, 17), who found it 'so distinctive, so intelligent, so
painfully harmonious, that it will confirm its author's
high place among his contemporaries'. Kermode developed
the idea that 'The Defence' belongs to a highly specialized
sub-genre, that of the chess-novel:

> 'The Defence' is a chess-novel so elaborate as to make
> up for the failure of everybody else to see the virtues
> of the subject; and there is nothing surprising about
> Nabokov's having written it.... The game becomes a
> powerful emblem of his aesthetic imperative: a harmony
> of occult forces, in which the wildly unexpected takes
> its place in a design. Figures from chess are frequent
> in his books; Fyodor in 'The Gift' devotes pages to it.
> And part of the propriety of the emblem is that it suits
> Nabokov's view of art as play.... The discontinuities
> between the game and life are part of the subject of
> this extraordinary book, and it is therefore precisely
> about one of the problems people are going to be pon-
> dering for many years, as they try to understand this
> surely great writer.

Such acknowledgements of Nabokov's greatness, from such
authoritative sources, are increasingly found. His translation of Pushkin's 'Eugene Onegin', however, published
in 1964 (revised edition 1977), reminds us that he had not
lost the capacity to excite literary controversy and to
participate in it directly. His four-volume edition,
extensively and eccentrically annotated, represents the
labour of many years; and of his profound learning in the
field of Pushkin scholarship, as well as of his sensitive-
ness to Pushkin's language, there could be no question.
What was debatable was his philosophy of verse translation,
especially his views on metre and his choice of diction in
rendering Pushkin's verse into English. Again, therefore,

we find critics ranged in opposite camps, with Nabokov
himself zestfully joining in the skirmishing on more than
one occasion.

   Christopher Ricks found the commentary 'crotchety' and
'opinionated' but 'brilliant' and 'hugely readable', as
well as informative on matters of poetic diction and a host
of lesser topics; it provided evidence that 'Nabokov has
considered the full implications of every word of his translation' (No. 44). Ronald Hingley described the edition as
'an extraordinary baroque monument' that makes 'a big
contribution to the study of Pushkin'; he was not the only
one, however, to wonder whether parts of it might be 'an
elaborate joke' (No. 45). John Wain found the translation
'delicious' and suggested an autobiographical element in
the entire undertaking:

   Nabokov has given us a full-length portrait of his own
   mind, complete with all its loves, hates, and prejudices. Just as, by the time we have finished the
   notes to 'Pale Fire', the figure of the commentator is
   as real to us as the figure of the poet, so, when we
   have finished the notes to 'Eugene Onegin', we are as
   securely in possession of the editor's personality as
   of Pushkin's. The only difference is that in the latter
   case Nabokov is working with material gathered not by
   the scholarship of the imagination but by the imagination of scholarship. ('Listener', 29 April 1965, 628)

Wain concludes that 'if the history of pedantry ever comes
to be written, its heroes will be the two writers who,
among their other achievements, raised pedantry to the
status of a branch of the art of literature: James Joyce
and Vladimir Nabokov'. Anthony Burgess also discerned a
continuity between this scholarly enterprise and the rest
of Nabokov's work:

   If 'Lolita' was a love affair with the English language,
   this new work is a massive act of copulation with scholarship.... These four volumes ... represent the very
   perfection of scholarship.... The Nabokov we know is
   very much here. I know of no other work which, ostensibly serving no higher purpose than to ease the way
   into an unknown piece of great art, itself approaches
   great art. ('Encounter', May 1965, 78).

Like some others, C.M. Bowra found it necessary to judge
the translation and the commentary separately: he praised
the latter, but remarked of the former that 'this kind of
experiment does either too much or too little. It intends

to be lively and precise; it ends by being pretentious'
('Sewanee Review', Spring 1965, 330). Robert Conquest
deplored Nabokov's choice of verse form for his translation as well as his 'unsuitable vocabulary' (No. 46). But
the fullest and most severe attack came from Nabokov's
friend of long standing, the American critic Edmund Wilson.
It has been said that 'the beginnings of Nabokov's second
literary career (as an American author writing in English)
can hardly be imagined without Wilson's help, advice and
literary contacts' (Simon Karlinsky, 'The Nabokov-Wilson
Letters' (1979), 1-2); but it is evident that by 1965
Wilson took the view that Nabokov no longer needed his
help. After admitting that the edition was 'something of
a disappointment' to him, he proceeded to attack the felicity ('the unnecessarily clumsy style') and even the accuracy of the translation (No. 47). The commentary he found
informative though 'overdone'. Nabokov responded to criticisms of his edition in the 'New York Review of Books'
(26 August 1965, 25) and again, more fully, in 'Encounter'
(February 1966, 80-9).

   In the year of Nabokov's death (1977), a new edition of
his 'Euguene Onegin' provoked further critical responses.
Clive James, dubbing it 'Nabokov's Folly', suggested that
'as a crib it is the best available' but that 'Nabokov's
ambitions as a scholar are thwarted by his creativity'
(No. 49). Henry Gifford praised the work's scholarly
integrity but judged the translation unsatisfying (No.
48). One of the most recent verdicts is, however, more
favourable, for John Bayley calls the commentary 'by far
the most erudite as well as the most fascinating ... in
English on Pushkin's poem' and finds the translation 'as
scrupulously accurate, in terms of grammar, sense and
phrasing, as it is idiosyncratic and Nabokovian in its
vocabulary' (Introduction to the Penguin Classics Edition
of 'Eugene Onegin' (1979), 17). Earlier Bayley had said
that both translation and notes 'convey the sheer density
as well as the delicacy of the novel' ('Pushkin: A Comparative Commentary' (1971), 236).

   Before the end of the 1960s, there followed three more
translations of Nabokov's Russian novels ('The Eye';
'Despair'; 'King, Queen, Knave') and, in 1969, a brand-new
English novel, 'Ada'. Signs of immaturity were detected
in 'The Eye', the Russian version of which dated back
thirty-five years. Stephen Koch found it 'obviously germinal' but containing 'the faults ... of the novice' (No.
50); and a reviewer in the 'Times Literary Supplement' said
that 'the initial device whereby Smurov is supposed to
believe that his suicide attempt has succeeded ... is
crude', but added that 'the progressive revelation of him

as a sad and self-deceiving man ... is elegant, witty and melancholy in Mr. Nabokov's best vein' (6 October 1966, 913). Roderick Cook, with greater enthusiasm, defended the apparently tricksy or jokey surface of Nabokov's fiction:

> Mr. Nabokov is a great kidder. He kids his characters, he kids his situations, and he kids the English language. But he always kids for real, as the saying is. He has always given his novels the form of an elaborate joke while underneath there are real flesh and blood and problems. This early novella ... is dry, witty, charming, and pointed, in his best vein.
> Above all, 'The Eye' has Nabokov's eye, and what his eye sees, the heart is not allowed to grieve over.... If Mr. Isherwood was a camera, Mr. Nabokov is a Polaroid. ('Harper's Magazine', January 1966, 100-1)

'Despair' had a distinctly mixed press. The 'Times Literary Supplement' reviewer found it 'fascinating' (No. 52); Ronald Hingley found the murder scene 'a minor masterpiece' (No. 53); and Bertram Root, noting 'a more distinctly Russian flavour than [in] most of his works', praised Nabokov's 'marvellous characterization and rich prose' ('North American Review', May 1966, 36). A reviewer in 'Newsweek' (16 May 1966, 122) seized the occasion to describe Nabokov as 'the last European, the last super-civilized man ... who somehow makes all other writers seem shaggy and thumb-tongued muddlers'. On the other hand, William Cooper found it governed more by 'whim' than by 'rule' (No. 54), and Robert Taubman suggested that, though Hermann Karlovich may be viewed as a first sketch for Humbert Humbert, the characters of 'Despair' lack solidity and reality as those of 'Lolita' do not:

> In the undifferentiated 'Despair' all is absurd — the minor characters, like cut-outs from faded daguerreotypes, hardly less than the main one. Sartre seems right to talk of the effect of exile on Nabokov at this period of his life, and of the emptiness of a *sujet gratuit*. ('New Statesman', 5 August 1966, 206)

(For Sartre's much earlier comment on 'Despair', see No. 4.) Paul Pickrel's praise was expressed with some uncertainty: 'the rather nasty fun of the book lies in its insane resourcefulness both in language and action' ('Harper's Magazine', June 1966, 99). Arthur Darack found more promise than fulfilment: 'a shadowy novel about a shadowy situation.... Other traits more highly developed in the

succeeding fifteen books are present embryonically in
this one' ('Saturday Review', 21 May 1966, 33). In a
double review of 'The Eye' and 'Despair', D.J. Enright
found the former 'a light and fairly light-hearted piece
of mild mystification' but judged the latter 'a more
substantial and characteristic work, although its central
deception falls short of Nabokov's usual elegance and in-
volution' ('New York Review of Books', 3 November 1966, 4).
   Reviewing 'King, Queen, Knave', Gillian Tindall consciously resisted the 'temptation to think of Nabokov's
early works mainly as dress rehearsals for his masterpieces', and stressed that 'this book is as polished as
any that have followed' (No. 57). Less generously, Denis
Donoghue found it somewhat laboured: 'effort keeps breaking in' (No. 58). For Henry Tube, on the other hand, it
was 'among the most sustained and successful examples of
his art'. Tube praised Nabokov's 'looking and seeing eye':
'to read a Nabokov novel is not so much to charge from
chapter to chapter in haste to discover the outcome, as
to linger one's way round a gallery of related paintings'.
He noted that Nabokov's subject-matter is cruelty, but
viewed 'with such fervent dispassion that it amounts to a
kind of passion' ('Spectator', 4 October 1968, 478).
   'Ada' quickly became a best-seller and achieved wide
circulation in paperback versions. (As a measure of
Nabokov's growing popularity during the early sixties,
the appearance of Penguin reprints of some of his novels
may be noted: 'Pnin', 1960; 'Laughter in the Dark', 1961;
'Invitation to a Beheading', 1962; 'The Real Life of
Sebastian Knight', 1964. Another index of popularity was
the appearance of excerpts from some of the later novels
in such wide-circulation magazines as 'Playboy' and the
'New Yorker'.) 'Time' (23 May 1969) bestowed on Nabokov
the accolade of a cover-portrait and devoted eight pages
to a survey of his work under the title Prospero's Progress; it noted, without fuss, that 'he has become, at
seventy, the greatest living American novelist, and the
most original writer and stylist since Joyce'. 'Ada'
itself provoked critical superlatives of a similar kind.
Matthew Hodgart considered that it 'contains Nabokov's
finest writing' (No. 62). The 'Times Literary Supplement' reviewer described it as 'the most Nabokovian novel
ever' (No. 64), while making it clear that this was not
necessarily a matter for rejoicing. Robert Alter opened
a long discussion in 'Commentary' (No. 63) by declaring
that Nabokov 'possesses what is probably the most finely
cultivated sense of form of any living writer', and concluded that 'few books written in our lifetime afford so
much pleasure'. Drawing attention to the element of teasing

gamesmanship in Nabokov, Alfred Kazin stated that 'probably
no author since Poe has so often consciously scored over
his readers' (No. 59). The same quality is examined in a
long review by John Updike, which opens in now-familiar
vein by hailing Nabokov as 'the best-equipped writer in
the English-speaking world' ('New Yorker', 2 August 1969,
67). Updike's superlatives accumulate as he describes the
'elaborateness' of Nabokov's prose in more detail: 'his
prose has never — not even in his haughty prefaces to
works resurrected from the Russian, not even in Humbert
Humbert's maddest flights — menaced a cowering reader
with more bristling erudition, garlicky puns, bearish
parentheses, and ogreish winks'. Asking himself whether
Nabokov's manner is 'just a game', he replies:

> Is art a game?... I think not. Art is part game, part
> grim exotic tussle with Things As They Are: the boxes
> must have holes where reality can look out and readers
> can look in.... And 'Ada', though aspiring to 'an art
> now become pure and abstract, and therefore genuine',
> is full of holes, stretches and pages and phrases
> whose life derives from life.

Updike's conclusion is that

> it is clear from 'Ada' and other evidences that Nabokov
> is a mystic ... in 'Ada', Nabokov has sought to con-
> struct, with his Hades and Nirvana, an Otherlife. Art
> begins with magic. Though Nabokov operates, it seems
> to me, without the sanctions, the charity and humility,
> that make a priest, he lays claim to the more ancient
> title of magician.

If 'Ada' aroused a louder chorus of enthusiasm than any
of Nabokov's novels except 'Lolita', there were some who
found it only too easy to forbear to cheer. Carol Johnson
opened her review with superlatives of a less approving
kind: 'Nabokov's "Ada" is a supremely literary product
of quite distinctly limited literary virtue' (No. 61).
Mary Ellmann found the style rather forced ('he seems to
be working for his words') and the teasing of the reader
'excessive' (No. 60). D.J. Enright commented sardonically
that 'to speak of the Master less than rhapsodically is to
incur the fury of the Nabokovites, a large and vocal and
merciless tribe'; but the fury of the addicts did not
deter him from finding in the novel 'further evidence that
great gifts can be put to small uses, a mountain of words
give birth to a mouse', though he admitted that 'there is
a mint of riddle-solving and parody-spotting to be enjoyed

here' ('Listener', 2 October 1969, 457). Even more dis-
missively, Gillian Tindall found the novel 'beyond a joke'
and diagnosed a radical technical weakness: 'the whole
account suffers grievously from being related in a retrospective leer, so that there is no momentum to carry it
along, no dramatic interest even within its own context'
('New Statesman', 3 October 1969, 461). The uncertainty
of the 'Times Literary Supplement's' reviewer perhaps
sums up the reception of 'Ada': 'This book is clearly the
author's Waterloo; it's less clear whether he figures as
Wellington or Napoleon' (No. 64). But the votes for
Nabokov as Wellington were certainly louder and probably
more numerous.

In a by now familiar sandwiching of old and new, Nabokov followed 'Ada' with two very early novels, 'Mary'
and 'Glory'. 'Mary', his first novel, was described by
Gillian Tindall as 'a small masterpiece, on the admittedly
minor theme of nostalgia' ('New Statesman', 19 February
1971, 244), and this view was fairly consistently held.
Auberon Waugh found it 'a slight but enchanting tale ...
straight, clean, and delightful in every way' but suspected
a Nabokovian joke, arguing that this alleged first novel
'has none of the feel of a prior novel' ('Spectator', 20
February 1971, 259). David J. Gordon noted 'foreshadowings of Nabokov's later interest in the figure of the
double and in complicated games' (No. 66). Anita Van
Vactor granted the 'prefigurations' but stressed the dis-
tinctiveness of the picture given in the book of 'the
sadness and awfulness of Russian émigré life in 1920s
Berlin' (No. 65). In his consideration of 'Glory', the
'Times Literary Supplement's' reviewer was struck by the
contrast between early and late Nabokov: beside the 'gross
and vital' American novels, the Russian ones possess a
'rather prim, faded texture' (No. 67). Brigid Brophy
praised the evocation of childhood in the early chapters,
and made a comparison (not a new one) with the neglected
novels of William Gerhardie (No. 68). V.S. Pritchett also
detected an affinity with 'the prickly worded yet nonchalant detachment of the best young European writing of
that period', instancing the novels of Henry Green and
the early work of Anthony Powell ('New York Review of
Books', 24 February 1972, 12).

'Glory' completed the long task of translating Nabokov's
Russian novels into English. His last years saw the appearance of two more short novels, 'Transparent Things'
(1972) and 'Look at the Harlequins!' (1974). Michael Wood
observed that 'Transparent Things' was 'Nabokov's first
work in English to have no Russian novel peering over its
shoulder, waiting for its chance', and suggested that

this seems to make a large difference in the writing.
The novel is brief, terse, oblique, abstract, almost
penitent, almost awkward, as if the glitter of earlier
works had to be atoned for, or as if the re-creation
of all the Russian novels in English had ended a cycle
and the author had to begin again, groping for a new
style. ('New York Review of Books', 16 November 1972,
12)

It says much for Nabokov's inexhaustible capacity to surprise his readers that a critic could claim, of a book
written by a man in his seventies, that it seemed to represent a new beginning. Wood commented on resemblances
to an earlier novel, 'The Defence', but insisted on a
significant difference, for the new novel

clearly suggests a hope, a chance of some kind of intel-
ligible hereafter, even if it lasts only a moment,
whereas 'The Defence' offered only an eternity of crippling paranoia as its only prospect. But the similarity will serve to remind us what to look for in the
rarefied air of Nabokov's mountains. Not human affections, or at least not much in that line, but a human
vertigo, an extraordinary perception of how we feel on
the edge of a metaphysical drop.

The 'Times Literary Supplement' reviewer also saw it as
a fresh start: the first new novel since 'Ada' could not
have been more different from that work, since it

leaves all that passionate encyclopedic faking behind
to emerge with a new lucidity, the bare boards at last.
Well, not quite. The imagined voice behind the novels
used to be saying, Look at my riches, my plots and con-
trivances, my looking-glass history and wonderland geography. Now the author comes forward with a different
sort of triumph in his eye, and says, Look at my poverty,
this mortal mess and these clumsy machines.... 'Transparent Things' is the best book there's been for a long
time about making and breaking fictions.... [Nabokov]
is a connoisseur, an insatiable student of the taste
and feel of mental events, someone who can speak with a
unique kind of tact and authority about the dizzy delights and pitiable humiliations of authorship.

Making a comparison that had by now become standard, the
reviewer compares Nabokov to Prospero, a 'weary wizard ...
taking his magic world apart and putting it all ... back
in the box' (4 May 1973, 488). Jonathan Raban concurred
in regarding this as 'a novel about the pathos of author-

ship', but was less convinced of its value: 'it is both
the least admirable, and the most revealing, of all Nabokov's novels' (No. 70).   Raban's view of the 'weary wizard'
Nabokov recalls what Lytton Strachey wrote about Shakespeare: that by the time he came to work on 'The Tempest'
he was bored with everything except poetry;   and Raban
finds 'none of life's resistance in this new novel.... He
is irritated with his characters even before he gives
them life'.   Mavis Gallant is also concerned with relating
this late novel to the rest of Nabokov's large *oeuvre*:

> Vladimir Nabokov, having spent his life building the
> Taj Mahal, has decided at the age of 73 — for his own
> amusement and incidentally for our pleasure — to
> construct a small mock replica.   The miniature is not
> flawed, no, but the most splendid features of the great
> model have been just slightly parodied, out of playful-
> ness almost.   'You see, the past is something of a
> joke,' he seems to be saying. ('New York Times Book
> Review', 19 November 1972, 1)

For a parallel, she turns to another 'semi-explanation',
Evelyn Waugh's 'The Ordeal of Gilbert Pinfold'.
     Martin Amis pursues a similar argument with respect to
'Look at the Harlequins!', which he sees as 'tricksy autobiography' and 'an appreciative review of the novelist's
middle years' (No. 73).   His verdict on the book is that
it represents a sad falling-off of Nabokov's powers;   but
he takes the opportunity of saluting those powers ('The
variety, force and richness of Nabokov's perceptions have
not even the palest rival in modern fiction').   Richard
Poirier found it 'an altogether coterie book ... resolutely
presumptuous about the commitment expected from its readers' (No. 72).   (Had Poirier forgotten the remark by James
Joyce, with whom Nabokov has so often been compared, that
he required of his reader that he should 'devote his whole
life to reading my works'?)   V.S. Pritchett was less
severe: 'not one of Nabokov's best fairy tales, but it is
good farce throbbing with his well-known obsessions;   there
is the usual mingling of tenderness and menace and underlying all the exile's stinging sense of loss' ('New York
Review of Books', 28 November 1974, 3);   and Eric Korn
observed that 'the fluency of the narrator is astounding'
('Times Literary Supplement', 18 April 1975, 417).
     Nabokov did not publish another novel, but in 'Details
of a Sunset and Other Stories' (1976) he completed the
task of 'Englishing' the Russian stories written at an
earlier period.   The foreword to that volume lists forty-
one translated stories in four volumes, the other three

being 'Nabokov's Dozen' (1958), 'A Russian Beauty' (1973)
and 'Tyrants Destroyed' (1975). In addition, he had written a considerable number of original stories in English.
The short stories attracted less critical attention than
the novels, and no account of their reception has been
included in the foregoing pages. An exception might be
made, however, for Angus Wilson's review of 'Nabokov's
Dozen' ('Spectator', 20 March 1959, 412), since Wilson
took the opportunity for a depreciation of Nabokov's
achievement in general as well as delivering an unfavourable verdict on his short stories. He found the latter
'a disappointment ... after "Lolita"': their range of themes
was limited ('the small change of competent short-story
writing') and the polished surface failed to conceal a
fundamental lack of originality. Wilson took issue with
the description of Nabokov (by his American namesake, Edmund Wilson) as 'a master of English prose': he himself
found Nabokov's prose 'very limited', and he commented
tartly that 'writers are not performing seals: we ask more
of them than the cleverness of writing a tongue other than
their own'. For most critics, however, Nabokov remained a
verbal magician, closer to Prospero than to a performing
seal. A more characteristic verdict is that of John Mellors
on the late and aptly titled collection, 'Details of a Sunset': 'an uneven collection in which the maestro is sometimes no more than tiresomely tricky.... However, there are
enough glimpses of the Nabokov magic to delight addicts'
('Listener', 16 December 1976, 799).

Nabokov's death on 2 July 1977 provided the occasion for
a number of obituary assessments, and these serve to remind
us that it is as yet too early for a critical consensus on
his achievement or for the relative importance of the various phases of his long career to be agreed on. But it
was at least possible to insist on his profound originality: as Richard Boeth put it, 'Leaving the matter of
greatness aside for fifty years or so, there is no question
that Nabokov was *sui generis*. Like his beloved Pushkin, he
derived from no other writer and leaves no true imitators'
('Newsweek', 18 July 1977, 42). Some obituarists expressed
their disappointment that Nabokov had not received the Nobel
Prize for literature: 'the Nobel Prize just sat there,
doing nothing, until our greatest living writer stopped
living and is now, presumably, instructing God on botany
and grammar' (John Leonard, 'New York Times Book Review',
14 August 1977, 22). R.Z. Shappard's explanation was that
'Nabokov crossed too many borders to have been a winner
in the geopolitics of the Nobel Prize' ('Time', 18 July
1977, 51). Anthony Burgess's suggestion that the period
of major achievement was initiated by 'Lolita' has already

been quoted ('Observer', 10 July 1977, 24). Francis King,
noting that most press announcements of Nabokov's death
referred to him as 'the author of "Lolita"', argued that the
novel is 'the least inhuman and the most compassionate' of
his books, and that after it

> the artificer became more and more adroit, but the
> artist seemed to falter and fade.... The kind of novel
> now fashionable, for good or ill, in this country and
> in the United States sets perception above performance,
> human interest above inhuman virtuosity. Thus Nabokov's
> kind of Fabergé Easter Egg is, for many, increasingly
> seen as a sterile, if impeccably fashioned, artefact
> rather than as a fertilising work of art. ('Sunday
> Times', 10 July 1977, 16)

W.L. Webb made a claim for the superiority of the early
work: 'I think one is beginning to see already that future
readers will probably be drawn most to those Russian novels
that he wrote as a young man, in the early years of his
exile in Berlin' ('Guardian', 5 July 1977, 10). Such variations of emphasis are inevitable in the face of a large
and varied body of work, much of which has appeared only
comparatively recently. But there was more general agreement on the extraordinary fineness and subtlety of Nabokov's
prose — 'a prose style', as Martin Amis said, 'equal to
the unique delicacy and richness of his perceptions' (No.
75); or, to quote 'The Times' obituarist once again,
'language which at its best had a flexibility and luminosity rarely found in prose narrative' (No. 74).
    Like the work of Joyce, to which it has so often been
compared, Nabokov's fiction lends itself readily to exegetical ingenuity; and it is not surprising that academic
critics set to work on Nabokov's *oeuvre* while it was still
incomplete. Page Stegner's 'Escape into Aesthetics'
appeared in 1966, and was followed by Andrew Field's
'Nabokov: His Life in Art' (1967), W.W. Rowe's 'Nabokov's
Deceptive World' (1971), Alfred Appel's 'Nabokov's Dark
Cinema' (1974), and other studies. More specialized are
Carl R. Proffer's 'Keys to Lolita' (1968) and Bobbie Ann
Mason's 'Nabokov's Garden: A Guide to "Ada"' (1974), the
latter published intriguingly by Ardis of Ann Arbor.
Andrew Field's bibliography appeared in 1973, and his un-
conventional biography, 'Nabokov: His Life in Part', in
1977. After Nabokov's abrupt rise to fame, interviewing
him became a minor industry, and more than two hundred
pages of interviews covering the period 1962-72 are included in the volume 'Strong Opinions' (1974).

So soon after Nabokov's death, it is hardly to be expected that any consensus will have emerged concerning his
stature as a writer or the relative merits of particular
works. The length of his career, the number of his books,
and the complexity of his role as a bilingual author make
him more than customarily difficult to see steadily and
whole even now that the *oeuvre* is virtually complete (a
volume of his Cornell lectures is promised in the week that
I write these words); and it seems likely that the disagreements, often sharp, registered in many of the items
assembled in this volume will not quickly be resolved. A
feature of Nabokov criticism is that the very qualities
that for some constitute the grounds of his excellence and
individuality are seen by others as grave defects and limitations. His technical virtuosity can also, less generously,
be regarded as mere tricksiness; his stylistic brilliance
as a collection of irritating mannerisms and an uncertain
grasp of the English language; his intelligence and learning as pedantry; his wit and humour as callousness and
perversity; his interest in obsessive states of mind as
morbidity; his passionate aestheticism as an indifference
to that moral earnestness that for some is the hallmark of
fictional quality; and so forth. Whether Nabokov will in
the long run be judged, as some critics greeted him during
his lifetime, to be one of the greatest of mid-century
novelists in English remains to be seen. His work (to use
George Steiner's vivid phrases) must now be a subject not
for 'the compulsive craft of the reviewer' but for 'the
meditative, re-creative art of the critic'. What seems
certain is that the debate will continue, and the books continue to be read and to produce in their readers, as their
author would have wished, both delight and exasperation.
The collection that follows contains, in whole or part,
more than seventy reviews of Nabokov's novels, ranging from
brief notes to substantial essays and written over a period
of more than forty years; and this introduction has had
occasion to quote from or refer to well over one hundred
additional items. At least since 'Lolita', however, the
reception of Nabokov's work on both sides of the Atlantic
has been very extensive; and the two hundred or so reviews
identified in this collection represent only a fraction of
the existing material, much of the remainder of which has
been examined but not used. My search has been greatly
assisted by the checklist, compiled by Jackson R. Bryer and
Thomas J. Bergin, Jr, of criticism for the novels up to and
including 'The Eye' (see Select Bibliography).

Chronological Table

Note: English titles in brackets are those under which the
novels subsequently appeared in an English translation and
are not necessarily an exact translation of the Russian
titles.

1899 Vladimir Vladimirovich Nabokov born on 22 April
   (10 April Old Style) at St Petersburg, Russia,
   the eldest child of Vladimir Dmitrievich Nabokov
   and his wife Elena Ivanovna.

1906 Begins to collect butterflies.

1908 Father, who was a founder of the Constitutional-
   ist Democratic Party and a member of the first
   Russian parliament, imprisoned for three months
   after protesting against the Tsar's dissolution
   of parliament in July 1906.

1911-17 Attends school in St Petersburg.

1916 A volume of Nabokov's poems in Russian is privately printed.

1919 The Nabokov family flees Russia and settles in
   Germany. (October) Nabokov enters Trinity
   College, Cambridge.

1922 Father assassinated in the Philharmonic Hall,
   Berlin, by Russian right-wing extremists. Nabokov graduates at Cambridge in French and Russian
   literature.

1922-37 Nabokov lives in Berlin.

1925 Marries Vera Evseevna Slonim.

1926 'Mashenka' ('Mary') published in Berlin.

1928 'Korol, Dama, Valet' ('King, Queen, Knave') published in Berlin.

1929-30 'Zaschita Luzhina' ('The Defence') serialized in
   an émigré journal published in Paris.

1930 'Zaschita Luzhina' published in volume form in
   Berlin. 'Soglyadataj' ('The Eye') serialized in

	Paris.
1931-2	'Podvig' ('Glory') serialized in Paris.
1932	'Kamera Obskura' ('Laughter in the Dark') published in Paris (also serialized 1932-3).
1933	'Podvig' published in volume form in Paris.
1934	Dmitri Nabokov (son) born. 'Otchayanie' ('Despair') serialized in Paris.
1935-6	'Priglashenie na kazn' ('Invitation to a Beheading') serialized in Paris.
1936	'Otchayanie' published in volume form in Berlin. 'Camera Obscura', an English translation by W. Roy of 'Kamera Obskura', published in London.
1937-40	Nabokov lives in Paris.
1937	'Despair' (Nabokov's English translation of 'Otchayanie') published in London.
1937-8	'Dar' ('The Gift') serialized in Paris.
1938	'Priglashenie na kazn' published in volume form in Paris. 'Laughter in the Dark' published in the USA (reprinted 1950, 1958, etc.; London, 1961).
1940	Nabokov goes to the USA
1941	'The Real Life of Sebastian Knight' published in the USA (London, 1945).
1941-8	Nabokov teaches at Wellesley College, Massachusetts.
1942-8	Nabokov is a Fellow of the Museum of Comparative Zoology at Harvard University.
1943	Nabokov receives a Guggenheim award (again in 1952).
1944	'Nikolai Gogol' published in New York.
1945	Nabokov becomes a US citizen.
1947	'Bend Sinister' published in New York.
1948-59	Nabokov is Professor of Russian and European Literature at Cornell University.
1949	'The Nearctic Members of the Genus Lycaeides Hübner' published.
1951	'Conclusive Evidence' published in New York.
1952	'Poems 1929-1951' published in Paris.
1955	'Lolita' published in Paris.
1957	'Pnin' published in New York and London. (June) Extract from 'Lolita' published in 'Anchor Review'.
1958	'Lolita' published in New York. 'Nabokov's Dozen' (short stories) published in New York (London, 1959).
1959	Nabokov moves to Montreux, Switzerland. 'Lolita' published in London. 'Invitation to a Beheading' published in New York (London, 1960). 'Poems' published in New York (London, 1961). 'The Real Life of Sebastian Knight' republished in New York (London, 1960).

1960	'Laughter in the Dark' republished in the USA (London, 1961). 'Bend Sinister' published in London.
1962	'Pale Fire' published in New York and London.
1963	'The Gift' published in New York and London.
1964	Translation of Pushkin's 'Eugene Onegin', with commentary, published in four volumes in Princeton and London. 'The Defence' published in New York and London.
1965	'The Eye' published in New York (London, 1966). (December 1965 - February 1966) Retranslated and revised version of 'Despair' serialized in 'Playboy'.
1966	'Speak, Memory' (retitled and revised version of 'Conclusive Evidence') published. New version of 'Despair' published in New York and London. 'Nabokov's Quartet' (short stories) published in New York (London, 1967).
1967	Nabokov's Russian translation of 'Lolita' published in New York.
1968	'King, Queen, Knave' published in New York and London.
1969	'Ada' published in New York and London.
1970	'Mary' published in New York (London, 197]).
1971	'Poems and Problems' published in New York and London.
1972	'Glory' and 'Transparent Things' published in New York and London.
1973	'A Russian Beauty and Other Stories' published in New York and London.
1974	'Look at the Harlequins!' published in New York and London.
1975	'Tyrants Destroyed and Other Stories' published in New York and London.
1977	(2 July) Nabokov dies in Montreux.

Note on the Text

The material in this volume follows the original texts in
all important respects, though obvious misprints have been
silently corrected. To avoid repetition and unnecessary
plot-summaries, many of the reviews have been shortened,
and all except very brief extracts from Nabokov's novels
have usually been omitted; these abbreviations and omis-
sions are indicated in the text.

Gleb Struve (born 1898 in Russia) taught at the University
of London and later at the University of California at
Berkeley. His publications include a study of Russian
literature in exile and an anthology of Russian prose and
verse 'from Pushkin to Nabokov'.

Until some years ago it could have been said with some show
of reason that the trouble with Russian literature outside
Russia was that it had no undergrowth. Since then the
position has changed; in spite of the unfavourable conditions (otherwise unfavourable than in Soviet Russia) several
young writers of promise have made their appearance (Vladimir Sirin, Nina Berberova, Gayto Gazdanov, Yury Felzen —
to speak only of the novelists), and some of them have already fulfilled that promise. The most original and accomplished among them is doubtless Vladimir Sirin, (this is
a nom-de-plume, his real name being Nabokov; he is the
eldest son of the late V.D. Nabokov, the well-known jurist
and politician assassinated in Berlin in 1922 by a political
fanatic of the Right).
    Sirin began his literary career as a poet by publishing,
in 1921, a book of mediocre youthful verse, slightly reminiscent of Fet and Alexey Tolstoy. His second book of
verse ('Cluster') [1923] showed a much higher level of
craftsmanship and had a strong personal accent; yet it
was still very far from foreshadowing his later works in

prose or even his later verse, among which there is a
delightful long poem about Cambridge, (he was educated at
Cambridge, reading simultaneously French literature and
zoology; butterflies are his passion, only second to
literature).

In 1923 he published translations of Lewis Carroll's
'Alice in Wonderland' and Romain Rolland's 'Colas Breugnon',
and after that there began to appear in various Russian
periodicals abroad his short stories, which from the very
outset revealed a striking ease and assurance of style, a
very keen instinct of observation, a predilection for
original plots and unexpected climaxes — rather unusual
in a Russian writer — and a peculiar care for construction,
also in contrast with the loose and formless structure of
a typical Russian story.

In 1926 appeared his first novel, entitled 'Mashenka'
['Mary'].(1) Though not yet a mature work, it contains
already the main elements of Sirin's technique. Novelists
can be divided into several categories according to their
attitude to the reality which they have to treat as their
artistic material. There are writers who merely tend to
reproduce photographically the reality they see; this way
of faithful and detailed reproduction can bear not only on
external, but on psychological processes. There are those
who shun that reality altogether and betake themselves to
the realm of pure fantasy. There are those who select
from reality and transform it artistically, who re-create
life, but hold to its laws and probabilities, giving the
illusion of naturalness without being photographic and
overfaithful, (this latter category would comprise such
writers as Balzac and Tolstoy). It seems hard to include
Sirin in any of these categories. He is a realist in the
sense that he uses material with which real life provides
him and is endowed with an exceptional visual keenness;
but what strikes us in him is the mixture of realism and
artificiality. He does not content himself with recreat-
ing the natural flow of life, he artificially organises
his real-life material. His artificiality is deliberate,
it is not a defect, it is not due to his inability to hit
the mark, so to speak — it is entirely desired, a part of
his artistic credo. Art must be artificial. An artist
must neither reproduce the reality just as he perceives
it, nor even transform it creatively and selectively and
yet obeying its laws; he must create on a plane parallel
to that of the real life. Real people and real life must
be his subject-matter, but he must not loosen his grip on
them, he must not let their world, the world of his novels,
have an independent verisimilar existence — as do Balzac
or Tolstoy, Dostoyevsky or Hardy; his world must obey the

laws established by him, its creator and arbitrary master;
the reader must be constantly aware of the author's will
directing and shaping the destinies of his characters.
Where other writers would deal with probabilities of life,
Sirin prefers to choose bare possibilities. It is not
accidental that coincidences play such an important part
in his novels. He uses them not as one of the many elements of reality, he emphasises and generalises them, makes
them a starting-point and a springboard of his novels, deliberately uses them as one of his artistic devices. This
gives an appearance of artificiality to his novels, though
they are peopled with real human beings and describe real
life.

Take 'Mashenka'. It deals with facts of real life,
definitely circumscribed in time and place, and that life
is described with masterful realism and truthfulness of
vision, (the humdrum life of an ordinary Russian boarding-
house in Berlin during the first years of the emigration and
the pastimes of a well-to-do youth in a pre-revolutionary
country house are excellently described) — yet many
people, on laying down the book, would probably say: 'How
unreal all this is, how untrue to life!' Does it mean that
Sirin has failed? Not at all, for he was out to describe
not a probable course of events, but one that is just
barely possible, though not improbable, one that without
being unreal is not natural and ordinary. Sirin loves
playing a sudden turn upon his readers, springing a surprise on them, winding up his story with a totally unexpected climax. 'Mashenka', for instance, ends in a quite
unexpected way, and this gives it a peculiar freshness
and originality. But those unexpected, and seemingly
unnatural, artificial climaxes always have a significance
on a different and deeper plane.

It is strange that Sirin's 'Mashenka' passed almost
unnoticed; it was fresh and original, very nearly perfect in construction — no looseness whatever about it, a
thing rather unusual in Russian literature, reminiscent
of Pushkin's and Lermontov's prose. One of its critics
laid particular stress on the mastery with which the everyday life of a Russian boarding-bouse in Berlin was drawn,
and hailed in Sirin the first 'bytopisatel' of the Russian
emigration, expecting the young author to follow up 'Mashenka' with something more in that line. Sirin's next novel,
however, belied that expectation. It did not contain a
single Russian character, its action was set in the German
bourgeois milieu, its theme was entirely psychological.

It is called 'King, Queen, Knave'. As the title suggests, Sirin chose here a trite, hackneyed subject, the
eternal triangle of husband, wife and lover. Yet so

original is his handling of this subject, so peculiar
the architectonic of the novel and so fresh and striking
its verbal texture, that the impression of freshness and
originality prevails despite the banal theme. There are
only three characters in the novel: Drayer, a wealthy
business man; Martha, his young and pretty wife; and
Franz, a poor relation of Drayer, a shy, self-conscious
young man. Drayer is a most curious, elusive person;
outwardly a perfect bourgeois, very sober and matter-of-
fact, he hides under this matter-of-factness a poetical
imagination, a passion for far-off wanderings, an interest
in things out of the ordinary, a subtly ironical (and yet
romantic) attitude to life. Martha, who is essentially
much more *terre à terre* than her matter-of-fact husband,
has long grown tired of Drayer's seeming indifference, of
his sudden and incomprehensible moods. She falls in love
with Franz and makes him fall in love with her. Gradually
she conceives the idea of putting Drayer out of the way.
The psychological interest of the novel lies in the presentation of the slow maturing of that idea in Martha's mind,
of the way she infects with it Franz, who becomes her passive and involuntary accomplice. She considers different
means of achieving her end, studies various methods of
poisoning, but they all prove impracticable. Then an opportunity presents itself to Martha. They all go to the sea-
side. Martha proposes an excursion in a boat, and conceives
an elaborate plan which is to end in the drowning of Drayer.
Though the whole thing does not look very natural, the reader is prepared to see it secceed. But with Sirin one never
knows what he has up his sleeve. The climax of the story
is again unexpected, though in a way quite usual. Whether
consciously or unconsciously (all the time we are left ig-
norant as to whether he is aware of Martha's affair with
Franz), Drayer thwarts Martha's plan. Martha catches a
bad cold and dies of pneumonia, and Drayer, who was seemingly so cold and indifferent, realises how he loved and
still loves her.

There is an air of deliberate unreality about Drayer,
Martha and Franz, which is further emphasised and enhanced
by the introduction of two queer, almost fantastic minor
personages. One is the old inventor of 'robot' mannequins
with whom Drayer is in business negotiations — there is
a subtly symbolical meaning in this bringing in of mannequins, it throws back a reflection on the living characters
of the story — they are themselves like mannequins or
those card figures they are supposed to impersonate; they
seem to move about in a flat, one-dimensional world. The
method of realistic description used by Sirin, his uncannily acute vision of the smallest external details and

his knack of putting his visions into striking verbal
shapes, gives a peculiar effect to this air of eerie unreality. Still queerer is the other fantastic personage —
Franz's landlord, a funny old juggler who calls himself
'Menetekelperes,' and gives us to understand that Franz,
Martha and the rest of them are but emanations of his mind.
In his person the author, who until then has kept aloof
from the world created by him (there is, indeed, very
little subjective element in Sirin, and from his novels
you never learn what are his feelings, views, likes or
dislikes), seems to peep into the novel and remind us that
he is the sole and arbitrary creator and master of this
world which he has at his mercy.

Sirin's short stories published after 'King, Queen,
Knave' (but in part written before it), in a volume entitled 'The Return of Chorb' (together with his later
poetry), reveal in miniature the same qualities which
characterise his novels — a predilection for unusual
situations, a great skill in handling them, an almost un-
canny visual keenness, and a great assurance of style.
Some of these short stories are little masterpieces. What
makes them so different from any other stories in Russian
literature (including Chekhov) is the amount of conscious
artistic effort you feel in them, of joyful resistance to
the material the author had to handle, of his pleasure in
twisting it this or that way, of making it flexible and sub-
missive. Seldom does one get from literature such an impression of the artist's own creative joy. The more unpleasant is the subject — and Sirin often chooses human
baseness for his subject, his characters are often repulsive, though in a way very different from Dostoyevsky's —
the more you are aware of that creative joy. One of the
best stories in the book is 'The Return of Chorb'.(2) A
very simple theme of a man's grief at the sudden loss of
a beloved person and the living-down of that grief is
treated in a most original way. In these short stories
Sirin shows his great versatility; there are no two of
them written in the same menner. Different influences may
be traced here and there, but they are welded into something quite original. There are, for instance, one or two
stories with a touch of Hoffmannesque element, but they also
contain something you will never find in Hoffmann. One
story (Podlets)(3) distantly resembles Chekhov in manner,
but it is a story Chekhov would never have written. An influence of Bunin can be traced in Sirin's language, in his
descriptions, in his visual acuity; but his art of composition, his skill in handling the plot, make him quite unlike Bunin. A comparison has sometimes been drawn between
Sirin and Proust, but 'creative memory' and attention to

details are, to my mind, the only things he has in common
with the great French writer.

In 1929 Sirin wrote a remarkable story called Pilgram.(4)
It is a study of the abnormal onesided mentality of an
otherwise rather commonplace German, owner of a small zoological shop in Berlin, who has a crazy passion for butterflies and is obsessed by a dream of travelling all over the
world, to see with his own eyes the exotic butterflies he
so much loves and of which he has such priceless collections
in stock. But this is only a dream, he is old and ailing,
business is bad in the post-war slump, and there is little
chance of his dream being realised. Then one day he has
a visit from a famous entomologist who, after some bar-
gaining, after keeping him for several days in suspense,
buys one of his most precious collections and pays a good
price for it. At last Pilgram's dream is going to come
true — he will go to Spain, thence over to Africa, to
India, to the Far East. He has a wife, a simple-minded
old creature, who has no sympathy with her husband's dreams
of exotic multi-coloured butterflies. He keeps her in the
dark about his plans, and on the day of his proposed departure, after completing all preparations, buying a ticket
for Madrid, etc., he sends her away on some errand, then
collects his things, the money — he intends taking all of
it, leaving his wife nothing. Pinned on the mantelpiece he
leaves a note for her, and is ready to start when he remembers that he has no small change, only banknotes. He goes
to fetch his money-box, and in opening it scatters the
coins on the floor. He stoops to pick them up. Here
Sirin, with his usual ingenuity, breaks the story, shifts
it, and tells us how Eleonora — Pilgram's wife — returned home to find their room in a state of complete disorder. Before she has time to think of a burglary she sees
the message left by her husband. Bewildered, puzzled, she
sits down on the bed, trying to compass what has happened,
unable to decide on some course of action, unable to grasp
the meaning of her husband's departure with all their
money, just after prosperity and happiness seemed to dawn
on them. I will quote in full the concluding passage of
the story to show the effective unexpectedness of its
ending:-

> Yes, Pilgram had gone far away. He probably visited
> Granada, and Murcia, and Albarracin; he probably saw
> the pale night moths turn round the tall, dazzling white
> street lamps in the Sevillan avenues; he probably got,
> too, as far as the Congo and Surinam and saw all those
> butterflies he had dreamt of seeing — the velvety black
> ones with crimson spots between their firm veins; the

rich blue ones, and the small mica-like ones with an-
tennæ resembling black feathers. And in a way it does
not matter in the least that, entering the shop in the
morning, Eleonora saw the valise and then her husband
sitting on the floor, amid scattered coins, his back
against the counter, his face set askew and grown blue,
long dead.

For sheer brilliance of writing and effectiveness of
construction, Pilgram is one of Sirin's masterpieces. And
in spite of the inhuman detachment with which the story
is told and the inhuman crankiness of Pilgram himself there
is a poignant human note in the impression it leaves on
us. To realise Sirin's loneliness in Russian literature,
one has merely to imagine the way in which, say, Gogol,
Turgenev, Tolstoy, Dostoyevsky or Chekhov would have
treated the same subject, (this is always a good test; in
his remarkable essay on Tolstoy's novels Constantine Leont-
yev imagined how Pushkin would have written 'War and Peace';
Mikhailovsky applied a similar test to the stories of Gleb
Uspensky).

In 1929, too, Sirin wrote his most ambitious and significant novel — 'Luzhin's Defence' (Zashchita Luzhina')
['The Defence']. It is also a study of abnormal, cranky
mentality and psychology, that of a chess wunderkind who
grows to become a sort of chess maniac. 'Luzhin's Defence'
lacks perhaps the compositional unity and simplicity of
'King, Queen, Knave'. Its psychological theme is more complex, and so is also its structure. Yet in a way Sirin
achieves here a still greater economy and simplicity —
instead of three characters, as in 'King, Queen, Knave', we
have only one who matters — Luzhin himself. But there is
a greater variety and a more detailed handling of secondary
characters. In harmony with its theme, the novel is constructed like a complicated game of chess, full of intricate combinations — this chess construction is introduced
intentionally, it is called upon to reflect the thematic
design and Luzhin's obsession, after a certain moment, with
the idea that life is but a game of chess played against
him.

The main interest of the novel lies in the inner tragedy
of Luzhin, who has no other interest in life but chess, and
in his one-sidedness, his lack of ordinary human qualities,
appears to us almost as a monster. Yet there is, behind
this monstrosity, something tragically and pathetically
human which makes a level-headed Russian girl fall in love
with him and, to her mother's horror, become betrothed to
him. But in the middle of an international tournament in
Berlin, in which Luzhin has to contest the world champion-

ship against the Italian champion Turati (the description
of their chess duel is a thing quite unique in literature),
Luzhin goes mad. His slow and gradual return to reason,
to the understanding of the outward world, which he perceives as a child and from which chess has disappeared
completely, is presented with great mastery. All goes well
till chess makes a sudden reappearance in his life, his
gift and passion return to him, and at the same time his
madness acquires a new turn, takes the form of chess perse-
cution, and he finally decides to 'drop out of the game';
he breaks the window of the bathroom and throws himself
out of it.

After 'Luzhin', Sirin wrote three more novels — he is
a prolific writer, and in this I perceive a certain danger
for him. 'The Spy' ('Soglyadatay') ['The Eye'] is a very
short novel, rather a longish short story, a weird and ultimately not very convincing study of multiplication of personality, of a man who, after committing suicide or failing
to commit it — it is not quite easy to make this out —
spies on himself in an after-death (or what he thinks to be
an after-death) life, but in an earthly environment, and
studies his mirror-like broken personality as reflected
in various personages he meets. There are some brilliant
passages in this story with its intermingling of the real
and the fantastic, but as a whole, as I say, it is not very
convincing. Through the mouthpiece of its hero Sirin expresses one of the important points in his artistic *credo*:
'I have realised that the only happiness in this world is
*in observing, in spying, in looking with wide-open eyes at
oneself, at others — in drawing no conclusions, in simply
gazing*.'

Sirin also voices here his philosophy of life, which is
somewhat akin to Tolstoy's historio-sophical ideas in 'War
and Peace':

There are no laws — a tootache loses a battle, a
rainy day cancels a proposed insurrection — everything
is vacillating, everything is due to chance, and vain
have been the efforts of that ramshackle and grumbling
bourgeois in Victorian check trousers, who wrotĕ the
obscure work called 'Capital' — a fruit of insomnia and
megrim. There is great fun is asking oneself, when one
looks back at the past: What would have happened if —
... in substituting one contingency for another, in
watching how from a grey minute of life, gone imper-
ceptibly and fruitlessly, buds forth a marvellous rosy
event which at its appointed hour had failed to bud, to
shine forth. Mysterious is this ramification of life;
in each past moment one feels one is at a crossing —

it was so, but it might have been otherwise; and the
countless flaming furrows stretch, doubling and trebling,
over the dark field of history....

Sirin's next novel, called 'The Feat' ('Podvig')
['Glory'] is somewhat disappointing, too. In sheer brilliance of style, of descriptions, of psychological portrayal
of minor characters, it can match with his best work. But
the figure of its hero lacks inner conviction. He is a
young Russian émigré who, after a few years spent at Cambridge (there is an obvious element of autobiographical
reminiscences in the outward skeleton of the work), a life
with his mother and stepfather in Switzerland, and a somewhat strange love affair with a Russian girl he met in
London, who is also loved by his English friend, Darwin,
decides, for no obvious reason, out of nostalgia or an
inborn passion for wanderings, to go somewhat mysteriously,
after elaborate preparations, to Russia, or rather to the
vague and unnamed country of his dreams and reminiscences.
With his disappearance into Russia the story ends.
Sirin's latest novel, 'Camera Obscura' ['Laughter in
the Dark'] has not yet been published in book form; in
it he tried his hand at a new genre — that of cinemato-
graphic dynamism.
Sirin's un-Russianness has been pointed out by several
critics. This is certainly true of his technique. His
interest in his plot, his careful construction, his in-
ventiveness and 'artificiality' make up a whole that is
very un-Russian, though separately these elements can
be found in individual Russian writers. Besides, Sirin
has no interest in ideas, in the social background, so
characteristic of the Russian traditional novel. Finally,
Russian literature has always been notorious for its interest in, and sympathy with, men, for its *humaneness*.
According to the Russian philosopher Berdiayev, Gogol
alone of the major Russian writers lacked that trait. I
think Pisemsky and among the moderns Sologub can be placed
on the same line. Sirin certainly belongs to it. Not that
he has no interest in men: 'every man is amusing,' says
the hero of his 'Spy'; but he certainly has no sympathy
with them, or rather does not allow that sympathy to inter-
fere with his artistic creative attitude. 'Only observe,
draw no conclusions' — is his artistic motto. One well-
known Russian novelist has said that Sirin is a writer who
has no God and probably no devil, and that in this, too,
he is very un-Russian. I am not sure it is so. Sirin is
an extremely chaste, reticent artist, in the sense that he
rarely reveals himself in his works. From his works you
will not learn what are his own views, ideas and feelings.

His attitude to his heroes is artistically objective and
ruthless, there is no invisible contact between him and
them, contact which you will find in the most 'objective'
Russian novelists. Yet Luzhin's tragic destiny moves us
as being genuinely and pathetically *human*. And is it not
a writer's greatest achievement, if he can move us while
himself remaining utterly detached.

Sirin's keen observant eye is sometimes ruthless in
picking out ridiculous details and in presenting his characters in the most unfavourable light. Yet you feel that
Sirin is no pessimist at all, that he delights in life,
that he is really in love with it; he knows what the joy
of creation is, and he is capable of communicating it to
his readers, notwithstanding his dismal themes and unpleasant characters.

Notes

1 Here and elsewhere the titles of the subsequent English
   translations of the works referred to by their Russian
   titles have been supplied.
2 The Return of Chorb is the title-story in a volume of
   short stories in Russian published by Nabokov in Berlin
   in 1930.
3 Podlets also made its appearance in 'The Return of
   Chorb'. It appeared as An Affair of Honour in 'A Russian Beauty' (1973).
4 Pilgram appeared in 'The Eye', a collection containing
   a novella and twelve short stories and published in
   Paris in 1938. Translated as The Aurelian, it appeared
   in Nabokov's 'Nine Stories' (1947) and subsequently in
   'Nabokov's Dozen' (1958).

2. P.M. BITSILLI IN 'SOVREMENNYE ZAPISKI'

1936

P.M. Bitsilli (1879-1953), émigré Russian scholar and
critic, lived in Bulgaria between the wars and wrote
studies of Dostoevsky, Chekhov and other authors. The
following review appeared in an émigré journal published
in Paris. Translation by D. Barton Johnson.

When one rereads an author straight through that one has
previously read at great intervals, it is easier to notice
in his work certain constantly recurring stylistic characteristics and through this to draw nearer to an understanding of his guiding *idea* — in the full sense of this
word, i.e., his vision of the world and of life —
insofar as 'form' and 'content' are identical in the case
of the writer in question. One such feature of Sirin's
work is his peculiar sort of 'word play,' the play of
like-sounding words: '...I kak *dym* ischezáet dokhódnyi
dom...' '...and like smoke vanishes the lucrative estate...'
('The Eye'), — as well as a multitude of similar combinations in 'Invitation to a Beheading'; combinations of words
with the same number of syllables and rhyming with each
other — '...Ot negó pákhlo muzhikóm, tabakóm, chesnokóm...'
'he smelled of muzhik, tobacco, and garlic...'; or word
groups which are 'symmetrical' in regard to sound —
'... v pes'ei máske s márlevoi pást'yu...' (*pm* — *mp*)
'...wearing a doglike mask with a gauze mouthpiece...';
cf. also '...Kartina li *kiski* krutógo kolor*ista*' '...is
it the painting of the brush of the abrupt colorist —';
alliterations plus assonances — 'test', opiráyas' na
trost'...' 'the father-in-law, leaning on his walking
stick...'; 'Tam tamózhnie kholmý tomlénie prudóv, támtam
dalékogo orkéstra...' 'There, the local hills, the languor
of the ponds, the tom-tom of a distant band...'; 'blevál
blédnyi bibliotékar'...' 'the livid librarian was vomit-
ing...'; — or as many more such cases as you like. It
seems as if the author himself is alluding to his own man-
nerism when he speaks of the novel that Cincinnatus is
reading where 'there was a page and a half long paragraph in which all of the words began with p.' But here
it is as if he were making fun of himself, consistent in
his striving to maintain the tone of irony; in another
place, speaking in the name of Cincinnatus, he provides a
foundation for this verbal device: '...sensing how words
are combined, what one must do for a commonplace word to
come alive and to share its neighbor's sheen, heat, shadow,
while reflecting itself in its neighbor and renewing the
neighboring word in the process...' The device which I
have noted is only one of the means of bringing a word to
life, of making it more expressive, of forcing one to *hear*
its sonority. But the sonority of a word is connected with
its *sense*: 'shelestiáshchee, vlázhnoe slóvo schást'e,
pléshchushchee slóvo, takóe zhivóe, rúchnoe, samó uly-
báetsia, samó plachet...' — 'the rustling, moist word
"happiness," a plashing word, so alive, tame, itself
smiling, itself crying...' ('The Eye'). 'Here too is the
interesting word "konéc" "end." Something like a "kon"

"horse" and "gonéc" "herald" in one...' (*Ib.*) Cf. also in
'Invitation to a Beheading': 'Tupóe tut, podpërtoe i zá-
pertoe chetóiu "tvérdo", temnaia tiur'má... dérzhit meniá
i tesnit' 'The *d*ull *tut* "here" propped up and locked up by
its pair of "t's," the *d*ark *d*ungeon, ... holds and constricts
me.' Thus it is that words which have similar sounds speak
about something common to all.

Of course, there is nothing new here in essence — since
in the wide use of bold metaphors, in the transfer, for
example, of physical qualities to concepts expressing
psychic qualities: '... zadúmalas' zhénskoi oblokóchennoi
zadúmannost'iu ('The Eye') '...she sank into meditation with
a feminine meditativeness which leaned its head on one el-
bow' or to concepts engendered by the perceptions of one
category, of qualities relating to the perceptions of
another category: 'bárkhatnaia tishiná plát'ya, rasshir-
yáyas' knízu, sliválas' s temotói' 'the velvet quiet of
her dress flaring at the bottom, blending with the darkness' ('Invitation to a Beheading'). Here the verbal
indications of separate perceptions are combined so that
instead of (discrete - DBJ) perceptions, a single integral
impression is imparted to us. Similar stylistic wonders
can be found as early as Gogol, and, subsequently, in a
number of other writers. The whole point is in the
function of these devices which is displayed by the degree
of boldness in their utilization. In this regard, Sirin,
it seems, goes farther than anyone before him — inasmuch
as such audacities are met in his work in contexts where
they strike one by their unexpectedness: not in lyric
poetry, but in 'narrative prose,' where, it would seem,
attention is directed toward the 'usual,' the 'everyday.'
In Sirin's case this is connected with the composition
where fantasy, the imaginary world, somehow creeps in
where we do not expect it. No matter how often this happens, as in 'Invitation to a Beheading,' we do not at all
expect it because just at the time it occurs, the tone
of narration is deliberately 'low-keyed,' calm, such as
that in which one customarily narrates the commonplace.
Nor is the introduction of fantasy into the vulgar commonplace new: it is found in Gogol, in Saltykov, and still
earlier in Hoffmann. But once having intruded, the imaginary world becomes primary in their works; the fantastic
motif is elaborated in detail in each bit of the narration
so that the commonplace constitutes, as it were, the
framework or the backdrop. In Sirin the elements of fantasy and reality are intentionally mixed; all the more in
that it is precisely the 'impossible' that is narrated *en
passant* just as are everyday trivialities upon which one's
attention does not linger: 'The footmen ... briskly served

the food, sometimes even leaping across the table with a
dish (somehow resembling a Chagall painting) and everyone
noticed the polite solicitude with which M'sieur Pierre
took care of Cincinnatus.' One could adduce as many such
examples as one likes. Sometimes, again by means of the
merest verbal hints, even that which relates to 'actuality'
assumes the character of some kind of stage prop: 'Lunú-
uzhe ubráli i gustýe báshni kréposti slivális' s túchami'
'The moon had already been removed and the dark towers of
the fortress blended with the clouds.' At first this seems
to be some sort of delirious perception of actuality. But
if you read anything of Sirin, through to the end, all at
once, so to speak — particularly 'Invitation to a Beheading' — it turns itself inside out. One begins to perceive 'reality' as 'delirium' and 'delirium' as 'actuality.'
Thus the 'word play' device performs the function of the reconstruction of an actuality concealed by the usual 'reality.'

All art, like culture in general, is the result of the
effort to free oneself from actuality and utilizing, nonetheless, the empirical data as *material*, to rework them so
as to touch another, an ideal, world. But these data are
perceived and conceived as real existence, as something
having their *own*, albeit very nasty *meaning* and as something, even though very nasty, none the less *established*
and this means, in and of itself, from a certain point of
view, also 'normal.' Sirin shows customary reality as a
'Whole collection of various negations,' i.e., of absolutely absurd objects: 'All sorts of such shapeless,
mottled, holey, spotted, pockmarked, knobby things...' In
such a situation the essence of creativity is the search
for 'an unintelligible and distorted mirror' in the reflection of which 'an unintelligible and distorted object'
would be transformed into 'a marvelous, shapely image.'
Wherein lies this illusoriness, this unreality 'of our
vaunted reality, of our bad dream,' where only 'from without penetrate the strangely, absurdly changing sounds and
images of the actual world which flows beyond the periphery of consciousness' (the words of Cincinnatus)? In
that the 'I' is not free in it — and *cannot* be free, for
man is not born of his own free will, ('...I am here
through an error — not in this prison, specifically — but
in this whole terrible striped world ...' *ib*.). And if
one is not M'sieur Pierre, for whom life is reduced to
'delights,' amorous, gastronomic, and so on, he is obli-
gatorily Cincinnatus, who, wherever he finds himself,
ultimately returns ever anew to his death cell.

But again: the theme 'life is a dream' and the theme of
man/prisoner are not new; they are well-known universal

themes and they have been touched upon in world literature a multitude of times and in the most diverse variants.
But in no one's work, so far as I know, have these themes
been exclusive nor have they been worked up till now with
such consistency, and with such perfection conditioned by
this consistency, with such mastery of reinterpretation of
the stylistic devices and compositional motifs going back
to Gogol, to the Romantics, to Saltykov-Shchedrin and to
Jonathan Swift. This is because no one has been so consistent in the elaboration of the *idea* underlying this
theme. 'Life is a dream.' Dream, as we know, has long
been considered the brother of Death. Sirin follows this
path to its end. Precisely, that life is death. This is
why, after the execution of Cincinnatus, one of the three
Fates standing by the scaffold bears off *not him* but 'the
tiny executioner,' 'like a larva' in her arms; Cincinnatus,
on the other hand, goes to a place where, 'judging by the
voices, stood beings akin to him,' i.e., 'impenetrable'
Leibnitzian monads 'which have been deprived of windows,'
pure souls, inhabitants of the Platonic world of ideas.

I have already had occasion to express the opinion that
the art of Sirin is the art of allegory. Why is the executioner 'tiny as a larva' at the final moment? Because,
probably, M'sieur Pierre is that which is proper to the
Cincinnatian monad in its earthly embodiment and because he
[M'sieur Pierre - DBJ] was *born* together with it and is
now returning to the earth. Cincinnatus and M'sieur
Pierre are two aspects of 'man in general,' the *everyman*
of the medieval English 'street drama,' of the mystery
play. The 'M'sieur Pierre' element is present in every
man while he lives, i.e., while he sojourns in that state
of the 'bad dream,' of *death*, which we consider life. To
die for 'Cincinnatus' means precisely to exterminate from
himself 'M'sieur Pierre,' that impersonal, 'universal'
element which therefore is *nameless* as it is embodied in
a second variant of M'sieur Pierre, (in the hero of the
story) Khvat, A Dashing Fellow ('The Eye'), who in just
such a way refers to himself as 'we,' or by the provi-
sional name 'just - Kostya.' But, of course, life is *not
only* death. In 'The Gift,' in the touching story Breaking the News ('The Eye'), Sirin is, as it were, not in
agreement with himself. But every person has moments when
that very same feeling of unreality, of the meaninglessness
of life, envelopes him and which in the case of Sirin
serves as the dominant motif of his creativity - amazement
mixed with terror before what usually is perceived as something comprehensible in and of itself, and as a dim vision
of something 'real' lying beyond all this. It is in this
that we find Sirin's Truth.

3. VLADISLAV KHODASEVICH, ON SIRIN, 'VOZROZHDENIE'

1937

On Khodasevich, see Introduction, p. 6. 'Vozrozhdenie'
('Renaissance') was an émigré journal published in Paris.
Translated by Michael H. Walker; translation edited by
Simon Karlinsky and Robert P. Hughes.

Art cannot be reduced to form, but without form it has no
existence and, consequently, no meaning. Therefore the
analysis of a work of art is unthinkable without an analysis of form.

Analysis of form would be a proper way of beginning
every judgment about an author, every account of him. But
formal analysis is so cumbersome and complicated that, in
speaking of Sirin, I should not venture to suggest that
you enter into that region with me. Besides, even I have
not produced a true and sufficiently complete analysis
of Sirin's form, real work in criticism under present conditions being impossible. All the same, I have made certain observations - and I shall permit myself to share the
results.

Under thorough scrutiny Sirin proves for the most part
to be an artist of form, of the writer's device, and not
only in that well-known and universally recognized sense
in which the formal aspect of his writing is distinguished
by exceptional diversity, complexity, brilliance and
novelty. All this is recognized and known precisely because it catches everyone's eye. But it catches the eye
because Sirin not only does not mask, does not hide his
devices, as is most frequently done by others (and in
which, for example, Dostoevsky attained startling perfection) but, on the contrary, because Sirin himself places
them in full view like a magician who, having amazed his
audience, reveals on the very spot the laboratory of his
miracles. This, it seems to me, is the key to all of
Sirin. His works are populated not only with the characters, but with an infinite number of devices which, like
elves or gnomes, scurry back and forth among the characters and perform an enormous amount of work. They saw and
carve and nail and paint, in front of the audience, setting
up and clearing away those stage sets amid which the play
is performed. They construct the world of the book and
they function as indispensably important characters.

Sirin does not hide them because one of his major tasks
is just that — to show how the devices live and work.

Sirin has a novel built entirely on the play of auto-
nomous devices. 'Invitation to a Beheading' is nothing
more than a chain of arabesques, patterns and images, sub-
ordinated not to an ideological, but only to a stylistic
unity (which, by the way, constitutes one of the 'ideas'
of the work). In 'Invitation to a Beheading' there is no
real life, as there are no real characters with the exception of Cincinnatus. All else is merely the play of the
stage-hand elves, the play of devices and images that fill
the creative consciousness or, rather, the creative delirium of Cincinnatus. With the termination of their playing the story comes to an abrupt end. Cincinnatus is not
beheaded and is not not-beheaded, since through the length
of the entire story we see him in an imaginary world where
no real events of any kind are possible. In the concluding
lines, the two-dimensional painted world of Cincinnatus
caves in over the collapsed backdrop: 'Cincinnatus made
his way,' says Sirin, 'amidst the dust, and falling things,
and the flapping scenery, in that direction where, to judge
by the voices, stood beings akin to him.' Here, of course,
is depicted the return of the artist from creative work to
reality. If you wish, the beheading is carried out at
that moment, but not the same one nor in the same sense as
that expected by the hero and the reader: with the return
into the world of 'beings akin to him,' the existence of
Cincinnatus the artist is cut off.

Peculiar to Sirin is the realization, or perhaps only a
deeply felt conviction, that the world of literary creativity, the true world of the artist, conjured through the
action of images and devices out of apparent simulacra of
the real world, consists in fact of a completely different
material — so different that the passage from one world
into the other, in whichever direction it is accomplished,
is akin to death. And it is portrayed by Sirin in the
form of death. If Cincinnatus dies, passing from the
creative world into the real one, then conversely, the
hero of the story Terra Incognita dies at that instant
when he finally plunges completely into the world of imagination. And although the transitions are accomplished
in diametrically opposed directions, both are equally depicted by Sirin in the form of a disintegration of the
stage set. Both worlds, in their relationship one to the
other, are for Sirin illusory.

In exactly the same way the butterfly dealer, Pilgram,
in the story The Aurelian, is dead for his wife, for his
customers, for the whole world, at that moment when he
finally sets out for Spain — a country not coincident

with the real Spain, because it has been created by his
fancy. In exactly the same way Luzhin dies at that moment
when, throwing himself out of the window onto the pale and
dark squares of a Berlin courtyard, he once and for all
slips out of reality and plunges into the world of his
chess creation — there where there are no wife, no acquain-
tances, no apartment, but where there are only the pure,
abstract relationships of creative devices.

If The Aurelian, Terra Incognita and 'Invitation to a
Beheading' are wholly devoted to the theme of the inter-
relationship of worlds, then 'The Defence' is the first
work in which Sirin rose to the full stature of his talent
(because here, perhaps for the first time, he found the
basic themes of his work) — then 'The Defence', belonging as it does to the same cycle, at the same time contains a transition to the second series of Sirin's writings, where the author poses different problems for himself — invariably, however, connected with the theme of
a creative work and the creative personality. These problems are of a somewhat more limited — one could even say
professional — character. In Luzhin's person the very
horror of such professionalism is shown; it is shown that
a permanent residence in the creative world, if the artist
is a man of talent and not of genius, will, as it were, suck
out his human blood, turning him into an automaton which
is not adapted to reality and which perishes from contact
with it.

'The Eye' depicts a charlatan of the arts, an impostor —
a man without gift and by nature a stranger to creative
work, but endeavoring to pass for an artist. Several mistakes committed by him are his ruin, although he of course
does not die, but only changes his profession, for he,
after all, has never been in the world of creative work and
there is in his story no passage from one world into the
other. However, in 'The Eye' the theme is already set
forth and it becomes central in 'Despair,' one of Sirin's
best novels. Here are shown the sufferings of a genuine,
self-critical artist. He perishes because of a single
mistake, because of a single slip allowed in a work which
devoured all of his creative ability. In the process of
creation he allowed for the possibility that the public,
humanity, might not be able to understand and value his
creation — and he was ready to suffer proudly from lack
of recognition. His despair is brought about by the fact
that he himself turns out to be guilty of his downfall,
because he is only a man of talent and not of genius.

The life of the artist and the life of a device in the
consciousness of the artist — this is Sirin's theme, revealing itself to some degree or other in almost every one

of his writings, beginning with 'The Defence.' However,
the artist (and more concretely speaking, the writer) is
never shown by him directly, but always behind a mask: a
chess-player, a businessman, etc. The reasons for this
are, I believe, manifold Foremost among them is that here,
too, we have to do with a device, though quite an ordinary
one. Russian formalists call it 'making it strange.' It
consists in showing the object in unexpected surroundings,
which place it in a new position, reveal new aspects of
it, and force a more direct perception of it. But there
are also other reasons. Had he represented his heroes
directly as writers, Sirin would have had, in depicting
their creative work, to place a novel inside a story or
a story within a story, which would excessively complicate
the plot and necessitate on the part of the reader a certain knowledge of the writer's craft. The very same would
come about, but with some other difficulties, if Sirin had
made them painters, sculptors or actors. He deprives
them of professional artistic attributes, but Luzhin works
on his chess problems and Hermann on plotting a crime in
exactly the same manner that an artist works on his crea-
tions. Finally, one should take into consideration the
fact that, except for the hero of 'The Eye,' all of Sirin's
heroes are genuine, inspired artists. Among them, Luzhin
and Hermann, as I mentioned, are only gifted men and not
geniuses, but even they cannot be denied a deep artistic
nature. Cincinnatus, Pilgram and the nameless hero of
Terra Incognita do not possess those detrimental traits
with which Luzhin and Hermann are marked. Consequently,
all of them, being shown without masks as undisguised
artists, would become (expressed in the language of
teachers of literature) positive types, which, as is
known, creates exceptional and, in the present instance,
unwarranted difficulties for the author. Moreover, in
such a case it would be too difficult for the author to
deliver them from that pompous and sugary tone which almost inevitably accompanies literary portrayals of true
artists. Only the hero of 'The Eye' could have been made
a man of letters by Sirin while avoiding these difficulties, for the simple reason that the hero is a fake writer.
However, I think — I am even almost convinced — that
Sirin, who has at his disposal a wide range of caustic
observations, will some day give himself rein and favor us
with a merciless satiric portrayal of a writer. Such a
portrayal would be a natural development in the unfolding
of the basic theme with which he is obsessed.

4.   JEAN-PAUL SARTRE IN 'EUROPE'

15 June 1939, 240-9

Jean-Paul Sartre (1905-80) was a French philosopher,
novelist and dramatist. In the previous year he had published his important novel 'La Nausée'. His review of
'La Méprise', a French translation of 'Despair', was reprinted in a collection of his prose writings, 'Situations I' (Paris, 1947). Sartre also refers to Nabokov
in his preface to Nathalie Sarraute's 'Portrait d'un inconnu' (Paris, 1957), reprinted in 'Situations IV' (Paris,
1964), where he links Nabokov's work with that of Evelyn
Waugh in the category of 'antinovels' — works which
'preserve the appearance and the contours of the novel' but
actually seek to 'destroy the novel before our eyes even
while appearing to create it'. He sees this as a sign
that 'we live in an age of reflexion and that the novel is
engaged in reflecting on itself'. Nabokov reviewed
Sartre's 'La Nausée' in the 'New York Times Book Review'
(24 April 1949).

...This author has plenty of talent, but he is the child of
old parents — by which I intend to refer only to his
spiritual parents, and specifically to Dostoevski: the
hero of this strange miscarriage of a novel bears a less
close resemblance to his double Felix than to the characters of 'A Raw Youth', 'The Eternal Husband', and 'Notes
from Underground'.... The difference is that, whereas
Dostoevski believes in his characters, Mr Nabokov no longer
believes in his, or for that matter in romantic art. He
makes no secret of borrowing Dostoevski's methods, but at
the same time he pokes fun at them.... In the history of
the novel, we must distinguish between the period in which
authors were devising the tools and that in which they
were reflecting on the tools that had been devised. Mr
Nabokov is an author of the second period; he deliberately
sets himself the task of reflection; he never writes without *watching himself* in the act of writing, just as others
listen to themselves speaking, and he is almost exclusively
interested in the subtle workings of his own reflective
consciousness....
     The result of all this is a curious work, the novel of
a self-critic and the self-criticism of the novel. One is
reminded of Gide's 'Counterfeiters'. In the case of Gide,

however, the critic is also an experimentalist: he tries
out new methods in order to ascertain their results.   Mr
Nabokov (is it through timidity or scepticism?) takes
great care not to invent a new technique.   He laughs at
the artifices of the traditional novel, but in the last
analysis uses nothing else.... Closing the book, one says
to oneself: what a fuss about nothing.   If Mr Nabokov is
so superior to the novels he writes, why does he write
them?   One could swear that he was impelled to do so by a
masochistic impulse.... I am quite willing to grant that
Mr Nabokov is right in dispensing with big scenes in the
romantic tradition;   but what does he give us in their
place?   Longwinded introductions, after which — when we
have been duly prepared — nothing happens;   excellent
thumbnail-sketches;   charming portraits;   literary essays.
Where is the novel?   It has dissolved in its own venom;
it is merely an example of what I call bookish literature.
The hero of 'Despair' confesses to us that, from the end
of 1914 to the middle of 1919, he read exactly one thousand and eighteen books.   I am afraid that Mr Nabokov, like
his hero, has read too much.

I perceive another resemblance between the author and
his character: both are victims of the war and of emigration.... There exists in our time a curious literature
written by Russian and other émigrés who are *rootless*. The
rootlessness of Mr Nabokov, like that of Hermann Carlovitch, is total.   They do not concern themselves with any
society, not even in order to revolt against it, because
they do not belong to any society.   Carlovitch is consequently reduced to committing perfect crimes, and Mr
Nabokov to writing in the English language on subjects of
no significance.

'The Real Life of
Sebastian Knight'

1941

Written in English; published in New York, 1941, 1959,
etc.; and in London, 1945, 1960, etc.

5. P.M.J. IN 'NEW YORK TIMES BOOK REVIEW'

11 January 1942, 7, 14

It is unfortunate that Mr Nabokov, who tries to combine
both methods [that of 'Cakes and Ale' and that of 'The
Quest for Corvo'], has neither the style of Maugham nor
the research of Symons.(1) It is much more unfortunate
that the person whom he writes of, this Sebastian Knight,
is a dull and tiresome fellow.... If the narrator had been
clever, the story could have been interesting. But the
fictional investigator is inept, and his final report does
nothing to suggest that the investigation was worthwhile.
Mr Nabokov's English style is interesting in a Walt Disney
sort of way. He describes a divan as 'sprawling', a writing desk as 'sullen and distant', a table lamp as having
a 'pulse', bookshelves as 'densely peopled', letters that
'swoon' under the 'torturing flame' of a fire. All of
this might sound nice in another language. It sounds
surrealist and rather silly in plain English, and I am
afraid that altogether this is a rather silly story.

Note

1 W. Somerset Maugham's novel 'Cakes and Ale' was pub-

lished in 1930, A.J.A. Symons's 'The Quest for Corvo'
(a biography of Frederick Rolfe, known as 'Baron
Corvo') in 1934.

6.   IRIS BARRY IN 'NEW YORK HERALD TRIBUNE BOOKS'

25 January 1942, 12

For all its apparent artlessness, this brief, intelligent
novel is an intricate piece of work indeed. On the surface, it is the earnest attempt of an unnamed man, the 'I'
of the narrative, to set down what he knows or can discover
about his recently dead brother, Sebastian, a gifted young
writer. The biographical facts, the remembrance of things
past, are recorded in a seemingly haphazard and innocent
manner, with some appetizing but almost over-cerebral
quotations from the dead author's novels to illuminate
fragments of information or recollection concerning the
childhood of Sebastian in 'old' Russia, the death of his
soldier-father in a duel, the strange character of his
English mother, the flight to Finland of the two boys with
Sebastian's stepmother in 1918, Sebastian's peculiar
friendships, painful love affairs, habits of living, of
writing, of thought.... A variety of opinions as to his
literary merit, fleeting hints that seem about to establish concrete facts about the central character promise
continually to lead towards that total discovery of the
essence of his personality to which the book is seemingly
directed.
     In fact, Mr. Nabokov most tantalisingly scatters, in-
stead of uniting, the small pieces of the puzzle: and
the small pieces themselves are made of mirror on both
sides, and confusingly reflect transient images which may
or may not have to be reckoned in with the total effect or
pattern. The 'real life' of Sebastian grows more mysterious, more enigmatic as the book proceeds. But the pattern
grows. Through all the mockery and mischief, the writer
continues to suggest not merely the total unknowableness
of any individual but, still more, to intimate the bewitched
loneliness of each single human being — one marble jostled
among many other marbles, but calling the impact by names
like 'love' — as well as the utter impossibility of recording the true biography of any writer.

Mr. Nabokov's book is full of barbs and pitfalls, and makes curious demands of the reader's attention and fancy, as when it 'lends' one of the minor characters a mask so that the man may not be identified as a real, recognizable person in actual life. It deludes the reader consciously. How exquisitely, for example, does it evoke a strange but ennobling pity in the scene, where the narrator sits silent in a darkened hospital room experiencing 'a sense of security, of peace, of wonderful relaxation' as he listens to the quick, soft breathing of his sick brother. But on the next page we find that there had been one of those idiotic, humiliating errors: the soft breathing had been that of a total stranger. Sebastian had been dead before his brother even reached the hospital.

To say that 'The Real Life of Sebastian Knight' is brilliantly, cunningly written and composed gets nowhere near the effect that the book makes. It is diabolically clever, not merely exotic in mood but as excitingly outside the main tradition of English story-telling as are Hans Andersen or Gogol. Written in the crispest and most lucid English, it somehow gives the effect of hearing the idiot's song from 'Boris Godunov' rendered by bellringers in an English village church, or 'Here we go gathering nuts and may' set to music by Stravinsky. As for the characters, all of them quite odd and very plausible, they evoke a host of half-memories culled from sources as various and un-English as Gerhardi, Balzac and Chekov. In its own most individual way this variation on the dual themes of real identity and of literary biography is a little masterpiece of cerebration and execution.

7. WALTER ALLEN IN 'SPECTATOR'

3 May 1946, 463-4

Walter Allen (born 1911) is an English novelist, critic and literary journalist. His books include several studies of fiction, including 'The English Novel' (1954).

Vladimir Nabokov is a Russian novelist who was educated at Cambridge and writes in English, French, German as well as Russian; the Sebastian Knight of his novel is a Russian

novelist who was educated at Cambridge and wrote in
English. Mr. Edmund Wilson contributes a blurb to the
book, in which he starts a hare in every sentence: 'If
I say that Nabokov is something like Proust, something like
Franz Kafka, and, probably, something like Gogol' — if
Mr. Wilson says any of these things he is, probably, leading the reader up the garden path. Mr. Nabokov, who is
certainly a most brilliant writer, is like none of these,
but resembles a lesser writer, Pirandello. Sebastian
Knight is a novelist of genius; Mr. Nabokov quotes from
his works, and, if he does not persuade us of his genius,
at least he is successful in suggesting an unusual talent
smacking of the nineteen-twenties. The narrator of the
novel is Knight's half-brother, a Russian in exile in
Paris, who sets out to reconstruct Sebastian's life after
his early death; a mysterious life, though possibly not
more so than most, obscured already by a cheap biography.
After a course of detective work, which takes in visits
to Cambridge, London, Paris, a small German spa, he amasses
the relevant facts. It is, in other words, an equivalent
in fiction of A.J.A. Symons' 'The Quest for Corvo'. And
what mystery do the facts enshrine? This, apparently:
'Whatever his secret was, I have learnt one secret too, and
namely: that the soul is but a manner of being — not a
constant state — that any soul may be yours, if you find
and follow its undulations. The hereafter may be the full
ability of consciously living in any chosen soul, in any
number of souls, all of them unconscious of their interchangeable burden. Thus — I am Sebastian Knight. I feel
as if I were impersonating him on a lighted stage....' A
belief which, if I understand it, I entirely disagree with.
    The metaphysical implications seriously damage 'The Real
Life of Sebastian Knight' as a novel. True, as a result,
perhaps, of the sense of identity, the narrator has in the
end produced a book as brilliant as any of Knight's, to
judge from the quotations from them; but since Mr. Nabokov wrote both that is not remarkable; so nothing is proved.
Nor do the careful reconstructions, the quotations from the
cheap 'Life of Knight', duly debunked by the narrator,
help to create an illusion of the reality of Knight; one
is merely left, as with Pirandello, thinking, 'It's all done
with mirrors,' and with the feeling of depression that technical virtuosity unaccompanied by adequate content so often
induces. Mr. Nabokov has performed the extremely clever
and extremely unsatisfying feat of writing a novel in which
nearly all the problems that the novelist must solve have
been evaded. His talent is obviously great; one joins with
the publisher in hoping that he will put his other novels
into English; but in the presence of this one, one can
only feel cheated and therefore aggrieved.

'Bend Sinister'

1947

Written in English; published in New York, 1947, and
London, 1960.

8. RICHARD WATTS, JR, IN 'NEW REPUBLIC'

7 July 1947, 26-7

The story of the free man under the totalitarian state is
still the classic tragedy of our age, and in 'Bend Sinister' it is given striking and original treatment, at once
impressive, powerful and oddly exasperating. This second
novel in English by Vladimir Nabokov, an American citizen
of Russian birth, a sardonic tale of an intellectual who
scorned his nation's tyrant, has an eerie, nightmare
quality and savage humor. They combine to make it considerably more than the warmed-over Arthur Koestler it
occasionally seems on the verge of becoming. 'Bend
Sinister' is written with a fluency which usually belies
its author's comparative unfamiliarity with the language,
but its chief fault is that an apparent fascination with
his own linguistic achievement sometimes causes Nabokov to
go in for verbal fanciness.
  As a dramatic fantasy of totalitarianism, 'Bend Sinister' is both simple and elaborate. It is simple in its
tragic story, which is merely that of a world-famous
philosopher — and it is one of the novel's successes
that Nabokov has drawn, in Professor Krug, an intellectual
hero whose status as an intellectual is completely credible — who is firmly convinced that his combination of

71

international fame and moral courage will protect him
against the outrages of the police state. It is elaborate
both in much of its style and in the manner in which
Nabokov has constructed an abstract, totalitarian land
which is both Russian and German in its language but de-
cidedly more National Socialist than Communist in its history, theory and practice....

Nabokov is at his best in his bitterly humorous thrusts
at the narrowness and stupidity of totalitarian thought
and action and in his flights of satirical scorn. His
scenes of horror, with their eerily distorted lights and
shadows, can also be powerful, and his account of the slow,
inexorable pressure exerted on Krug captures the terror of
the police state in a manner not easy to forget. Then,
after his friends have been dragged off to prison as warn-
ings, when the philosopher's son has been taken from him,
tortured and then killed by mistake just as Krug offers to
give in, an atmosphere of pity and terror is created with
shocking forcefulness. It is because Nabokov can achieve
some of the ominous and comic effects he manages in 'Bend
Sinister' that his puckish weakness for affectation seems
so outrageous.

9. NATHAN L. ROTHMAN IN 'SATURDAY REVIEW'

2 August 1947, 33

Mr. Nabokov is a writer of tremendous technical powers,
and it goes almost without saying that the actual plot of
the book at hand is its least important part. We can
come to that in a moment. Nabokov has mastered every kind
of virtuosity that has been developed in this century.
Naturally he owes a great deal to Joyce; it is there to
be seen in the asides and the several (and simultaneous)
depths of consciousness, in the bardic phrases, in the
incessant literary recalls (which is all right here since
the hero, Adam Krug, is a university professor).

And there is, of course, the final definitive signature — a conscious tribute to the master, I should say —
when Nabokov stops his narrative cold, to insert a long
and fanciful dialogue on Shakespeare and 'Hamlet,' as
Joyce did in 'Ulysses.' I do not, of course, speak of
imitation. This is a matter of proceeding from the source.
Nabokov is an artist in his own right, entirely and easily

at home in the worlds of the conscious and the subconscious, lighting them with a display of literary fireworks that must delight every literate reader.

He is not Joyce's equal, and does not need to be, but there is no harm in pointing out that 'Ulysses' contained also, behind its fireworks and within its intricacies, a spirit in profound agony. I miss the spirit in Nabokov's book, particularly in view of its announced program: a novel of man under the tyrant state. Krug is the man: a stalwart anarchist throwing his weight about uncompromisingly within a parental state. He is unconcerned, he is contemptuous, he is foolhardy. He knew Paduk, the dictator, when they were schoolmates, and regards him still as the repulsive toad he was then. Krug's thoughts, his involved and highly expressive mental life, are the only commentary upon Paduk and his fascist regime (in this nameless country, with its very language created by Nabokov for the occasion). This is the book: Krug against the state.

It is a drama we know only too well. And, as we read it here it seems somehow desiccated, fleshless, a distant clash remembered and echoed in contempt. Or, to suggest another analogy, it seems to have receded too deeply into too remote, if meticulously formed, an image. The thing has the dimensions of a fantasy seen through the small end of a telescope. Krug, the observer, is real, but not Paduk, not his minions, not his crimes and his victims, not the whole panorama of his evil state. Not even Krug's bereavements, his tears, his fears. There is the shadow of a fear, and the echo of an outcry — but it is all in the disembodied and fathomless memory of the beholder Krug. And when Nabokov himself steps in deliberately at the end, like the puppet-master, and draws up his strings and removes Krug, why then the disillusion is complete. Brilliant, brilliant, but after all it was not real, he was not hurt, we need not be concerned, there is the puppet hanging, and here is the master himself, large as life, smiling at us.

10. V.S. NAIPAUL IN 'NEW STATESMAN'

26 March 1960, 461-2

V.S. Naipaul (born 1932) is a novelist; his books include 'A House for Mr Biswas' (1961).

'Bend Sinister' was published in America in 1947 and was
the second novel in English by Vladimir Nabokov. Though
clearly a work of distinction, it is easy to see why this
novel has had to wait so long for publication in this
country. It is bizarre, puzzling and difficult.... It
is not realistic, satirical or prophetic; it is not
'Darkness at Noon' or 'Animal Farm' or 'Nineteen-Eighty-
Four'. It is not political. The police state with its
theatrical machinery seems to be used only as a setting
for a contemporary tale of mystery and imagination. And
as a fantasy it does not seem to me to be a success. There
are too many puzzles. What is the value of the amusing,
but disproportionately long, Thurberish interpretation of
'Hamlet'? Who is the 'I' who steps from time to time between the reader and the novel? Is it Mr Nabokov, or is it
the insane Krug himself, breaking from the third person
into the first, as children do when they write stories?
The skill with which Mr Nabokov creates his effects of
fantasy is remarkable: an oblique narrative method coupled
with a minute exploration of small scenes, precise detail
upon precise detail, again and again dissolves reality into
nightmare. But the effort is too cerebral to arouse immediate response. Too much has to be worked out; there
are too many distractions.
  Mr Nabokov's style is almost too good for the novel.
His vocabulary calls too much attention to itself, and
his botanical words continually send the simple bulb-
burier to the dictionary. He is incapable of lightness;
his sentences are overloaded and the very precision with
which he gets his effects is in the long run fatiguing.
At times he is as ponderous as the proverbial sports-
writer: the moon is 'our siliceous satellite', press-
clippings are 'indigenous allusions', to use a blotter is
to 'apply the leech'. 'Bend Sinister' is not easy to
read, and not sufficiently rewarding. For all its brilliance, it is only an exercise.

11.   MALCOLM BRADBURY IN 'PUNCH'

20 April 1960, 562

Malcolm Bradbury (born 1932), English novelist and critic,
is Professor of American Studies at the University of East

Anglia. His books include 'The Social Context of Modern
English Literature' (1972) and 'The Novel Today' (1977).

The harsh comic voice, the wry view of things, has a special importance in our day and age. Finding a voice, a
way of writing, when there are so many available in the
tradition yet when no one seems quite *right*, is the problem, and when Mann parodies, when Auden turns buffoon,
when Beckett finds farce in the problem of a faithless
age, we see a sophisticated answer. The comic tone represents our lack of sureness, our rejection of Victorian
high-seriousness, our need to wrap things up. 'Bend
Sinister' is, in fact, a comedy about totalitarianism;
hideous events are seen through the screen of farce. Adam
Krug, leading philosopher in a small state, tries to with-
draw himself from the problem of a *coup d'état* which has
placed the Ekwilist party in power. Here the satire turns
on the west, on America, for the Ekwilists seek to do away
with discrimination by intelligence or individual superiority — yet paradoxically they need the blessing of
their one great intellect for their new régime. The fable
is handled with a rhetorical zest that is occasionally
offensive; Nabokov plays with his tale, does tricks,
stands on his head. The story hasn't quite evolved from
the study, where the writer can put in personal jokes.
Yet the strain between style and fable is meaningful; it
is a moral fable told in an amoral voice.

12. FRANK KERMODE IN 'ENCOUNTER'

June 1960, 81-6

Frank Kermode (born 1919) has held chairs at Manchester,
Bristol and University College, London, and is now King
Edward VII Professor of English Literature at Cambridge.
His books include 'Romantic Image' (1957), 'The Sense of
an Ending' (1967) and 'The Genesis of Secrecy' (1979).

Mr. Nabokov is a major novelist; the proof of this exists,
but is only gradually becoming available, as the old novels

are released in Britain. Probably he will not be greatly
loved; the personality that presides over his work is
not amiable. We do not much care to be the objects of
an author's contempt, and — to simplify for a moment —
that is the way Nabokov seems to feel about us. It is
not very common for a man of really overpowering intelligence to write novels; and, especially if he is also
an impatient man, he is likely, when he does so, to encounter special problems. The medium itself may irk him,
because of its associations with base entertainment, and
because it traditionally encourages the reader to 'identify' with its characters. The reader is even more of a
problem. A kind of thinking, and the pleasure that accompanies it, no longer go on in happy privacy but have
to be made available to others, some or many of whom have
no hope of understanding and experiencing them. The
novel insults the intelligence of its author; and the
author thinks of his reader as being morally deaf, like
the boarding-house keeper in Mr. Pinter's play, who is so
committed to the belief that what goes on is nice that she
hardly registers an attempt to strangle her.

In his apologia for 'Lolita' Nabokov tosses us an
aesthetic:

> For me the work of fiction exists only in so far as
> it affords me what I shall bluntly call aesthetic
> bliss; that is, a sense of being somehow, somewhere,
> connected with other states of being where art (cur-
> iosity, tenderness, kindness, ecstasy) is the norm.
> There are not many such books. All the rest is topi-
> cal trash coming in huge blocks of plaster that are
> carefully transmitted from age to age until someone
> comes along with a hammer and takes a good crack at
> Balzac, at Gorki, at Mann.

This is loosely expressed, and not extraordinary anyway, but we note 'affords *me*'; also 'states of being'
which suggests that others can participate in the bliss.
(The strange inclusion of 'curiosity' as a gloss on 'art'
helps, by the way, to explain the association in Nabokov
of passionate excitement with flourishes of recondite
learning.) The list of plaster-novelists — in which he
would also place Conrad — is more interesting. The
novel is too easy. It can be stuffed with facts or doctrine, a photograph or a tract; or it can be laboriously
moulded to the shape of some moralistic obsession. Nabokov finds all this contemptible and an obstacle to aesthetic bliss. And that is why his fiction is uniformly fantastic; everything in it is a kind of joke. He uses a

hot-house prose, its improbable loops and blooms are
themselves a mockery of prevailing narrative styles;   when
it moves briskly it is with an effect of farce, when it is
fine it parodies itself.   The moral *données* of the novels
are absurdly ambiguous, hence our slow bewilderment with
'Lolita'.   Humbert displays great delicacy, is disgusted
with visitors whose modesty won't allow them to flush the
lavatory, or with Quilty's phoney British accent and the
'thick gore' that comes from him as the bullets sink in;
but this delicacy will not survive Lolita's delicious
crumbiness.   The nastiness *we* are likely to sense vulgarly
in the affair with the girl is transferred, with a show of
fastidious indignation, to behaviour *we* very probably
approve: 'There is nothing wrong, say both hemispheres,
when a brute of forty, blessed by the local priest and
bloated with drink, sheds his sweat-drenched finery and
thrusts himself up to the hilt into his youthful bride.'
Humbert is not a brute, nor forty, nor drunk or dirty or
married.   He is, like his creator's novels, morally isolated in the interests of bliss.   And although the treatment of 'normal' relationships is disgusted or farcical,
this isolation is unavoidably tragic.   Nabokov's genre is,
in fact, tragic farce.   There is here a slight resemblance
to Graham Greene, who also has the power to see through
a joke into an abyss;   but a much stronger resemblance
to Sterne.

In 'Bend Sinister' this is very strong, partly because
of a coincidence of theme;   for 'Bend Sinister' treats, as
Sterne did, of a 'clash between the world of learning and
that of human affairs' (Douglas Jefferson).   The hero is
a famous philosopher called Adam Krug, a somewhat Nabokov-
like man with his own superior powers.... He is a tragic
Shandy;   the fate of his son is a consequence of an obsession with intellect, the habit of expecting matters to
fall out in accordance with intelligent prediction, just
as his father's preoccupation with book-learning, and the
obsessive researches of Uncle Toby, brought disaster to
Tristram.   The difference between Sterne's comedy and
Nabokov's tragedy is simply that the hard facts upon
which the Shandys bruise themselves are orderly and to be
respected;   whereas Krug's victors are aimless and banal,
and their policy the corruption of a philosophy.

This material difference does not detract from the impressive linguistic and formal resemblances between Nabokov
and Sterne.   Both, for example, use scientific language for
farce....

Nabokov plays the devil with his narrative, just in the
Sterne manner.   Little notes are addressed to the author
himself.   'Describe the bedroom.... Last chance of des-

cribing the bedroom.' The author intervenes out of pity:
'it was then that I felt a pang of pity for Adam and slid
towards him along an inclined beam of pale light — causing instantaneous madness.' He introduces long digressions, including a long one on 'Hamlet' which undoubtedly
attempts to overgo the Scylla and Charybdis episode in
'Ulysses'. 'The real plot of the play,' according to
Professor Hamm, a scholar acceptable to the new régime,
'will be readily grasped if the following is realised:
the Ghost on the battlements of Elsinore is not the ghost
of King Hamlet. It is that of Fortinbras the Elder.' He
has come to soften the morale of the Danes and prepare the
way for the succession of Fortinbras the Younger. Krug
listens to the argument, to 'these intricate convolutions
of sheer stupidity' which remind him of the new régime.
Then he sketches the scenario (pre-Olivier) of a film on
'Hamlet': unweeded garden set, 'Hamlet at Wittenberg,
always late, missing G. Bruno's lectures,' 'lusty old King
Hamlet smiting with a poleaxe the Polacks,' 'a liberal
shepherd on marshy ground where *Orchis mascula* grows.'
Then the etymological game: Ophelia is quite possibly
'an anagram of Alpheios, with the "S" lost in the damp
grass — Alpheus the rivergod, who pursued a long-legged
nymph until Artemis changed her into a stream (*cp.* Winnipeg
Lake, ripple 585, Vico Press edition).' Finally there are
translations of 'Hamlet' into the newly-invented language.
After all this two organ-grinders appear outside, and extraordinarily horrible police officers arrive to arrest
Krug's friend.

The function of this digression is extremely complicated. It is a civilised way of not talking about Krug's
wife, who has just died. It is a useless but agreeable
exercise of intellect, and will contrast with the smooth
bestiality of the police. It is funny. The translations
are not just a wanton exhibition of glossolalia but another
link with the main theme, just before the police arrive.
Paduk, the dictator, has promoted the use of a writing-
machine, a sort of typewriter which reproduces one's hand-
writing. Is the heartbreaking labour of translation, since
it 'presupposes a voluntary limitation of thought in sub-
mission to another man's genius' compensated by the pleasure it gives, or is it no more than 'an exaggerated and
spiritualised replica of Paduk's writing-machine?' Here
is a theological issue of importance, the border territory
between Krugs and Paduks. It is not settled; it is
interrupted by the sinister duality of organ-grinders and
the entry of the police.

There is wantonness here; there is wantonness also in
the large-screen cardiograph in which medical minions

study the action of Paduk's heart, in the parrot which
carries police messages, in the conclusion of the novel
where, with the bullets ripping into the mad Krug, the
author switches off the story and turns his attention to
the moths at his window. But it is easy to distinguish
between this kind of wantonness and, say, Mr. Bratby's.(1)
Merely to write centrifugally, to torment the narrative
line, to destroy the illusion by inconsistencies of presentation, all this is within the scope of any rudimentary,
slightly sophisticated talent. It might be done by anyone who thinks, as many do, that the structure of a work
of art is the business not of the artist but of the observer.

But this is not Nabokov's way. 'Bend Sinister' is not
finally wanton, any more than Sterne was. There is a
pretty rigorous subordination of all these stunts and
rhetorical exercises to the shape of the whole. Nabokov
uses, and never abuses, familiar devices to establish
'spatial' design — what Mr. Forster calls 'rhythms.' The
'spatulate puddle' of the first paragraph is one such;
Krug's wife taking off her jewels, the treacherous pro-
verb of a trimming professor, are two more. And the
tragic movement of the narrative seems hardly to be interrupted. The book opens with a self-consciously superb
evocation of grief, a sort of virtuoso development of
Rossetti's woodspurge; it goes on to the parable of Krug
on the bridge, patient and humorous with the unreasonable
peasant soldiers. Krug will not save his university nor
himself, nor, in the end, his own son from the dictator
because he will not see that stupidity and venality can
become omnipotent; because he earned the right at school
to sit on the head of Paduk, the Average Man.... Hurling
himself on Paduk, he does not die only because the author
intervenes — to tell us that Krug died well, and left his
spatulate mark 'in the intimate texture of space.' He
describes a moth outside his window: 'a good night for
mothing,' he concludes. We are kept right out of Krug,
right out of Nabokov. We are placed, at best, in respect
of this author, where Krug places his bourgeois friend
Maximov.

When Krug mentioned once that the word 'loyalty'
phonetically and visually reminded him of a golden fork
lying in the sun on a smooth spread of pale yellow silk,
Maximov replied somewhat stiffly that to *him* loyalty
was limited to its dictionary denotation. Common-
sense with him was saved from smug vulgarity by a delicate emotional undercurrent, and the somewhat bare and
birdless symmetry of his branching principles was ever

so slightly disturbed by a moist wind blowing from
regions which he naively thought did not exist.

We have to be as good as Maximov to be fit for Nabokov.
We may not like this; but when reading 'Bend Sinister'
it is vital to remember that its author would label a
book about the oppression of the human spirit by a stupid
and brutal government 'topical trash.' It is a work of
art or nothing.

Note

1 In the same article Professor Kermode briefly reviewed
John Bratby's novel 'Breakdown'.

'Lolita'

1955

Written in English; published in Paris, 1955; New York, 1958; and London, 1959.

13. JOHN HOLLANDER IN 'PARTISAN REVIEW'

Autumn 1956, 557-60

John Hollander (born 1929) is Professor of English at Hunter College, City University of New York. He is the author of many volumes of criticism and poetry. Professor Hollander tells me that his review, apparently the first to appear in the USA, was 'written from a copy of the Olympia Press edition given to Harry Levin by Nabokov'.

In the bizarre mixture of vintage 1830 sham editorial note and parody 'Saturday Review' piece that serves as an introduction to this remarkable book, we are earnestly informed that 'As a case history, "Lolita" will become no doubt a classic in psychiatric circles.' There is no doubt that it will not. The shades of Stavrogin, Lewis Carroll, Tiberius, Popeye, or worse hinted at in the foreword, the pornographic promises implicit in its publication by a Parisian erotica house, seem only ghosts to be dispelled almost in the very first chapter. Even to state that the book is *about* a cultivated European emigré in love with a twelve-year-old girl is misleading: modern readers cannot help but refer such a theme to the wrong novelistic con-

ventions. There is no clinical, sociological, or mythic
seriousness about 'Lolita,' but it flames with a tremendous perversity of an unexpected kind. Readers of Mr.
Nabokov's earlier work will be more prepared than most to
relate such a theme to a style weird enough to support it
in a new way. They may understand what it means to say
that this book often suggests a terrifyingly semi-serious
parody of 'Manon Lescaut' by James Thurber. Nearly everything about 'Lolita' is parodic, save for the primary love
story, which ridicules only itself....

[A plot-summary follows.]

Throughout all this, Mr. Nabokov's attention is fixed on
the sentimental treatment of the love affair itself, and
the satiric portrayal of the American *kitsch* through which
the lovers peregrinate. It is Humbert's own amazingly
flexible rhetoric, primarily, which permits of rapid
switches back and forth from: 'and feeling as I did her warm
weight on my lap (so that, in a sense, I was always with
Lolita as a mother is with child)' to: 'We had breakfast in
the township of Soda, pop. 1001.' Much of the book's
comic genius lies in the style, which alternates elements
of Turgenev and mock Proust, rigorous Constant-like *ana-
lyse de l'amour* and parody and pastiche. There are moments of surrealoid super-clarity, but unlike true surrealism, these glimpses never stake all on the effect of
the moment, abandoning any further dramatic utility. They
seem to spring from the kind of Dickensian eye which lets
Esther Summerson in 'Bleak House' notice, before any more
concrete signs of familial disorder, the fact that one of
Mrs. Jellyby's curtains is secured with a fork. But the
most pervasive single device of style is the verbal diddle.
Humbert fiddles with his own name ('Hamburg,' 'Humbug,'
'Homburg,' etc.) and indeed, with everything else. 'Guilty
of killing Quilty,' he mutters toward the beginning of the
narrative, 'Oh my Lolita, I have only words to play with.'
Usually the games are even more Joycean, especially in a
long section in which are described the recondite *noms de
guerre* with which his pursuing rival, the more to pique him,
fills out motel registers. One thinks of Thurber's mad
fixation on the linguistic games with which he avoids social confrontations. But in 'Lolita,' the word-play leads
back to the love-play always: it is a little like an extended trope on the pathetic fallacy, in which verbal hocus-
pocus makes the obsessive object light up, in intellectual
neon, everywhere.
The problem of what to make of 'Lolita' has led certain
of the book's admirers to beg off its sexual and literary

outlandishness by remarking that the whole thing is *really*
Mr. Nabokov's love affair with America. Certainly Dolores
herself, with her outrageous jargon and tastes, is part of
what Auden has called the 'heterogeneous dreck' of the
American landscape through which she and her doting lover
move. But there is something more here, surely, some
better way for the reader to escape (if he must) the too-
serious acceptance of the suburb of heterosexuality in
which Humbert dwells. His particular Lecherville has, as
far as I know, no well-known clinically respectable name
of long standing (Old Can't-tell-the-players, without-a-
scorecard Krafft-Ebing has to resort to 'violation of persons under the age of fourteen' for his map). This is
important, I feel. Humbert himself tells us: 'I am not
concerned with so-called "sex" at all. Anyone can imagine
these elements of animality. A greater endeavor lures me
on: to fix once and for all the perilous magic of nymphets.'
Indeed, the 'sex' in this book is all subject to tender
exegesis (after one rare moment of melodramatic tenderness
from Lolita: 'It may interest physiologists to learn, at
this point, that I have the ability — a most singular
case, I presume — of shedding torrents of tears throughout the other tempest'). The not-quite-teen-age-girl
herself, of course, providing her learned lover with duties
involving the procurement of sundaes and movie magazines,
is the only plausible modern *femme fatale*. She is elusive,
perverse, and, above all, *transient* (each nymphet has but
a few years of affinitive power). Indeed, there *is* a
moral term for the moral condition that is the subject of
this book, but it comes from the lexicon of purely literary
pathology. 'Nympholepsy,' the frenzy of attachment to an
unattainable object, was a common word for a commonly cultivated romantic state. I rather think that Mr. Nobokov's
strategy was to literalize the word's metaphor, and to write
of a class of real nymphets who could produce in their
palely loitering admirers the rhetorical action whose
fruit is romantic writing. Swinburne and Poe provide the
names for the two lost loves, and the lost child and the
Lady of Pain unite, for Mr. Nabokov himself, in one 'fair,
nasty nymph.' 'Lolita,' if it is anything '*really*,' is the
record of Mr. Nabokov's love affair with the romantic novel,
a today-unattainable literary object as short-lived of
beauty as it is long of memory. It is also, not to change
the subject for a minute, just about the funniest book I
remember having read.

14.   F.W. DUPEE IN 'ANCHOR REVIEW'

1957, 1-3, 5-13

F.W. Dupee (born 1904) taught at Columbia University and has
published books on Henry James and other authors.   The
same issue of the 'Anchor Review' included substantial
extracts from 'Lolita' and also Nabokov's essay On a Book
Entitled 'Lolita' (see Introduction, p. 11).

In 'Lolita' Vladimir Nabokov has made a notable tale out
of notably forbidding matter and breathed fresh virulence
into the great tradition, recently languishing, of the
roman noir.   The author of several novels, a first-rate
memoir of his Russian childhood and exilic youth, a cranky
study of Gogol, and some learned monographs on the subject
of Lepidoptera, Mr. Nabokov is an experienced and no doubt
widely read man of letters.   But none of his previous
ventures has quite prepared us for the impact of 'Lolita.'
The impact of 'Lolita' on American publishers — the
several who saw it in manuscript — was such that the book
was finally brought out by a small press in Paris.   American publishers are not greatly to blame.   There is a real
challenge in 'Lolita,' and to say there is not would do the
book itself an injustice.   A largely sympathetic critic
writing in 'Partisan Review' (Mr. John Hollander) declares
that 'Lolita' 'flames with a tremendous perversity of an
unexpected kind.'   It does, and the flame would definitely
singe a sleeve;   and for just this reason 'Lolita' is not
for the mere fancier of erotica or consumer of pornography,
if there are such people and if they matter.   'Lolita'
applies its heat to the entire sensibility, including the
sense of humor.   Instead of putting the desires in an
agreeable simmer, it acts on them almost like a cautery,
sterilizing them with horrid laughter.   Between the horror
and the hilarity of it, 'Lolita' is a fascinating but very
special sort of experience.   It is a tale for the adult
public;   and should it sometime be published in the United
States, it could be trusted, I think, to make its mark with
that public as an original work of literature.
      Meanwhile Mr. Nabokov's terrible infant circulates over
here in its Paris format, gets itself reviewed in advanced
periodicals and acquires a small celebrity.   But this celebrity, if it is of the kind I think it is, could do the book
a subtler injury than censorship can do, insisting as it

mostly does that 'Lolita' is no more than a very brilliant
joke or literary burlesque. Mr. Hollander gives good
reason for being of this opinion. He suggests that the
book has, besides its tremendous perversity, a wealth of
uproarious parody but 'no clinical, sociological or mythic
seriousness.'

'Lolita' is very funny, very full of burlesque intentions, but the supreme laugh may be on the reviewers for
failing to see how much of everyone's reality lurks in its
fantastic shadow play. Surely the ways listed by Mr.
Hollander — clinical, sociological, mythic — are not
the only ways of making perversity pay off in literature;
there are simpler ways of being serious. Mr. Nabokov has
devoted much art to making 'Lolita' yield reactions which
I can only describe as 'human.' True, his hero is a
thorough creep and no pitiable sick man or aspiring sick
soul. He is contrived in such a way that he resists the
charity of the clinic and refuses to be vaporized into
allegory. Entangled in some of the most intricately sordid situations ever presented by a novelist, his hero tends
to be in fact what some of Joyce's characters become in
their guilty fantasies: a 'sex fiend' pursued by angry
bodies of righteous citizens. Incongruously, however, his
situations are always assuming familiar forms, his horrid
scrapes become our scrapes. The book's general effect is
profoundly mischievous, like that of some diabolical distorting mirror in some particularly obscene amusement
park. The images of life that 'Lolita' gives back are
ghastly but recognizable. If Mr. Nabokov's methods are
the usual methods of comedy, they are here carried to new
extremes....

[A plot-summary follows.]

Such a summary of the action naturally excludes most of
the values that give subtlety to 'Lolita' in the reading
of it. These values mainly inhere in what Mr. Nabokov
makes of Humbert Humbert. In the falsest of false posi-
tions, Humbert has enough decency to feel his position as
what it is. He impersonates the hero of a novel, even
though he isn't a hero by nature; and by some curious law
he is more interesting as his actions become more outrageous.
The prologue, recounting his early life, rings with a
Frenchy sort of jocularity and is the least convincing part
of 'Lolita,' just as it is the most innocent part. The
jocular tone of the prologue probably arises from its
being in some measure a burlesque of those Freudian flash-
backs resorted to by many novelists in order to make clear
how the hero 'got that way.' However Humbert got that way,

we are made to see that he has become something which, in
its grimness, quite defies explanation. It defies statis-
tics, too, although his psychiatrist has informed him that
'at least 12% of American adult males — a "conservative"
estimate according to Dr. Blanche Schwarzmann (verbal communication) — enjoy yearly, in one way or another, the
special experience "H.H." describes with such despair.'
He is the impossible sort of person whom Freud can't help,
or Kinsey either: cocky, humorous, perceptive, fastidious,
and almost too well read, to articulate ('You can always
count on a murderer for a fancy prose style'). His qualities are pretty much at the command of his obsession, but
he naturally seeks to avoid the implications of his servi-
tude and, like any Vautrin or Raskolnikov, he plays his
roles, assumes his masks. Yet these impostures are not
so much chosen by him as thrust upon him by the conditions
of his life; and brutally, one after another, they are
snatched away, exposing an awkward grin. His very name
lends itself to indiscriminate garbling and tends to re-
solve itself into Humburg. He marries the full-sized
woman in Paris under the consoling impression that he is
irresistible to her (he thinks all adult women are mad
about him, and some are). But off she goes with a poor
specimen of a White Russian taxi driver and Humbert is left
with another interrupted relationship on his record, another
shattered mask at his feet.

    With his entry upon the American scene his impersona-
tions become more profound and his story takes on the true
stature. Indeed 'Lolita' at this point begins to impersonate an 'international novel' (of the journalistic
Graham Greene or Koestler type rather than the Henry James
type). The deep unreality within Humbert is complemented
by another kind of unreality in the place of his destiny.
He becomes subject to the preposterous chances and changes
of a wide-open society, a culture madly on the move. His
fate hangs on the godlike motions of the motorcar and the
wayward oracle of the telephone. There is an ambiguous
promise in the friendliness of small towns, the lush convenience of omnipresent hotels and motels, the defiant
come-on of little girls in blue jeans, the suggestive innocence of the instruction they receive at school and the
literature they read. '"Mr. Uterus (I quote from a girls'
magazine) starts to build a thick soft wall on the chance
a possible baby may have to be bedded down there."'

    'It's a free country!' Lolita cries when her mother
tries to send her to bed. Humbert is an ironic portrait
of the visiting European, and the Hazes help to complete
the likeness. He is to them the prince of a lost realm —
actually a luxury hotel kept by his father on the Riviera.

He seems to have the superior sexual acumen and appeal so often assumed by Europeans and envied by Americans — but his sexuality is as peculiar as we know. Mrs. Haze's husband, a hazy figure at best, has long been dead, and she and her daughter have made their pointless way from the Middle West to this New England town where Humbert arrives to be their boarder, ostensibly with the idea of writing a book in a peaceful retreat. The Haze women and their appurtenances are familiar enough; they have been portrayed in many satirical novels and problem plays of modern manners. There is the arty, career-bent, unloving mother; the defiant unloved daughter with her eternal blue jeans, her deplorable manners and secrets, her loud cries of 'You dope!' and 'I think you stink!'; and there is the litter of lamps, sofas, coffee tables, magazines, Van Gogh prints, and pink toilet-seat tidies amid which they irritably and insubstantially live. But the observations and machinations of Humbert, the sinister outsider, project a fierce glare on this trite house and its trite occupants, re-creating them and investing them with a sour pathos. 'The poor lady [Charlotte Haze] was in her middle thirties, she had a shiny forehead, plucked eyebrows, and quite simple but not unattractive features of a type that may be defined as a weak solution of Marlene Dietrich.... Her smile was but a quizzical jerk of one eyebrow; and uncoiling herself from the sofa as she talked, she kept making spasmodic dashes at three ash trays and the near fender (where lay the brown core of an apple); whereupon she would sink back again, one leg folded under her.'

Charlotte Haze will soon uncoil herself for a more urgent reason and then dash impulsively into eternity. She is an ominous figure, a resonant type. With her 'principles' which bulk large but weigh little, her vacuous animation, her habit of asserting herself although she has next to nothing in her to assert, Charlotte is the immoral moralist, the loveless romantic, the laughless comic — whatever it is that spoils the party and dampens the honeymoon all across America. Once married to Humbert she naturally imagines herself to be deeply attractive to him. She looms alluringly in slacks or bathing suit, coils and uncoils herself with more nervous abandon than ever, buys the pair of them a brand-new bed, cooks up fetching little messes for dinner, and in a frenzy of mis-placed homemaking decides to redecorate the entire house. But her taste in these matters, which she owes to her cul-ture, is no more attractive to Humbert than her robust femininity, for which nature is to blame. Her diluted Dietrich charms are lost on him, preoccupied as he is by the skinny charms of Lolita; but so would Dietrich at full

strength be lost on him. Thus Charlotte is made to act out
a timeless travesty of Woman, and of Sex itself with the
rigid specializations and fetishisms that attend it in its
capitalized form, or whenever it is an end in itself.
Noting Humbert's gravitation towards Lolita and away from
Charlotte, we can only wonder at the small affective range
of *anyone's* desires. Why the one female rather than the
other? Can a few years more or less, an inch or two of
flesh at thigh or bosom, make *that* much difference? Then,
as we learn, there is Humbert's rich distaste for fully
developed co-eds — those much publicized love objects —
and his horror at realizing that Lolita herself will soon
be just another woman. ('I see, maybe, the coffin of coarse
female flesh in which my nymphets are buried alive.') One
man's meat is another man's mummy. Humbert is heir to the
merry old European tradition of libertinage but he has
forgotten the point of it. Rather, he has reduced it to
absurdity and is himself reduced to all kinds of anxious
fantasies and substitutive pleasures. Where the Marquis
de Sade, that other specialized libertine, fed poisoned
bonbons to his victims in the hope of seeing them writhe,
Humbert avails himself of sleeping pills which only leave
his victim thoroughly awake.

The scene at the Enchanted Hunters, the suburban hotel
where Humbert and Lolita finally seduce one another, is one
long spasm of comic horror — though now with a different
drift from the Charlotte scenes — and Nabokov spares us
nothing of Humbert's soft misery and dubious triumph. The
famous scene in Proust in which Charlus pays to have himself flogged by personable young men who are only turning
an honest penny in the interim of caring for their families
and fighting for *la Patrie* — that scene appears heroically
comic, almost like some adventure of Falstaff or Don
Quixote, compared to the mean ironies that beat upon Humbert Humbert through the long night, while a religious convention is in progress in the hotel, and the corridors
creak and the toilets groan familiarly, and Lolita refuses
to give up her restless spirit to sleep.

Their historic night at the Enchanted Hunters is an
initiation into the impostures and discomfitures of the
motel-hopping life that awaits them. '"The name," I said
coldly [to the the room clerk], "is not Humbert, and not
Humbug, but Herbert, I mean Humbert, and any room will do,
just put in a cot for my little daughter. She is ten and
very tired."' Humbert's guilty fears constantly stalk him.
An inspector at the state line peers suspiciously into the
car and says, 'Any honey?' Tires go flat with an accusing
plap-plap beneath them. All hostelries seem hostile,

whether they are merely called the Kumfy Kabins or are elaborate affairs with notices on the wall that read:

*We wish you to feel at home while here. All equipment was
carefully checked upon your arrival. Your license number
is on record here. Use hot water sparingly. We reserve
the right to eject without notice any objectionable person.
Do not throw waste material of ANY kind in the toilet bowl.
Thank you. Call again. The Management. P.S. We consider
our guests the Finest People in the World.*

In the course of this insane journey, Humbert undergoes
a reversal of roles and in so doing registers more and more
sharply the real horror and the real significance of his
partnership with Lolita. He first impersonated her father
in order to elude the authorities, but in time he comes to
feel more and more like her actual father. Towards the end
he begins to reflect on the whole affair in the spirit of
a parent who has disappointed his child and been disappointed by her in turn. 'I often noticed that, living as we did,
she and I, in a world of total evil, we would become
strangely embarrassed whenever I tried to discuss anything
she and an older friend, she and a parent, she and a real
healthy sweetheart ... might have discussed.... She would
mail her invulnerability in trite brashness and boredom,
whereas I, using for my desperately detached comments an
artificial tone of voice that set my own last teeth on
edge, provoked my audience to such outbursts of rudeness
as made any further conversation impossible, oh, my poor,
bruised child.'
Humbert's remorse is more effective for not clothing
itself in abstractly moral terms. He feels, not that he has
betrayed a 'trust' of the kind that traditionally inheres
in parenthood, but that he has horribly let Lolita down as
lover, friend, and fellow human being, as well as in his
capacity as father. The consequence has been a complete
sundering of human relations with her. Lolita herself, we
learn at their last meeting, has not been destroyed; indeed, she has exhibited the strange capacity of the young
to survive the worst abuses (other things being equal).
Nor is any forgiveness of him on her part in question at
this final meeting. Her career with him, so painfully
vivid in his own memory, has for her fallen into place in
a world of experience which she views as 'just one gag
after another.' If she originally called him Dad in bitter
irony, she now calls him Dad in sad earnest. But she
doesn't mean anything by it, any real affection, and it's
too late anyway. His betrayal, not of a trust but of her,
has done its work. For of course he did betray her unspeak-

ably. It did not constitute any justification of Humbert
that she was his willing mistress at first and already knew
the ropes. On the contrary this only deepened and complicated his guilt. Outright rape would conceivably have
counted for less than this queasy collusion, especially
considering the orphaned state of Lolita, to whom he was
after all her only excuse for a parent.

In all this, the distorting mirrors have been contin-
uously at work, giving back a monstrous picture of what
is again, like the grim sexual comedy of the Charlotte
episode, a desperately common experience. The perverse
partnership of Humbert and Lolita reflects some of the
painful comedy of family relations in general. There is,
on Lolita's side, the recurrent childhood feeling of being
misunderstood, abused, betrayed by one's parents until at
last — if one is lucky enough to grow up to that stage —
one can accept them as part of the gag that life is, or
even love them if one is luckier than Lolita. From Humbert's point of view, which is the predominating one, the
situation is even more complicated, in fact, quite hopeless.
He is the parent who sadly suspects that communication has
broken down between himself and his child. Instead of
conversation there is only a weary compulsive banter. Mutual
trust is replaced by a shameful system of bargains and
bribes: the 'normal' man's form of collusion with his
child. Desiring an affectionate and willing compliance
with his wishes, he is fortunate if he can purchase a temporary docility with gifts of money, clothes, or chocolate
sundaes. In his own eyes he becomes a mere purveyor of
such material favors, and day after day he pays the,too
large bills at the endless motels of life. All the time,
his suffering over the failure of love in his child is enhanced by his suspicion that it is all his fault. While
trying to count up the blessings he has bestowed on her he
remembers, as he fears that *she* remembers, only his acts
of cruelty or indifference. He attempts now and then to
repair the damage, restore communications. But he is
quickly rebuffed in some unexpected way which confirms his
original fears. '"A penny for your thoughts," I said, and
she stretched out her palm at once.' Those inaccessible
thoughts, that outstretched palm! Such are the cares of
a family man.

Considering the weird shapes of sexuality that 'Lolita'
assumes, the novel might appear to invite Freudian interpretations of the usual kind. Fathers want to sleep with
their daughters, daughters with their fathers. The reverse of any such intention is the burden of 'Lolita.'
By parading the theme of incest, with drums and banners,
Mr. Nabokov makes it ridicule itself out of existence so

far as 'Lolita' is concerned; and the same holds for the
other evidences of popular Freudianism with which the tale
is strewn. 'Lolita,' far from being mythic, is anti-mythic
in this respect. Mr. Nabokov cultivates the groans and
guffaws of the recalcitrant fact, the embarrassment that
yields to neither myth nor clinic, the bitter commonplaces
of life's indestructible surface.

To say this, however, is to take 'Lolita' at its best.
The novel has its less than superlative moments, when the
ribald fantastication gives way to a thin facetiousness or
a pastiche of Joyce. In confessional novels of the intensity of 'Lolita,' moreover, there is frequently a dis-
quieting note of unresolved tension. It is present even in
the great narratives of this character by Constant and
Proust. The hero of such self-scrutinizing novels is both
the culprit and the judge, an unlikely situation, and he
must strain and strain to persuade us that he is at once
bad enough to sin and good enough to repent. Humbert's
'world of total evil' seems out of character, or at least
in conflict with his idiom. It is the author intervening
on Humbert's behalf and playing the role straight in order
to make a vital point. So, too, with Humbert's belated
love cries for his Lolita, which seem to be dictated by
some principle of compensation and ring a little false (to
me). 'I was a pentapod monster, but I loved you. I was
despicable and brutal and turpid, and everything, *mais je
t'aimais, je t'aimais!*' 'Lolita' is partly a masterpiece
of grotesque comedy, partly an unsubdued wilderness where
the wolf howls — a real wolf howling for a real Red Riding
Hood.

15.   HOWARD NEMEROV IN 'KENYON REVIEW'

Spring 1957, 320-1

Howard Nemerov (born 1920) is an American poet, critic,
novelist and short-story writer. His 'Collected Poems'
were published in 1977. For another extract from this
review, see p. 109.

Nabokov's own artistic concern, here as elsewhere, I should
say, has no more to do with morality than with sex; with

either or both only incidentally, as problem, as offering
poignant particular illuminations of what it is to live.
His subject is always the inner insanity and how it may
oddly match or fail to match the outer absurdity, and this
problem he sees as susceptible only of *artistic* solutions.
He may well be the accountant of the universe — in My Poor
Pnin, the narrator recalls a speck of dust extracted from
his eye in 1911: 'I wonder where that speck is now? The
dull, mad fact is that it *does* exist somewhere' — but he
is not its moral accountant, and his double entries seek
only the exact balance between inside and outside, self
and world, in a realm — 'aurochs and angels, the secret
of durable pigments, prophetic sonnets, the refuge of art'
— to which morality stands but as a dubious, Euclidean
convenience; that balance is what in the arts is traditionally called *truth*.

'Lolita' is nevertheless a moral work, if by morality
in literature we are to understand the illustration of a
usurious rate of exchange between our naughty desires and
virtuous pains, of the process whereby pleasures become
punishments, or our vices suddenly become recognizable as
identical with our sufferings. In some dream-America,
'Lolita' would make a fine test case for the Producers'
Code, for if Humbert Humbert is a wicked man, and he is,
he gets punished for it in the end. Also in the middle.
And at the beginning.

16. LIONEL TRILLING IN 'ENCOUNTER'

October 1958

Lionel Trilling (1905-75), one of the leading American
critics of his generation, spent most of his teaching
career at Columbia University. His many books include 'The
Liberal Imagination' (1950) and 'Sincerity and Authenticity' (1973).

...This, then, is the story of 'Lolita' and it is indeed
shocking. In a tone which is calculatedly not serious, it
makes a prolonged assault on one of our unquestioned and
unquestionably sexual prohibitions, the sexual inviolability
of girls of a certain age (and compounds the impiousness
with what amounts to incest).

It is all very well for us to remember that Juliet was fourteen when she was betrothed to Paris, and gave herself, with our full approval, to Romeo.   It is all very well for us to find a wry idyllic charm in the story of the Aged David and the little maid Abishag.   And to gravely receive Dante's account of being struck to the heart by an eight-year-old Beatrice.   And to say that distant cultures — H.H. gives a list of them to put his idiosyncrasy in some moral perspective — and hot climates make a difference in ideas of the right age for female sexuality to begin.   All very well for us to have long ago got over our first horror at what Freud told us about the sexuality of children;   and to receive blandly what he has told us about the 'family romance' and its part in the dynamics of the psyche.   All very well for the family and society to take approving note of the little girl's developing sexual charms, to find a sweet comedy in her growing awareness of them and her learning to use them, and for her mother to be open and frank and delighted and ironic over the teacups about the clear signs of the explosive force of her sexual impulse.   We have all become so nicely clear-eyed, so sensibly Coming-of-Age-in-Samoa. But let an adult male seriously think about the girl as a sexual object and all our sensibility is revolted.

The response is not reasoned but visceral.   Within the range of possible heterosexual conduct, this is one of the few prohibitions which still seem to us to be confirmed by nature itself.   Virginity once seemed so confirmed, as did the marital fidelity of women, but they do so no longer.   No novelist would expect us to respond with any moral intensity to his representing an unmarried girl having a sexual experience, whether in love or curiosity;   the infidelity of a wife may perhaps be a little more interesting, but not much.   The most serious response the novelist would expect from us is that we should 'understand,' which he would count on us to do automatically.

But our response to the situation that Mr. Nabokov presents to us is that of shock.   And we find ourselves the more shocked when we realise that, in the course of reading the novel, we have come virtually to condone the violation it presents.   Charles Dickens, by no means a naive man, was once required to meet a young woman who had lived for some years with a man out of wedlock;   he was dreadfully agitated at the prospect, and when he met the girl he was appalled to discover that he was not confronting a piece of depravity but a principled, attractive young person, virtually a lady.   It was a terrible blow to the certitude of his moral feelings.   That we may experience the same loss of certitude about the sexual behaviour that

'Lolita' describes is perhaps suggested by the tone of my
summary of the story — I was plainly not able to muster
up the note of moral outrage. And it is likely that any
reader of 'Lolita' will discover that he comes to see the
situation as less and less abstract and moral and horrible,
and more and more as human and 'understandable.' Less
and less, indeed, do we see a *situation*; what we become
aware of is people. Humbert is perfectly willing to say
that he is a monster; no doubt he is, but we find ourselves less and less eager to say so. Perhaps his depravity is the easier to accept when we learn that he deals
with a Lolita who is not innocent, and who seems to have
very few emotions to be violated; and I suppose we naturally incline to be lenient towards a rapist — legally and
by intention H.H. is that — who eventually feels a death-
less devotion to his victim!

But we have only to let the immediate influence of the
book diminish a little with time, we have only to free
ourselves from the rationalising effect of H.H.'s obsessive passion, we have only to move back into the real
world where twelve-year-olds are being bored by Social
Studies and plagued by orthodonture, to feel again the
outrage at the violation of the sexual prohibition. And
to feel this the more because we have been seduced into
conniving in the violation, because we have permitted our
fantasies to accept what we know to be revolting.

What, we must ask, is Mr. Nabokov's purpose in making
this occasion for outrage?

I have indicated that his purpose cannot be explained
by any interest in the 'psychological' aspects of the story;
he has none whatever. His novel is as far as possible from
being a 'study of' the emotions it presents. The malice
which H.H. bears to psychiatry is quite Mr. Nabokov's own;
for author, as for character, psychiatric concepts are
merely occasions for naughty irreverence. Psychiatry and
the world may join in giving scientific or ugly names to
Humbert's sexual idiosyncrasy; the novel treats of it as
a condition of love like another.

And we can be sure that Mr. Nabokov has not committed
himself to moral subversion. He is not concerned to bring
about a sexual revolution which will make paedophilia a
rational and respectable form of heterosexuality. Humbert's 'ferocity and jocularity,' what we might call his
moral facetiousness reaching the point of anarchic silli-
ness, make the pervasive tone of the narrative, and that
tone does have its curious influence upon us, as does the
absoluteness of Humbert's passional obsession. Yet any
anarchic power to which we may respond in the novel is
quite negated when, near the end of the history, H.H. re-

flects, in a tone never used before, on the havoc he has
made of Lolita's life.

It is of course possible that Mr. Nabokov wanted to
shock us merely for shocking's sake, that he had in mind
the intention of what might be called general satire, the
purpose of which is to make us uneasy with ourselves,
less sure of our moral simplicity than we have been: this
he brings about by contriving the effect I have described,
of leading us to become quite at ease with a sexual situation that should outrage us and then facing us with our
facilely-given acquiescence.

And then of course Mr. Nabokov may be intending a more
particular satire, upon the peculiar sexual hypocrisy of
American life. I have in mind the perpetual publicity we
give to sexuality, the unending invitation made by our
popular art and advertising to sexual awareness, competence,
and competition. To what end is a girl-child taught from
her earliest years to consider the brightness and fragrance
of her hair, and the shape of her body, and her look of
readiness for adventure? Why, what other end than that
she shall some day be a really capable air-line hostess?
Or that she shall have the shining self-respect which, as
we know, underlies all true virtue and efficiency? Or
that her husband and her children shall not be ashamed of
her, but, on the contrary, proud to claim her as their own?
So say the headmistresses, the principals, the deans of
women, the parents. But in every other culture that Mr.
Nabokov is aware of, which is a good many, the arts of the
boudoir were understood to point to the bed, and if they
were taught early, they were understood to point to the
bed early.

But I think that the real reason why Mr. Nabokov chose
his outrageous subject matter is that he wanted to write
a story about love.

'Lolita' is about love. Perhaps I shall be better understood if I put the statement in this form: 'Lolita' is
not about sex, but about love. Almost every page sets
forth some explicit erotic emotion or some overt erotic
action and still it is not about sex. It is about love.

This makes it unique in my experience of contemporary
novels. If our fiction gives accurate testimony, love has
disappeared from the western world, just as Denis de Rougemont said it should. The contemporary novel can tell us
about sex, and about sexual communion, and about mutuality,
and about the strong fine relationships that grow up between men and women; and it can tell us about marriage.
But about love, which was once one of its chief preoccupations, it can tell us nothing at all.

My having mentioned Denis de Rougemont and his curious, belated, supererogatory onslaught on love will indicate that I have in mind what I seem to remember he calls passion-love, a kind of love with which European litera-ture has dealt since time immemorial but with especial intensity since the Arthurian romances and the code of courtly love. Passion-love was a mode of feeling not available to everyone — the authorities on the subject restricted it to the aristocracy — but it was always of the greatest interest to almost everyone who was at all interested in the feelings, and it had a continuing in-fluence on other kinds of love and on the literary con-ventions through which love was represented.

The essential condition of this kind of love was that it had nothing to do with marriage and could not possibly exist in marriage. Andreas Capellanus in his manual on courtly love set it down as perfectly obvious doctrine that a husband and wife cannot be lovers. The reason was that theirs was a practical and contractual relationship, hav-ing reference to estates and progeny. It was not a relation of the heart and the inclination, and the situation of the lady made it impossible for her to give herself in free-will because it was expected that she give herself in obedience. That the possibility of love could exist only apart from and more or less in opposition to marriage has been, by and large, the traditional supposition of the European upper classes, which have placed most of their expectations of erotic pleasure outside of marriage.

It was surely one of the most interesting and important of cultural revisions when the middle classes, which had been quite specifically excluded from the pleasure and dig-nity of love (one cannot be both busy and a lover), began to appropriate the prestige of this mode of feeling and to change it in the process of adopting it. For they assi-milated it to marriage itself, and required of married love that it have the high brilliance and significance of passion-love. Something of that expectation still per-sists — it is still the love-poetry and the love-music and the love-dramas of passion-love in its later forms that shape our notions of what the erotic experience can be in intensity, in variety, in grace.

But inevitably the sexual revolution of our time brought the relationship between marriage and passion-love to a virtual end. Perhaps all that the two now have in common is the belief that the lovers must freely choose each other and that their choice has the highest sanctions and must not be interfered with. Apart from this, every as-pect of the new relationship is a denial of the old ideal of love. If one can rely on the evidence of fiction to

discover the modern idea of the right relation between a
man and a woman, it would probably begin with a sexual
meeting, more or less tentative or experimental, and go on
to sexual communion, after which marriage would take place.
There would follow a period in which husband and wife
would each make an effort to get rid of their *merely
symbolic* feelings for the other *partner* in the marriage
and to learn to see each other *without illusion* and as
they are *in reality*. To do this is the sign of *maturity*.
It enables husband and wife to *build a life together*. In
the *mutuality* and *warmth* of their *togetherness* the children
are included. Towards each other, as towards their children, they show *tolerance* and *understanding*, which they
find it easier to do if they have a *good sexual relationship*.

The condition towards which such a marriage aspires is
health — a marriage is praised by being called a *healthy*
marriage. This will suggest how far the modern ideal of
love is from passion-love. The literal meaning of the
word *passion* will indicate the distance. Nowadays we use
the word chiefly to mean an intense feeling, forgetting
the old distinction between a passion and an emotion, the
former being an emotion before which we are helpless,
which we have to *suffer*, in whose grip we are *passive*. The
passion-lover was a sick man, a *patient*. It was the convention for hims to say that he was sick and to make a show
of his physical and mental derangement. And indeed by any
modern standard of emotional health what he was expected to
display in the way of obsessional conduct and masochism
would make his condition deserve some sort of pretty grave
name. His passion filled his whole mind to the exclusion
of everything else;   he submitted himself to his *mistress* as
her *servant*, even her *slave*, he gloried in her *power* over
him and expected that she would make him suffer, that she
would be *cruel*.

Obviously I am dealing with a convention of literature,
not describing the actual relationship between men and
women. But it was a convention of a peculiar explicitness
and force and it exerted an influence upon the management
of the emotions down through the 19th century. At that
time, it may be observed, the creative genius took over
some of the characteristics of the lover: his obsessive-
ness, his masochism, his noble subservience to an ideal,
and his antagonism to the social conventions, his propensity for making a scandal.

For scandal was of the essence of passion-love, which
not only inverted the marital relationship of men and
women but subverted marriage itself. It could also sub-
vert a man's social responsibility, his honour. In either
case, a scandal resulted, the extent of which measured the

force of the love. Typically it led to disaster for the
lovers, to death. For one aspect of the pathology of love
was that it made of no account certain established judgments, denying the reality and the good of much in the
world that is indeed real and good. In this respect
lovers were conceived of much as we conceive of the artist —
that is, as captivated by a reality and a good that are not
of the ordinary world.

Now it may well be that all this is absurd, and really and
truly a kind of pathology, and that we are much the better
for being quite done with it, and that our contemporary
love-ideal of a firm, tolerant, humorous, wry, happy marriage is a great advance from it. The world seems to be
agreed that this is so — the evidence is to be found in
a wide range of testimony from the most elementary fiction
and the simplest handbook of marriage up to psychoanalysis
and the works of D.H. Lawrence, for whom 'love' was ana-
thema. But the old ideal, as I have said, still has its
charm for us — we still understand it in some degree;
it still speaks to us of an intensity and grace of erotic
emotion and behaviour that we do not want to admit is
entirely beyond our reach.

   If a novelist wanted, for whatever strange reason, to
write a novel about the old kind of love, how would he go
about it? How would he find or contrive the elements that
make love possible?

   For example, if love requires scandal, what could the
novelist count on to constitute a scandal? Surely not —
as I have already suggested — adultery. The very word is
archaic; we recognise the possibility of its use only in
law or in the past. Marital infidelity is not thought of
as necessarily destructive of marriage, and, indeed, the
word *unfaithful*, which once had so terrible a charge of
meaning, begins to sound quaint, seeming to be inappropriate to our modern code. A few years ago William Bar-
rett asked, à *propos* the effect of 'Othello' on a modern
audience, whether anyone nowadays could really comprehend
and be interested in the spectacle of Othello's jealousy.
I think that both comprehension and interest are possible.
There are more than enough of the old feelings still left —
nothing is ever thrown out of the attic of the mind — to
permit us to understand perfectly well what Othello feels.
Here we must be aware of the difference between life and
literature. It is of course not true that people do not
feel sexual jealousy; it is still one of the most intense
of emotions. But they find it ever harder to believe that
they are justified in feeling it, that they do right to
give this emotion any authority. A contemporary writer

would not be able to interest us in a situation like
Othello's because, even if he had proof in his own experience of the actuality of jealousy, he could not give intellectual credence, or expect his readers to give it, to
an emotion which in Shakespeare was visceral, questionable,
of absolute authority.

But the breaking of the taboo about the sexual unavail-
ability of very young girls has for us something of the
force that a wife's infidelity had for Shakespeare. H.H.'s
relation with Lolita defies society as scandalously as did
Tristan's relation with Iseult, or Vronsky's with Anna. It
puts the lovers, as lovers in literature must be put, beyond the pale of society.

Then the novelist, if he is to maintain the right conditions for a story of passion-love, must see to it that
his lovers do not approach the condition of marriage.
That is, their behaviour to each other must not be touched
by practicality, their virtues must not be of a kind that
acknowledges the claims of the world. As soon as mutuality
comes in, and common interests, and co-operation, and
tolerance, and a concern for each other's welfare or prestige in the world, the ethos of the family, or marriage,
has asserted itself and they lose their status of lovers.
Their behaviour to each other must be precisely not what
we call 'mature' — they must see each other and the world
with the imperious absolutism of children. So that a man
in the grip of an obsessional lust and a girl of twelve
make the ideal couple for a story about love written in
our time. At least at the beginning of his love for
Lolita there are no practical moral considerations, no
practical personal considerations, that qualify H.H.'s
behaviour. As for Lolita, there is no possibility of her
bringing the relation close to the condition of marriage
because she cannot even imagine the female rôle in marriage.
She remains perpetually the cruel mistress; even after her
lover has won physical possession of her, she withholds the
favour of her feeling, for she has none to give, by reason
of her age, possibly by reason of her temperament.

Then the novelist must pay due attention to making the
lover's obsession believable and not ridiculous. Nowadays
we find it difficult to give credence to the idea that a
man might feel that his reason and his very life depended
on the response to him of a particular woman. Recently I
read 'Liber Amoris' with some graduate students and found
that they had no understanding whatever of Hazlitt's obsessive commitment to Sarah Walker. They could see no
reason why a man could not break the chains of a passion
so unrewarding, so humiliating. I later regretted having
been cross at their stupidity when I found myself doubting

the verisimilitude of Proust's account of the relation of
Swann to Odette. But our doubts are allayed if the obsession can be accounted for by the known fact of a sexual
peculiarity, an avowed aberration. Pathology naturalises
the strange particularity of the lover's preference.

I may seem to have been talking about 'Lolita' as if in
writing it Mr. Nabokov had undertaken a job of emotional
archaeology. This may not be quite fair to Mr. Nabokov's
whole intention, but it does suggest how regressive a book
'Lolita' is, how, although it strikes all the most approved
modern postures and attitudes, it is concerned to restore
a foredone mode of feeling. And in nothing is 'Lolita'
so archaic as in its way of imaging the beloved. We with
our modern latitude in these matters are likely to be amused
by the minor details of his mistress's person that caught
the lover's fancy in the novels of the 19th century — the
expressiveness of the eyes, a certain kind of glance, a
foot, an ankle, a wrist, an ear, a ringlet; with our
modern reader's knowledge of the size and shape of the
heroine's breasts, thighs, belly, and buttocks, these seem
trifling and beside the point. Yet the interest in the
not immediately erotic details of the female person was
not forced on the lover or the novelist by narrow conventions; rather, it was an aspect of the fetishism which
seems to attend passion-love, a sort of synecdoche of desire, in which the part stands for the whole, and even the
glove or the scarf of the beloved has an erotic value. This
is the mode of H.H.'s adoration of Lolita, and against the
background of his sexual greed, which he calls 'ape-like,'
it comes over us as another reason for being shocked, that
in recent fiction no lover has thought of his beloved with
so much tenderness, that no woman has been so charmingly
evoked, in such grace and delicacy, as Lolita; the description of her tennis game, in which even her racket has
an erotic charm, is one of the few examples of rapture in
modern writing.
    It seems to me that it is impossible to miss the *parti
pris* in Mr. Nabokov's archæological undertaking, the impulse to mock and discredit all forms of progressive ra-
tionalism not only because they are stupid in themselves
but because they have brought the madness of love to an end.
But Mr. Nabokov is not partisan to the point of being dis-
honest about the true nature of love. It is H.H., that
mixture of ferocity and jocularity, who reminds us that
'Love seeketh only self to please.... And builds a Hell in
Heaven's despite.' The passages in which Humbert gives
voice to this judgment are not as well done as one might
wish; they stand in an awkward relation to the tone and

device of the book. Yet perhaps for that very reason they
are the more startling and impressive (if we do not read
them in a mood which makes them seem to verge upon the
maudlin).

And in the end H.H. succumbs, and happily, to the dia-
lectic of the history of love. I have represented passion-
love as being the antithesis of marriage and as coming to
an end when the conditions characteristic of marriage impose themselves, by whatever means, upon the lovers. Yet
it is always to marriage that passion-love aspires, unique
marriage, ideal marriage, marriage available to no other
pair, but marriage nonetheless, with all the cramping
vows and habitualness of marriage. And it is just this
that H.H. eventually desires. Mr. Nabokov is, among his
other accomplishments, an eminent entomologist and I shall
leave it to some really rigorous close-reader of fiction
to tell us what an entomological novelist wants us to do
with the fact that *nymph* is the name for the young of an
insect without complete metamorphosis. Probably nothing.
But he is also a scholar of languages and he knows that
nymph is the Greek word for *bride*. He does not impart
this information to us, yet he is at pains, as I have remarked, to put us in mind of the rapturous, tortured marriage of Poe and Virginia, and one of his last meditations
on Lolita is of the constancy she evokes from him despite
the ravages of time having destroyed the old incitements
to lust:

[Trilling quotes a passage from Chapter 29 of the novel,
'There she was with her ruined looks ... still auburn and
almond'.]

I am not sure just how I respond to the moral implication of this passage — I am not sure that with it, as with
other passages in which H.H. speaks of the depth and wild
solemnity of his love and remorse, Mr. Nabokov has not
laid an emotional trap for the reader, that perhaps H.H.'s
last intensities ought not to be received with considerably
more irony than at first they call for. I don't say this
with the least certitude. It may be that Mr. Nabokov really
wants us to believe with entire seriousness that we are
witnessing the culmination of H.H.'s moral evolution. Perhaps he even wants us to believe that his ascent from 'ape-
like' lust to a love which challenges the devils below and
the angels up over the sea to ever dissever his soul from
the soul of the lovely Annabel Lee constitutes the life-cycle
of the erotic instinct. I can, I think, manage to take
seriously a tragic Humbert, but I find myself easier with
Humbert the anti-hero, with Humbert as cousin-german to
Rameau's nephew.

I don't want to put my uneasiness with the tragic Humbert as an objection. Indeed, for me one of the attractions of 'Lolita' is its ambiguity of tone — which is pretty well exemplified in the passage I have quoted — and its ambiguity of intention, its ability to arouse uneasiness, to throw the reader off balance, to require him to change his stance and shift his position and move on. 'Lolita' gives us no chance to settle and sink roots. Perhaps it is the curious moral mobility it urges on us that accounts for its remarkable ability to represent certain aspects of American life.

17.   KINGSLEY AMIS IN 'SPECTATOR'

6 November 1959, 635-6

Kingsley Amis (born 1922) is a novelist, poet and critic, and a frequent reviewer of Nabokov. He achieved success with the publication of his first novel, 'Lucky Jim' (1954). He has edited the 'Oxford Book of Light Verse' (1978).

Few books published in this country since the King James Bible can have set up more eager expectation than 'Lolita,' nor, on the other hand, can any work have been much better known in advance to its potential audience. The interest of this first British issue, indeed, is likely to be less in what the thing is actually like — you and I had already got hold of it somehow, hadn't we? — than in what 'they' will say about it. 'They' in this case covers a far wider spectrum than usual, all the way from the inevitable big-review-plus-leader-plus-interminable-correspondence in the 'Times Literary Supplement' to the stern clashes of personality and taste round the local Boots counter; and somewhere in the middle will come Richard Hoggart, Cassandra, Lord Montgomery, two or three bishops, Dame Edith Sitwell, the chairman of the Bournemouth East Conservative Association, Dr. Bronowski, Professor Ayer, John O'London, Mr. Bevan and every last one of the couple of hundred thousand people in Britain who have, or can scrounge, access to some public medium. It is encouraging to see all this concern for a book of serious literary pretension, even if some of the concern, while serious enough, is not literary

in the way we ordinarily think of it. One would be even
more encouraged if the book in question were not so thoroughly bad in both senses: bad as a work of art, that is, and
morally bad — though certainly not obscene or pornographic.

At that last qualification I suspect I shall lose quite
a number of my readers, even if they are 'Spectator' readers — though I cannot see anything wrong in enjoying the
kind of hot book that so many acquirers of 'Lolita' will
have found to their chagrin that it is not. But I take
it as fairly probable that these are the kind of people who
kept the book at the top of the American best-seller lists
week after week, and who will doubtless do the same or better over here. Perception of this probability, together
with an understandable desire to protect serious literature from the assaults of official and unofficial wowsers,
has had its share in evoking the wild hosannas of praise
for 'Lolita' that have been ringing round the civilised
world. As things are, it is not enough that such a book
should be declared non-obscene in the eyes of any reasonable person; it must be declared great as well if it is
to be quite safe. The issue is further complicated by the
fact that what really offends the wowsers is not just pre-
sumptive obscenity, but this in combination with an insufficiently reverent attitude in sexual matters. Thus in
the case of 'The Philanderer,' an instructive semi-pre-
cedent to that of 'Lolita,' what got the thing into the
courts was the theme of philandering as such, rather than
any corruptive power imaginable as residing in individual
passages and expressions. Actually there can have been
few books of overtly sexual content written out of stronger
moral conviction or in purer terms (or with duller impact).
If only the hero had been properly 'in love,' his bedroom
antics could have been detailed down to the last twitch
without anyone taking much notice.

'Lolita,' accordingly, reaches the British public preceded by a sort of creeping barrage of critical acclaim:
I expect great things from the jacket, which I have not
yet seen. Meanwhile, I note a nine-page appendix in which
thirty-one critics from nine countries fire off their
commendatory salvoes. Only a few of these are content to
assert the mere inoffensiveness of the work; the majority,
from Lord Boothby via Heikki Brotherus in the Finnish
'Soumen Kuvalehti' down to Dorothy Parker, go on to extol
its high moral seriousness and/or (usually and) its outstanding literary merits: distinguished — beauty — beauty
— brilliant — great — major — masterpiece — power —
great — beautiful — beautiful — masterpiece. That ought
to be enough to roll up both flanks of any local bench or
libraries committee of even the highest wowser morale, not

to speak of more elevated powers, and this is fine as far
as it goes. But it would be a pity if all the 'masterpiece' stuff got treated seriously, especially in view
of the critical direction it takes. *Beauty* and *beautiful*
and their synonyms set the tone here, and there is much
talk of *style*. The long battle against style still hangs
in the balance, and a reverse over 'Lolita' could be damaging.

Style, a personal style, a distinguished style, usually
turns out in practice to mean a high idiosyncratic noise-
level in the writing, with plenty of rumble and wow from
imagery, syntax and diction: Donne, Pater, Virginia Woolf.
There is, however, a good deal of nostalgia for style
nowadays among people of oldster age-group or literary
training; it shows in snorting accusations of graceless-
ness levelled against some younger novelists and merges
into the hankering for 'experiment' that still dies hard.
Those interested will have noticed a connection here with
that yearning for uplift, or rich man's Billy Graham, which
masquerades as reasoned antipathy to modern British philosophy. If we have not got Kant or Nietzsche, at least we
have Colin Wilson. And if we have not got Ruskin or Car-
lyle, at least we have Nabokov:

> She adored brilliant water and was a remarkably
> smart diver. Comfortably robed, I would settle down
> in the rich post-meridian shade after my own demure
> dip, and there I would sit, with a dummy book or a bag
> of bonbons, or both, or nothing but my tingling glands,
> and watch her gambol, rubber-capped, bepearled, smoothly
> tanned, as glad as an ad, in her trim-fitted satin
> pants and shirred bra. Pubescent sweetheart! How
> smugly would I marvel that she was mine, mine, mine,
> and revise the recent matitudinal swoon to the moan of
> the mourning doves, and devise the late afternoon one,
> and slitting my sun-speared eyes, compare Lolita to
> whatever other nymphets parsimonious chance collected
> around her for my anthological delectation and judgment;
> and today, putting my hand on my ailing heart, I really
> do not think that any of them ever surpassed her in
> desirability, or if they did, it was so two or three
> times at the most, in a certain light, with certain
> perfumes blended in the air — once in the hopeless
> case of a pale Spanish child, the daughter of a heavy-
> jawed nobleman, and another time — *mais je divague*.

No extract, however, could do justice to the sustained
din of pun, allusion, neologism, alliteration, *cynghanedd,*
apostrophe, parenthesis, rhetorical question. French,

Latin, *anent, perchance, would fain, for the nonce* — here
is style and no mistake. One will be told, of course, that
this is the 'whole point,' that this is the hero, Humbert
Humbert, talking in his own person, not the author, and
that what we are getting is 'characterisation.' All right;
but it seems ill-advised to characterise logomania by
making it talk 120,000 words at us, and a glance at Nabokov's
last novel, 'Pnin,' which is not written in the first person, establishes that this is Nabokov talking (there is non-
stylistic evidence too). The development of this *émigré*'s
euphuism is a likely consequence of Nabokov's having had
to abandon his natural idiom, as he puts it, his 'untram-
melled, rich and infinitely docile Russian tongue for a
second-rate brand of English, devoid of any of those
apparatuses — the baffling mirror, the black velvet backdrop, the implied associations and traditions — which the
native illusionist, frac-tails flying, can magically use
to transcend the heritage in his own way.' This, which
enacts the problem with characteristic tricksy indirection,
also implies its solution as the laborious confection of
equivalent apparatuses in the adoptive language: the whole
farrago of imagery, archaism, etc., which cannot strike
even the most finely tuned foreign ear as it strikes that
of the native English-speaker. The end product sadly
invokes a Charles Atlas muscle-man of language as opposed
to the healthy and useful adult.

We know well enough that every style has a way of in-
filtrating what is being presented, so that, offered as
the vehicle of Humbert's soliloquy, this style is involved
with the entire moral tenor of the book. Thus Humbert is
not only decadently sophisticated and tortuously imaginative and self-regardingly detached, he is also all of
these things as he describes his seduction of the twelve-
year-old Lolita and his long history of cohabitation with
her. All this is arguably Humbert himself, and so is his
account, 'delightfully witty' in implication, of his murder of a rival; but the many totally incidental cruelties
— the bloody car wreck by the roadside that brings into
view the kind of shoe Lolita covets, the wounding of a
squirrel, apparently just for fun — bring the author into
consideration as well, and I really don't care which of them
is being wonderfully mature and devastating when Lolita's
mother (recently Humbert's wife) is run over and killed....

There comes a point where the atrophy of moral sense,
evident throughout this book, finally leads to dullness,
fatuity and unreality. Humbert's 'love' for Lolita is a
matter of the senses, even of the membranes; his moments
of remorse are few, brief and unconvincing; it never
really occurs to him to ask himself just what the hell he

thinks he is up to. There is plenty of self-absorption
around us, heaven knows, but not enough on this scale to
be worth writing about at length, just as the mad are
much less interesting than the sane. And — here again
the author heaves into view — the human circuit of 'Lolita,'
for all its geographical sweep, is suffocatingly narrow: the
murderee is Humbert over again, Humbert's old queer pal is
Humbert and unnecessary, Lolita's mother talks like Humbert,
writes letters in Humbert's style, so does Lolita's girl-
chum — the whole affair is Humbert gleefully meditating
about Lolita, looking up to be ever so European about some
American thing, then gleefully meditating again. There is,
further, an appalling poverty of incident and even of narrative: the central episode of the book, a long illicit
motel-tour round the States, is related in catalogue,
without scenes, as near as possible without the singling-
out of individual occasions; meditation again, an exercise
in the frequentative imperfect tense — there's one you
missed, Nabokov/Humbert boy.

The only success of the book is the portrait of Lolita
herself. I have rarely seen the external ambience of a
character so marvellously realised, and yet there is seldom
more than the necessary undertone of sensuality.... The
pity is that Humbert could not care less about the darkness
of her life at home, and although the teenage vulgarity of
Lolita's behaviour is caught with an equal precision he could
not care less either about what she was really like. She
is a 'portrait' in a very full sense, devotedly watched and
listened to but never conversed with, the object of desire
but never of curiosity. What else did she do in Humbert's
presence but play tennis and eat sundaes and go to bed with
him? What did they talk about? What did they actually get
up to? Apart from a few sentences of elegant hot-book
euphemism — reminding us that the work first saw the light
under the imprint of the Olympia Press, Paris — we are
not even told that. Do not misunderstand me if I say that
one of the troubles with 'Lolita' is that, so far from being
too pornographic, it is not pornographic enough.

As well as *moral* and *beautiful*, the book is also held
to be *funny*, often *devastatingly* so, and *satirical*. As
for the *funny* part, all that registered with me were a
few passages where irritation caused Humbert to drop the
old style-scrambler for a moment and speak in clear. The
satirical thing is a bit better, but it has been rather
foisted on to 'Lolita' as a result of the eagerness of
Americans to hear the worst of themselves. V.S. Pritchett's
comparison with 'The Loved One' is apt in a different way
from that intended: both books score the expected points
with great gusto, neither is nearly as devastating as dozens

of books by Americans, neither is acceptable as a picture
of America. Perhaps only native-born Americans can provide this, which leads one to reflect that Nabokov's tragedy has been his separation from Europe, the source of
his natural subject-matter as well as of his natural language. There is nothing in 'Lolita' as fine as the seven
pages of Colette, a story of his dating from 1948 in which
the germ of 'Lolita' is clearly discernible. Here is the
same little monkey with the long-toed bare feet and the
bruise on her tender skin, inciting the author to a reminis-
cence of 'Carmen' — in 'Lolita' this reappears in the
eerie modernised disguise of a pop song. The Biarritz
world of pre-1914 is evoked with a tender intensity that
none of the Middle West travelogues or Virginia moteliana
can match; and here the hero, being like the heroine ten
years old, allows his love to slip away from him down a
path which Humbert, out of solipsistic brutality, and
Nabokov, out of a deficiency of good sense, denied to
Lolita....

18. WALTER ALLEN IN 'NEW STATESMAN'

7 November 1959, 632

...'Lolita', then, is the record precisely of a 'humiliating, sordid, taciturn love life', told as by a narrator
who knows himself inside out, whose wits, one might even
say whose very moral sense, have been sharpened to razor-
keenness by the compulsion to which he is a victim. Inevitably, character and subject being what they are, there
are two or three passages, of varying length, which some
people might consider obscene. Now that we are allowed
under the Jenkins Act to consider the book 'as a whole',
these surely fall into their proper perspective. The
novel is told with sparkling brilliance. But here one must
distinguish between Nabokov's brilliance and that which is
postulated to Humbert. On Nabokov's part the creation of
Humbert is a feat of impersonation only comparable in our
time, it seems to me, with Joyce Cary's turning himself
into the crotchety, dotty, semi-senile lawyer, Tom Wilcher,
in 'To Be a Pilgrim'. But Humbert's brilliance, the inso-
lent ease with which he manipulates the English language,
is part of his character. It becomes at times almost a
form of exhibitionism, a manic showing-off, which by con-

trast heightens the intensity of the moments of self-discovery, whether realised as perceptions of beauty or as
perceptions of moral truth; as in the almost unbearably
poignant passage towards the end of the novel when Humbert,
after a period of years, confronts Lolita living in a shack
in a small-town slum, a new Lolita, a woman at 17, married and pregnant. It is as though he — and the reader —
are seeing the real Lolita for the first time; all his
defences are down, and in that moment he realises imagi-
natively the full extent of the evil he has done her.

But Humbert's mannered, sophisticated, intellectually
clowning style (and one calls it Humbert's rather than
Nabokov's because comparison with the style of 'Speak,
Memory' and 'Pnin' shows that it is a conscious device on
the author's part) has another function: it is the vehicle
of Humbert's comic perception of American life. The novel
is often very funny indeed, and some aspects of the United
States, the hotels, the motels, the small-town drug stores
and gas stations of the tourist, are caught and exactly
pinned down as never before. At times, Humbert's progress
across the continent reads like learned burlesque of Whitman or, for that matter, Wolfe; at times, the satire nar-
rows down into extraordinarily comic character-studies.
But always it is essentially the satire of a cosmopolitan
European in the presence of a civilisation which even as
he falls in love with it, he finds wildly improbable.

'Pnin'

1957

Written in English; published in New York and London, 1957.

19. HOWARD NEMEROV IN 'KENYON REVIEW'

Spring 1957, 314

The various episodes are charmingly told, by turns funny
and pathetic, sometimes though rarely falling into that
rich, warm humanity so admired by certain book reviewers
and detested by Nabokov, who wrote of Gogol's death that
'the scene is unpleasant and has a human appeal which I
deplore' ('Gogol,' New Directions, 1944). As a novel,
this book looks somewhat accidental, though held together
(if it is) by one pretty device emerging at the finish,
where the first-person narrator appears on the scene to
take Pnin's job and incidentally reveal that most of what
he knows about Pnin is gathered at second hand from people
who impersonate him.

20.   PAMELA HANSFORD JOHNSON IN 'NEW STATESMAN'

21 September 1957, 361

Pamela Hansford Johnson (Rt Hon. Lady Snow) (1912-1981) was
an English novelist and critic.

...Nabokov writes in the tradition of Chekhov, Svevo,
William Gerhardi. Some passages in 'Pnin' are, in fact,
startlingly like passages in those books of Gerhardi's
which plucked a literary nerve thirty years ago, much in
the way that Nabokov's are plucking one now. Both these
men were young in Russia before the Revolution: and it
seems as though that experience has endowed them with a
sadness at the same time nostalgic and facetious. Nabokov's
art — and this is true to some extent of the others I have
just mentioned — is the art which elaborates the causes of
weeping. Here are no great tragedies, unless it is a tragedy for the hero to be too small, too fat, too preposterous for tragedy: but behind every tenderness and
hilarity there is a complexity of sorrow....
   The real virtue of this book is in its sweetness. It
is very funny. It creates a type-hero, in this case The
Eternal Refugee, to stand with (and be much more interesting than) Oblomov — we shall all be recognizing Pnins from
now on. The comic style is catching, and is flattering
to the reader's detective sense — here is Kafka, here is
Proust, here, in the adjectives preceding proper names, is
Joyce. But without the sweetness, this book would be not
much more than a first-class Third Programme comic strip.
As it is, a hero who is at one level absurd is simultaneously endowed with dignity and moral grace. That is a remarkable feat.

21.   KINGSLEY AMIS IN 'SPECTATOR'

27 September 1957, 403

The reading of literary works is an arduous, puzzling business for it may entail the exercise of independent judgment.

No wonder, then, that a sympathetic hearing greets the
writer who lets you know as plainly as possible what his
book is doing and how you are to respond to it. The
works of D.H. Lawrence, for instance, would hardly have
made such an impact without their author's stentorian
conviction that they were uniquely important and truth-
telling, with a rider thrown in to the effect that disagreement on this point was tantamount to an admission of
indulgence in nasty habits. Most readers are only too
eager to take the will for the deed and a novelist has
only himself to blame if insufficiently blatant affirmation of his will results in disappointed bafflement about
his deed.

The above applies not only to books that are supposed
to be profound, but also to those that are supposed to be
funny. The work under review is very very clearly supposed to be funny. The action — various small-scale
misadventures of a White Russian scholar in the American
university world — is a thin trickle between prodigious
banks of whimsical commentary and ejaculatory, parenthesis-
ridden description: on every page there are little fire-
work displays about Pnin's trouble with his radiator, Pnin
under his sunlamp, Pnin's difficulties with English, Pnin
bathing, Pnin learning to drive, Pnin's 'sparse auburn
beard (today only white bristles would sprout if he did not
shave — poor Pnin, poor albino porcupine!).'

Yes, it *must* be funny! And it must be brilliantly
satirical too, by virtue of being set on the campus, and
having professors' wives in it. And it must be rather
profound, somehow, because there are lots of literary and
artistic allusions. And sad, because we aren't allowed
to forget for a moment that Pnin is a permanent exile
from Mother Russia. And, finally, it establishes itself
as belonging to a tradition ... the little man ... innocence ... beset by circumstances, but ... eyes of a child
... tender ... rich humanity ... pathos ... clown....

That this limp, tasteless salad of Joyce, Chaplin, Mary
MacCarthy and of course Nabokov (who should know better)
has had delighted noises made over it by Edmund Wilson,
Randall Jarrell and Graham Greene is a mystery of some dimensions. The last-named whose comment in its entirety
reads: 'It is hilariously funny and of a sadness...' was
presumably overcome by emotion before he could finish.
The Wilson view that Nabokov is 'probably' like Gogol is
also arresting. It just goes to show, doesn't it?

'Invitation to a Beheading'

1959

Originally written in Russian as 'Priglashenie na kazn';
serialized in 'Sovremennye Zapiski' (Paris), 1935-6, and
published in volume form in Paris, 1938. Translated by
Dmitri and Vladimir Nabokov; published in New York, 1959,
and London, 1960.

22. PAUL PICKREL IN 'HARPER'S MAGAZINE'

November 1959, 104, 106

Paul Pickrel (born 1917) is Professor of English at Smith
College, Northampton, Mass. He has published essays, reviews and a novel.

The immense success of 'Lolita' was almost certain to increase interest in the other works of Vladimir Nabokov, and
that interest is now rather generously rewarded with the re-
publication of 'The Real Life of Sebastian Knight', Nabokov's
first novel in English ... and the first translation of a book
by Nabokov from the Russian, 'Invitation to a Beheading'....
   It is unlikely that either book will win anything like
the audience that has responded to 'Lolita,' chiefly because neither has the sexual interest it has, though one
of them, the 'Invitation,' has an engaging nymphet in a
minor role. But in fact neither book has the richness of
invention or the wonderful comedy of 'Lolita.'
   But the books have a fascination beyond the fact that
they illustrate earlier phases of an important writer's

work, at least for anyone who takes the art of fiction
seriously, for they show Nabokov almost as much a theorizer
of fiction as a practitioner. In the 'Invitation' the
young man who is to be beheaded attempts to while away his
time in prison by reading an interminable novel called
'Quercus,' which is written from the point of view of an
oak tree; it tells of all the conversations that take place
under the tree through the centuries, and when nothing
else is happening pads out the interstices with accounts
of various sciences dealing with trees.

Presumably 'Quercus' is exactly the kind of novel that
Nabokov finds unbearable; certainly it is the very opposite of the kind of novel he likes to write. With its
emphasis on external detail, its slow, meticulous, and
mechanical account of the passage of time, its preference
for literal-minded reporting to the imagination's bolder
flights, its tendency to take itself seriously, 'Quercus'
obviously stands for the stolid, well-made book, and
Nabokov's impatience with it recalls Virginia Woolf's
impatience with the novels of Arnold Bennett. Not that
Nabokov and Virginia Woolf have much in common (I cannot
imagine that they would even care to read each other's
books), but they share the opinion that the writing of
fiction requires more than conscientious hard work.

'Invitation to a Beheading' can perhaps be best described as a surrealistic novel. It pays no attention to
any probability except the psychological; the most unlikely events occur — the setting changes itself, when
a man starts undressing he does not stop with his clothes
but takes off his shoulder-blades and ribs and other parts
as well, another man sometimes goes out leaving his beard
and hair behind, etc., etc. Some of this is delightful,
some of it seems simply willful, and a little of it goes
a long way. One difficulty with the book is that a reader
does not always know where the Russian setting leaves off
and the surrealism begins; in older Russian fiction there
are often details that seem to the Western reader surrealistic but probably are not — the character in one of
Turgenev's stories who wears two neckties, for instance,
or the dish of radishes stewed in honey that is served
somewhere in Gogol....

'The Real Life of Sebastian Knight' is much more like
a conventional novel, though it too is a book much concerned with the art of fiction. The Sebastian Knight
of the title was a novelist when he was alive, and in the
course of the book his various novels are described. They
are wonderful books, quite impossible to write, but wildly
inventive, turning the novel form upside down and inside
out in all sorts of unlikely ways.

The narrator of 'The Real Life of Sebastian Knight' ...
has one wonderful interview with his late brother's secre-
tary — one Mr Goodman — who himself has written an account of the 'real' Sebastian Knight. The quotations from
Mr Goodman's book are a masterly take-off on the affecta-
tions of vapid literary biography.

'The Real Life of Sebastian Knight' has wit and style;
the theme of the ambiguity of identity — by this time
not the most original of themes in modern fiction — is
extremely well handled.

23.   JOHN WAIN IN 'NEW REPUBLIC'

21 December 1959, 18-19

John Wain (born 1925) has written novels, short stories,
poetry, criticism, biography and autobiography. He was
Professor of Poetry at Oxford, 1973-78.

...Nabokov has expended a lifetime's devoted effort on
the task of developing and refining an absolutely individual style, which will convey the thousand and one idiosyncratic *nuances* suggested by his imagination; both
in English and (according to Marc Slonim) in Russian, he
has brought this linguistic instrument to the pitch of
utter perfection. And yet it is remarkable that he has
never troubled to develop a style in which ordinary
generalized thought (political opinions, for instance) can
be conveyed. When he modulates from distilled impres-
sions into the ordinary statement of an opinion, his writing
plummets abruptly from the height of felicity into vague-
ness and fumbling....

He has always been a favorite writer of mine, and yet,
when I came to read a number of his books one after another in preparation for this article, I found the experience fatiguing and had to make frequent stops; it was
like exercising one set of muscles while keeping the rest
of my body still. There is too little bread to his in-
tolerable deal of sack. The author's passion for analyzing
the minutiae of sensation and emotion will not allow him
to go in a straight line from A to B. In the midst of an
account of his studies at Cambridge, in those first years

of exile in which he was haunted by the fear of losing
'the only thing I had salvaged from Russia — her language,'
he will break off to describe the exact process of 'drawing'
a coal fire with a sheet of newspaper.

> ...I would heap on more coals and help revive the
> flames by spreading a sheet of 'The London Times'
> over the smoking black jaws of the fireplace, thus
> screening completely its open recess. A humming noise
> would start behind the taut paper, which would acquire
> the smoothness of drum-skin and the beauty of luminous
> parchment. Presently, as the hum turned into a roar,
> an orange-coloured spot would appear in the middle
> of the sheet, and whatever patch of print happened to
> be there (for example, 'The League does not command a
> guinea or a gun,' or '...the revenges that Nemesis has
> had upon Allied hesitation and indecision in Eastern
> and Central Europe...')stood out with ominous clarity —
> until suddenly the orange spot bursts. Then the flam-
> ing sheet, with the whirr of a liberated phoenix, would
> fly up the chimney to join the stars.

It is superb, of course, and to open a book of Nabokov's
and come upon such a passage (as one never fails to do before reading far) is to feel a tingle of delight. But that
tingle, endlessly repeated, becomes a kind of Chinese torture.
I don't, however, want to present a picture of Nabokov,
as a mere aesthetic trifler. He may not be very interested
in opinions, but a strong set of *attitudes* is clearly
visible in his work, and the fatiguing, cloying flavor
of his books is due more to an over-elaborate surface
than to an inner emptiness. In 'real life,' Mr. Nabokov
is a well-known lepidopterist, and he has picked up one
habit from his pets: he cannot fly in a straight line.
A butterfly's purposes are as serious as yours and mine,
but it is condemned to give this impression of frivolity
by the protective wavering of its flight. So with Nabokov.
He cannot, under any circumstances, 'get on.' There are
moments when the most patient reader longs to say to him
(as some-body is supposed to have said to Henry James),
'Cough it up in papa's hand!'
Nothing, I suppose, will change him, and indeed the
idea of so delightful an author's being changed is an
unwelcome one. But, change or not, there is certainly a
development. It is a little hard to be certain without
having read everything he has written, and for this we
must wait until al the Russian novels, published in the
thirties under the name of 'Sirin,' are translated and

reissued, like this one.   But I fancy that when Mr. Nabokov's *oeuvre* can be seen as a whole, the books of his
'American period' will prove to have more substance, less
of a ghost-like quality, than his 'European' work.   For
one thing, America has given Mr. Nabokov a more stable
and workaday life.   Academic society may be artificial,
but it can hardly be as artificial as the life of the
émigré Russian colony in Berlin in the twenties, or the
more dispersed and etiolated version of the same life in
Paris a decade later.   There is, in America, nothing
strange about being an expatriate.   The society is not
yet tightly-woven enough to present a hard, impenetrable
surface to the 'foreigner';   even an Englishman can assimilate, and a cosmopolitan European more easily still.
This means that Mr. Nabokov has now, in middle life,
something definite to write about.   'Lolita,' for example,
has all the fanciful quality of his earlier books, but it
is also a substantial work of social satire.... In the same
way, 'Pnin' (perhaps the most perfect of Nabokov's books)
is not only the funniest of that curious sub-category of
novels dealing with campus life, but also an unforgettable
picture of a profound commentary on racial character: an
old-fashioned liberal Russian patiently building a life
on the alien planet of modern America.   It is not satire;
Pnin is homeless not because America cannot provide homes,
but because for him the very idea of home has vanished —
or rather, he carries the idea wherever he goes, but the
reality to which it corresponds has been destroyed.   That
is why Pnin can be absurd, touching and lovable, while
never ceasing to have genuine grandeur.

From what I have said up to now, a reader unfamiliar
with Nabokov might have the impression of a dreamy, insub-
stantial writer, strong on the psychology of memory, on
the less familiar reaches of the emotional life, and on
certain imponderables such as the confrontation of different temperaments, racial and otherwise.   All this is
true, but there is one strong — indeed, blazing — emotion of a straight-forward, non-refined character that
glows through all Nabokov's work, and that is hatred of
tyranny.   I use the word 'tyranny' rather than some more
20th-Century term such as 'totalitarianism,' because the
quality of Nabokov's feeling here seems to me immemorial,
even archaic;   as an artist (i.e. an individual who will
cease to exist if he abandons his individuality) he hates
the thought of a world in which the individual is denied
the right to live and develop in his own way.   An early
short story, Cloud, Castle, Lake (1937), concerns a mild
and thoughtful little man who is forced by a whimsical
chance to accompany a party of hearty, leather-breeched

tourists on a trip through Rhineland beauty spots;   they
arrive at one particular place where he feels an unearthly
peace and serenity;   he announces his intention of staying
there for ever, but his touring companions will not hear
of it, and drag him away, beating him up at the same
time, just for luck.

'There will be beer at Ewald,' said Schramm in a cares-
sing voice. 'Five hours by train. Hikes. A hunting
lodge. Coal mines. Lots of interesting things.'
    'I shall complain,' wailed Vassili Ivanovich. 'Give
me back my bag. I have the right to remain where I want.
Oh, but this is nothing less than an invitation to a
beheading.'

The phrase forced from Vassili's lips as they drag him
away is like a sign-post pointing backward to the novel,
written three or four years previously. Evidently the
theme is one that haunts Nabokov's imagination, or did
until he exorcised it. 'Invitation to a Beheading' is, on
a first reading, less technically interesting than Nabokov's
later work;   'Sirin' was evidently a devotee of Kafka
(though Nabokov denies that he knew Kafka at the time
of the composition of this work) with whom he had many
imaginative qualities in common. One senses a literary
debt to 'The Trial' and 'The Castle.' But 'Invitation to
a Beheading' is a book that haunts the memory;   it is only
a few weeks since I first read it, but already I am beginning to suspect that it will stay in my mind, with a
rather disconcerting tenacity....

24. UNSIGNED REVIEW, 'TIMES LITERARY SUPPLEMENT'

10 June 1960, 365

...Something of the atmosphere of 'Invitation to a Beheading', with its sense of being involved in a nightmare
that has as yet run only a fraction of its course, remains indissociably linked with Berlin of the 1930s, but
the style of writing throughout is still extremely fresh
and Mr. Nabokov shows in his use of words an inventive
mastery that keeps them always alive, and which also bears
out his claim that in his son he had found a 'marvellously
congenial translator'. Yet somehow in the end 'Invitation

to a Beheading' does not entirely carry conviction.   Is it
because the immediacy of the danger, against which Mr.
Nabokov is warning, is for the moment less apparent, or
that Cincinnatus himself comes out as a rather colour-
less creature, or because there is in Mr. Nabokov's writing
a displeasing element of rather arrogant pretension that
can at times seem simply silly, as when in his preface he
describes his book as 'a violin in a void'? For all that
Mr. Nabokov will undoubtedly find the few readers of whom
he declares himself in search, who, after reading his
book 'will jump up, ruffling their hair'.

25.   BURNS SINGER IN 'ENCOUNTER'

January 1961, 77

Burns Singer (1928-64) was born in New York of British
parents. His 'Collected Poems' was published in 1970.

Utopia has become a bad word. Ever since Kafka introduced us to the unfortunate K., literature has sprouted
a multitude of imaginary societies, each ruled by some
more or less abstract principle and each more hideous
than those which preceded it.
    Vladimir Nabokov evidently had the idea of adding to
this literature of a tortured Utopia when he wrote 'Invitation to a Beheading' in Russian back in the 1930s and
my chief complaint is that he has shirked the opportunity.
By setting the entire novel in the prison where the condemned man awaits his executioner, he obscures the social
background to such an extent that it remains as impenetrable
as Cincinnatus C. is accused of being. He does not even
bother to establish the precise nature of C.'s crime and,
except that in some vague way it has to do with being
human, we are told no more about it. All we can be sure
of is that C. is too ineffectual, too weak and too pusil-
lanimous to be a dangerous revolutionary and this does
give us some slight insight into a régime which feels
that it must break such a butterfly upon a wheel. Then,
too, in the figure of the vulgar, jovial little executioner Mr. Nabokov does create a singularly memorable
grotesque who, if he is taken as a representative of the

outside world, does that world very little credit. C.'s
wife and mother, on the other hand, a stupid trollop and
a shy, nice woman respectively, might belong to any
society and are to be found plentifully in our own. That
their characters should be so little affected by the
totalitarian régime in which they live is a central in-
consistency for which C.'s moaning over his inarticulate-
ness cannot compensate. After having been told about
the dehumanising vigour of the government, it is somewhat
of a disappointment to discover that it has not succeeded
in stamping out any single human vice or pettiness. Nor
even human courage and virtue, for these remain intact in
C.'s mother.

'Laughter in the Dark'

1960

Originally written in Russian as 'Kamera Obskura'; serialized in 'Sovremennye Zapiski' (Paris), 1932-3; published in volume form in Paris, 1932. Translated by W.
Roy as 'Camera Obscura' (London), 1936. Translated by
Vladimir Nabokov as 'Laughter in the Dark' (New York,
1938; reprinted 1950, 1958, 1960, 1961; London, 1961;
etc.).

26. ANTHONY BURGESS IN 'YORKSHIRE POST'

23 March 1961, 4

Anthony Burgess (born 1917) is an English novelist and
critic. His novels include 'A Clockwork Orange' (1962);
among his critical works are studies of Shakespeare and
Joyce.

While awaiting a successor to 'Lolita', we continue to be
fed with odd old bits out of the fridge....
    'Laughter in the Dark' confirms me in the belief that
'Lolita' was one of those rare miraculous fusions: the
subject-matter of a perverse obsession justified an or-
nate lyricism and a feverish concern with detail ('a fancy
prose style', as naughty Humbert calls it).
    In this pre-war work ... we may note occasional grace,
as well as an eye for patches of cloud in a window, the
faint flue on a female spine, but the story is mere

cliché, unredeemed by 'a fancy prose style' into anything
more significant.

A married Berliner ruins his life by taking a mistress —
that's about all.   It's rather a nasty little story, really,
made to seem all the nastier for the live and learned intelligence that glistens through it.   And we don't really
like to think of Nabokov as a nasty writer.

27.   NICHOLAS BLAKE IN 'SUNDAY TELEGRAPH'

2 April 1961, 7

Nicholas Blake was the pseudonym of Cecil Day-Lewis (1904-
72), English poet.   He was Professor of Poetry at Oxford
(1951-6) and Poet Laureate (1968-72).   Under his pseudonym
he published detective stories.

First published just before the war, this reads like a
dummy-run at 'Lolita.'   True, Margot is a few years older
than that heroine when she is picked up by the Berlin
art-expert, Albinus.   But she is the same mischievous,
vulgar, on-the-make type of waif....

'Laughter in the Dark' spares us the excruciating
knickerbocker-glory style of Vladimir Nabokov's most recent
study in infatuation, though addicts are allowed a few
spoonfuls — e.g., 'The fire of this kiss was still around
him like a coloured glory when he returned home.'

Albinus, bumbling, timid, ecstatic, absurd, like a
Thurber dog in love, almost commands our sympathy at
times.   Almost: but Mr. Nabokov's extraordinary talent
for modulating emotional frenzy into farce just at the
moment when it is getting out of hand (a Brechtian alienation?) saves the day.

It also prevents me from taking this novel — funny,
astute, brilliantly constructed and fashionably heartless
though it is — altogether seriously.

28.   UNSIGNED REVIEW, 'TIMES LITERARY SUPPLEMENT'

7 April 1961, 218

To say that Mr Nabokov is the most gifted Russian novelist
now living, while true, is not particularly high praise:
Russian literature, what with one thing and another, has
been on the thin side since the 1920s.   However, since
'Laughter in the Dark', originally written in Russian, is
now before us in the author's own English, it is just possible to consider it as a product of his second, American,
literary career;   and in that case there is a wider field
within which to look for comparisons.
   Why, it may be asked, bother to make comparisons at
all?   Simply in order to enable the reviewer, fresh from
'Laughter in the Dark', to state his conviction that there
is no writer in English today who in sheer literary talent
is Mr. Nabokov's superior: more, that it would be hard
to name his peer.   If he is not what is termed a 'great'
writer, it is for moral reasons: Mr. Nabokov does not
take people seriously enough....
   The story is told swiftly, ruthlessly, with no concessions.   Within a tight frame Mr. Nabokov reveals a
rich diversity of gifts.   Like most good novelists, he is
sparing of landscape;   what he gives of it is masterly:

   It was a bright windy day in mid-April.   On the sunlit
   wall of the opposite house the fast shadow of smoke
   ran sideway from the shadow of a chimney.   The asphalt
   was drying patchily after a recent shower, the damp still
   showing in the form of grotesque black skeletons as if
   painted across the width of the road.

The characters are firmly drawn, above all the three
principals.   Most care has been spent on the inhuman Rex,
a crueller, more brilliant Basil Seal....(1)
   'Laughter in the Dark' is a cruel little masterpiece,
one of those books ('Les Enfants Terribles' is another)(2)
from which nothing could be taken away and to which nothing
could be added without damage done.
   But is Mr. Nabokov quite as cool and as tough as he
obviously would like people to believe?   At times one
experiences (in his words) 'eerie doubts'.   When you come
to think about it, in 'Pnin' he revealed genuinely sympathetic understanding.   Could it be that the mockery of
Albinus in 'Laughter in the Dark' is just part of a pose,
that behind the smart tweed jacket and the silk shirt

beats the heart of a *grand sentimental*? Hardly that. And
yet there is something odd about Mr Nabokov's ruthlessness.
It reminds one, somehow, of the two-edged cruelty of
Pechorin.(3)

Notes

1 Character in Evelyn Waugh's novel 'Black Mischief'
   (1932).
2 Novel by Jean Cocteau, published in 1929.
3 Character in Lermontov's novel 'A Hero of Our Time'.

'Pale Fire'

1962

Written in English; published in New York and London,
1962.

29. MARY McCARTHY IN 'NEW REPUBLIC'

4 June 1962, 21-7

Mary McCarthy (born 1912) is an American novelist, essay-
ist, journalist and reviewer.

'Pale Fire' is a Jack-in-the-box, a Fabergé gem, a clockwork toy, a chess problem, an infernal machine, a trap to
catch reviewers, a cat-and-mouse game, a do-it-yourself
novel. It consists of a 999-line poem of four cantos in
heroic couplets together with an editor's preface, notes,
index, and proof-corrections. When the separate parts
are assembled, according to the manufacturer's directions,
and fitted together with the help of clues and cross-
references, which must be hunted down as in a paper-chase,
a novel on several levels is revealed, and these 'levels'
are not the customary 'levels of meaning' of modernist
criticism but planes in a fictive space, rather like
those houses of memory in medieval mnemonic science,
where words, facts, and numbers were stored till wanted
in various rooms and attics, or like the Houses of astrology into which the heavens are divided.

The poem has been written by a sixty-one-year-old American poet of the homely, deceptively homely, Robert Frost type who teaches at Wordsmith College in New Wye, Appalachia; his name is John Shade, his wife is called Sybil, née Irondell or Swallow; his parents were ornithologists; he and his wife had a fat, plain daughter, Hazel, who killed herself young by drowning in a lake near the campus. Shade's academic 'field' is Pope, and his poem, 'Pale Fire,' is in Pope's heroic measure; in content, it is closer to Wordsworthian pastures — rambling, autobiographical, full of childhood memories, gleanings from Nature, interrogations of the universe: a kind of American 'Prelude.' The commentator is Shade's colleague, a refugee professor from Zembla, a mythical country north of Russia. His name is Charles Kinbote; he lives next door to Shade in a house he has rented from Judge Goldsworth, of the law faculty, absent on sabbatical leave. (If, as the commentator points out, you recombine the syllables of 'Wordsmith' and 'Goldsworth,' you get Goldsmith and Wordsworth, two masters of the heroic couplet.) At the moment of writing, Kinbote has fled Appalachia and is living in a log cabin in a motor court at Cedarn in the Southwest; Shade has been murdered, fortuitously, by a killer calling himself Jack Grey, and Kinbote, with the widow's permission, has taken his manuscript to edit in hiding, far from the machinations of two rival Shadians on the faculty. Kinbote, known on the campus as the Great Beaver, is a bearded vegetarian pederast, who has had bad luck with his youthful 'ping-pong partners'; a lonely philologue and long-standing admirer of the poet (he has translated him into Zemblan), he has the unfortunate habit of 'dropping in' on the Shades, spying on them (they don't draw theirs) with binoculars from a post at a window or in the shrubbery; jealous of Mrs. Shade, he is always available for a game of chess or a 'good ramble' with the tolerant poet, whom he tirelessly entertains with his Zemblan reminiscences. 'I don't see how John and Sybil can stand you,' a faculty wife hisses at him in the grocery store. 'What's more, you are insane.'

That is the plot's ground floor. Then comes the *piano nobile*. Kinbote believes that he has inspired his friend with his tales of his native Zembla, of its exiled king, Charles the beloved, and the Revolution that started in the Glass Works; indeed, he has convinced himself that the poem is *his* poem — the occupational mania of commentators — and cannot be properly understood without his gloss, which narrates Zemblan events paralleling the poet's composition. What at once irresistibly peeps out from Kinbote's notes is that he himself is none other than

Charles the Beloved, disguised in a beaver as an academic;
he escaped from Zembla in a motor boat and flew to America
after a short stay on the Côte d'Azur; an American sym-
pathizer, a trustee of Wordsmith, Mrs. Sylvia O'Donnell,
has found him a post on the language faculty. His col-
leagues (read 'mortal enemies') include — besides burly
Professor Hurley, head of the department and an adherent
of *'engazhay'* literature — Professor C., a literary
Freudian and owner of an ultra-modern villa, a certain
Professor Pnin, and an instructor, Mr. Gerald Emerald, a
young man in a bow tie and green velvet jacket. Meanwhile the Shadows, the Secret Police of Zembla, have hired
a gunman, Jakob Gradus, alias Jacques d'Argus, alias
Jacques Degré, alias Jack Grey, to do away with the royal
exile. Gradus' slow descent on Wordsmith synchronizes,
move by move, with Shade's composition of 'Pale Fire'; the
thug, wearing a brown suit, a trilby, and carrying a
Browning, alights on the campus the day the poem is
finished. In the library he converges with Mr. Gerald
Emerald, who obligingly gives him a lift to Professor
Kinbote's house. There, firing at the king, he kills the
poet; when the police take him, he masks his real purpose
and identity by claiming to be a lunatic escaped from a
local asylum.

This second story, the *piano nobile*, is the 'real'
story as it appears to Kinbote of the events leading to
the poet's death. But the real, real story, the story
underneath, has been transpiring gradually, by degrees,
to the reader. Kinbote is mad. He is a harmless refugee
pedant named Botkin who teaches in the Russian department
and who fancies himself to be the exiled king of Zembla.
This delusion, which he supposes to be his secret, is
known to the poet, who pities him, and to the campus at
large, which does not — the insensate woman in the grocery
store was expressing the general opinion. The killer is
just what he claims to be — Jack Grey, an escaped criminal lunatic, who has been sent to the State Asylum for
the Insane by, precisely, Judge Goldsworth, Botkin's
landlord. It is Judge Goldsworth that the madman intended
to murder, not Botkin, alias Kinbote, alias Charles the
Beloved; the slain poet was the victim of a case of
double mistaken identity (his poem too is murdered by its
editor, who mistakes it for something else). The clue
to Gradus-Grey, moreover, was in Botkin's hands when, early
in the narrative, he leafed through a sentimental album
kept by the judge containing photographs of the killers
he had sent to prison or condemned to death: '...a
strangler's quite ordinary-looking hands, a self-made
widow, the close-set merciless eyes of a homicidal maniac

(somewhat resembling, I admit, the late Jacques d'Argus),
a bright little parricide aged seven...' He got, as it
were, a preview of the coming film — a frequent occur-
rence in this kind of case. Projected onto Zembla, in fact,
are the daily events of the campus. Gradus' boss, Uzum-
rudov, one of the higher Shadows, met on the Riviera in
a green velvet jacket is slowly recognized to be 'little
Mr. Anon.,' alias Gerald Emerald, alias Reginald Emerald,
a teacher of freshman English, who has made advances to
(read in reverse 'had advances made to him by') Professor
Botkin, and who is also the author of a rude anonymous
note suggesting that Professor Botkin has halitosis. The
paranoid political structure called Zembla in Botkin's
exiled fantasy — with its Extremist government and secret
agents — is a transliteration of a pederast's persecu-
tion complex, complicated by the 'normal' conspiracy-mania
of a faculty common room.

But there is in fact a 'Zembla,' behind the Iron Curtain. The real, real story, the plane of ordinary sanity
and common sense, the reader's presumed plane, cannot be
accepted as final. The explanation that Botkin is mad
will totally satisfy only Professors H. and C. and their
consorts, who can put aside 'Pale Fire' as a detective
story, with the reader racing the author to the solution.
'Pale Fire' is not a detective story, though it includes
one. Each plane or level in its shadow box proves to be
a false bottom; there is an infinite perspective regression,
for the book is a book of mirrors.

Shade's poem begins with a very beautiful image, of a
bird that has flown against a window and smashed itself,
mistaking the reflected sky in the glass for the true
azure. 'I was the shadow of the waxwing slain / By the
false azure of the window pane.' This image is followed
by another, still more beautiful and poignant, a picture
of that trick of optics whereby a room at night, when the
shades have not been drawn, is reflected in the dark landscape outside.

> Uncurtaining the night I'd let dark glass
> Hang all the furniture above the grass
> And how delightful when a fall of snow
> Covered my glimpse of lawn and reached up so
> As to make chair and bed exactly stand
> Upon that snow, out in that crystal land!

'That crystal land,' notes the commentator, loony Professor Botkin. 'Perhaps an allusion to Zembla, my dear
country.' On the plane of everyday sanity, he errs. But
on the plane of poetry and magic, he is speaking the simple

truth, for Zembla is Semblance, Appearance, the mirror-
realm, the Looking Glass of Alice. This is the first
clue in the treasure-hunt, pointing the reader to the
dual or punning nature of the whole work's composition.
'Pale Fire', a reflective poem, is also a prism of reflections. Zembla, the land of seeming, now governed by
the Extremists, is the antipodes of Appalachia, in real
homespun democratic America, but it is also the *semblable*,
the twin, as seen in a distorting glass. Semblance becomes resemblance.
    The word Zembla can be found in Pope's 'Essay on Man'
(Epistle 2, v); there it signifies the fabulous extreme
north, the land of the polar star.

> But where the Extreme of Vice was ne'er agreed.
> Ask where's the North? At York, 'tis on the Tweed;
> In Scotland, at the Oroades, and there,
> At Greenland, Zembla, or the Lord knows where;
> No creature owns it in the first degree,
> But thinks his neighbor farther gone than he.

Pope is saying that vice, when you start to look for it,
is always somewhere else — a will-o'-the-wisp. This
somewhere else is Zembla, but it is also next door, at your
neighbor's. Now Botkin is Shade's neighbor and vice versa;
moreover, people who live in glass houses.... Shade has a
vice, the bottle, the festive glass, and Botkin's vice
is that he is an *invert*, *i.e.*, turned upside down, as the
antipodes are, relative to each other. Further, the
reader will notice that the word Extreme, with a capital
(Zemblan Extremists) and the word degree (Gradus is degree in Russian), both occur in these verses, in the neigh-
borhood of Zembla, pre-mirroring 'Pale Fire', as though by
second sight. Reading on, you find (lines 267-268), the
following lines quoted by John Shade in a discarded
variant:

> See the blind beggar dance, the cripple sing,
> The sot a hero, lunatic a king...

The second line is 'Pale Fire' in a nutshell. Pope continues (lines 269-270):

> The starving chemist in his golden views
> Supremely blest, the poet in his muse.

'Supremely Blest' is the title of John Shade's book on
Pope. In this section of the poem, Pope is playing on
the light and shade antithesis and on what an editor calls

the 'pattern of paradoxical attitudes' to which man's dual
nature is subject. The lunatic Botkin incidentally, playing king, *inverts* his name.

To leave Pope momentarily and return to Zembla, there
is an actual Nova Zembla, a group of islands in the Arctic
Ocean, north of Archangel. The name is derived from the
Russian Novaya Zemlya, which means 'new land.' Or *terre
neuve*, Newfoundland, the New World. Therefore Appalachia = Zembla. But since for Pope Zembla was roughly
equal to Greenland, then Zembla must be a green land, an
Arcadia. Arcady is a name often bestowed by Professor
Botkin on New Wye, Appalachia, which also gets the epithet
'green,' and he quotes '*Et in Arcadia ego*,' for Death has
come to Arcady in the shape of Gradus, ex-glazier and killer, the emissary of Zembla on the other side of the world.
Green-jacketed Gerald Emerald gives Death a lift in his
car.

The complementary color to green is red. Zembla has
turned red after the revolution that began in the Glass
Factory. Green and red flash on and off in the narrative
like traffic signals and sometimes reverse their message.
Green appears to be the color of death, and red the color
of life; red is the king's color and green the color of
his enemies. Green is pre-eminently the color of seeming
(the theatrical greenroom), the color, too, of camouflage,
for Nature, being green at least in summer, can hide a
green-clad figure in her verdure. But red is a color that
is dangerous to a wearer who is trying to melt into the
surroundings. The king escapes from his royal prison
wearing a red wool cap and sweater (donned in the dark) and
he is only saved by the fact that forty loyal Karlists,
his supporters, put on red wool caps and sweaters too (red
wool yarn - yarn comes from Latin 'soothsayer' — is protective Russian folk magic) and confuse the Shadows with
a multitude of false kings. Yet when the king arrives
in America he floats down with a green silk parachute
(because he is in disguise?), and his gardener at New
Wye, a Negro whom he calls Balthasar (the black king of
the three Magi), has a green thumb, a red sweater, and is
seen on a green ladder; it is the gardener who saves
the king's life when Gradus, alias Grey, appears.

Now when Alice went through the looking-glass she
entered a chess game as a white pawn. There is surely a
chess game or chess problem in 'Pale Fire,' played on a
board of green and red squares. The poet describes his
residence as 'the frame house between / Goldsworth and
Wordsmith on its square of green'; the Rose Court in the
royal palace in Onhava (Far Away), the Zemblan capital, is
a sectile mosaic with rose petals cut out of red stone

and large thorns cut out of green marble. There is much
stress, in place-descriptions, on framing, and reference
is made to chess problems of 'the solus rex type.' The
royal fugitive may be likened to a lone king running away
on the board. But in problems of the solus rex type, the
king, though outnumbered, is, curiously enough, not always at a disadvantage; for example, a king and two
knights cannot checkmate a lone king — the game is stale-
mated or drawn. All the chess games played by characters
in the story are draws. The plot of the novel ends in a
kind of draw, if not a stalemate. The king's escape from
the castle is doubtless castling.

Chess is the perfect mirror-game, with the pieces
drawn up confronting each other as in a looking-glass;
moreover, castles, knights, and bishops have their twins
as well as their opposite numbers. The piece, by the way,
called the bishop in English, in French is *le fou* or
madman. In the book there are two opposed lunatics at
large: Gradus and Kinbote. The moves made by Gradus
from the Zemblan capital to Wordsmith in New Wye parallel
spatially the moves made in time by the poet toward the
completion of his poem; at the zero hour, there is a con-
vergence of space and time. What is shadowed forth here
may be a game of three-dimensional chess — three simultaneous games played by a pair of chess wizards on three
transparent boards arranged vertically. A framed crystal
land, the depth-echo of the bedroom projected onto the snow.

The moves of Gradus also hint some astrological pro-
gression. The magnum opus of old John Shade is begun
July 1, 1959, at the dead center of the year. The poem
is completed (except for the last line) the day of Gradus'
arrival, July 21, on the cusp between Cancer and Leo.
Botkin arrived at Judge Goldsworth's 'chateau' on February
5, 1959; on Monday, February 16, he was introduced to the
poet at lunch at the Faculty Club; on March 14, he dined
at the Shades', etc. The fateful conjunction of three
planets seems to be indicated, and the old astrological
notion of events on earth mirroring the movements of the
stars in the sky.

The twinning and doubling proliferate; the multiplication of levels refracts a prismatic, opaline light on
Faculty Row. Zembla is not just land but earth — 'Terra
the Fair, an orbicle of jasp,' as John Shade names the
globe; a Zemblan feuilletonist had fancifully dubbed
its capital Uranograd — 'Sky City.' The fate of Charles
the Beloved is a rippling reflection of the fate of Charles
II of England on his travels, of Bonnie Prince Charlie
and of the deposed Shakespearean rulers for whom streets
are named in Onhava — Coriolanus Lane, Timon Alley.

Prospero of 'The Tempest' pops in and out of the commentary,
like a Fata Morgana, to mislead the reader into looking
for 'pale fire' in Shakespeare's swansong. It is not there,
but 'The Tempest' is in 'Pale Fire': Prospero's emerald
isle, called the Ile of Divels, in the New World, Iris and
Juno's peacock, sea caves, the chess game of Ferdinand
and Miranda, Prospero's enchantments, his lost kingdom,
and Caliban, whom he taught language, that supreme miracle
of mirroring.

Nature's imitations of Nature are also evoked — echo,
the mocking-bird perched on a television aerial ('TV's
huge paperclip'), the iridescent eyes of the peacock's
fan, the cicada's emerald case, a poplar tree's rabbit-
foot — all the 'natural shams' of so-called protective
mimicry by which, as Shade says in his poem, 'The reed
becomes a bird, the knobby twig / An inchworm and the
cobra head, a big / Wickedly folded moth.' These disguises are not different from the exiled king's red cap
and sweater (like the markings of a bird) or the impersonation of an actor. Not only Nature's shams but
Nature's freaks dance in and out of the lines: rings
around the moon, rainbows and sun dogs (bright spots of
light, often colored, sometimes seen on the ring of the
solar halo), the heliotrope or sun-turner, which, by a
trick of language, is also the bloodstone, Muscovy glass
(mica), phosphorescence (named for Venus, the Morning
Star), mirages, the roundlet of pale light called the *ignis
fatuus*, fireflies, everything speckled, freckled, curiously
patterned, dappled, quaint (as in Hopkins' poem, Pied
Beauty). The arrowy tracks of the pheasant, the red
heraldic barrings of the Vanessa butterfly, snow crystals.
And the imitation of natural effects in manufactures:
stained glass, paperweights containing snowstorms and
mountain views, glass eyes. Not to mention other curios
like the bull's eye lantern, glass giraffes, Cartesian
devils. Botkin, the bearded urning, is himself a prime
'freak of Nature,' like Humbert. And the freakish puns
of language ('Red Sox win 5/4 on Chapman's Homer'), 'mus-
cat' (a cat-and-mouse game), anagrams, mirror-writing,
such words as versipel. The author loves the ampersand
and dainty diminutives ending in 'let' or 'et' (nymphet).
Rugged John Shade is addicted to 'word-golf,' which he
induces Botkin to play with him. Botkin's best scores
are hate-love in three (late-lave-love), lass-male in
four (last-mast-malt-male), live-dead in five. If you
play word-golf with the title words, you can get pale-hate
in two and fire-love in three. Or pale-love in three and
fire-hate in three.

The misunderstandings of scholarship, cases of mistaken
word-identity, also enchant this dear author. *E.g.*,
'alderwood' and 'alderking' keep cropping up in the gloss
with overtones of northern forest magic. What can an
alderking be, excluding chief or ruler, which would give
king-king, a redundancy? 'Erle' is the German word for
alder, and the alder tree, which grows in wet places, has
the curious property of not rotting under water. Hence
it is a kind of magic tree, very useful for piles sup-
porting bridges. And John Shade, writing of the loss of
his daughter, echoes Goethe's 'The Erl-King.'

Who rides so late in the night and the wind?
It is the writer's grief. It is the wild
March wind. It is the father with his child.

Now the German scholar, Herder, in translating the elf-
king story from the Danish, mistook the word for elf (*elle*)
for the word for alder. So it is not really the alderking
but the elf- or goblin-king, but the word alder touched
by the enchanted word elf becomes enchanted itself and
dangerous. Goethe's erl-king, notes Kinbote, fell in love
with the traveler's little boy. Therefore alderking means
an eerie, dangerous invert found in northern forest-
countries.

Similar sorcerer's tricks are played with the word
stone. The king in his red cap escaping through the
Zemblan mountains is compared to a *Steinmann*, which, as
Kinbote explains, is a pile of stones erected by alpinists
to commemorate an ascent; these stonemen, apparently,
like snowmen, were finished off with a red cap and scarf.
The *Steinmann*, then, becomes a synonym for one of the
king's disguised followers in red cap and sweater (*e.g.*,
Julius Steinmann, Zemblan patriot). But the *Steinmann* has
another meaning, not divulged by Kinbote; it is the *homme
de pierre* or *homme de St. Pierre* of Pushkin's poem about
Don Giovanni, in short the stone statue, the Commendatore
of the opera. Anyone who sups with the stone man, St.
Peter's deputy, will be carried off to hell. The mountain
that the *Steinmann*-king has to cross is wooded by Mandevil
Forest; toward the end of his journey he meets a disguised
figure, Baron Mandevil, man of fashion, catamite, and
Zemblan patriot. Read man-devil, but read also Sir
John Mandeville, medieval impostor and author of a book
of voyages who posed as an English knight (perhaps a chess
move is indicated?). Finally the stone (glancing by glass
houses) is simply the stone thrown into a pool or lake
and starting the tremulous magic of widening ripples that
distort the clear mirroring of the image — as the word

stone itself, cast into the pool of this paragraph has
sent out wavelets in a widening circle.

Lakes — the original mirrors of primeval man — play
an important part in the story. There are three lakes
near the campus, Omega, Ozero, and Zero (Indian names,
notes Botkin, garbled by early settlers); the king sees
his consort, Disa, Duchess of Payn (sadism; theirs was a
'white' marriage) mirrored in an Italian lake. The
poet's daughter was drowned herself in Lake Omega; her
name ('...in lone Glenartney's hazel shade') is taken
from 'The Lady of the Lake.' But a hazel wand is also
a divining-rod, used to find water; in her girlhood, the
poor child, witch Hazel, was a poltergeist.

Trees, lakes, butterflies, stones, peacocks — there is
also the waxwing, the poet's alter ego, which appears in
the first line of the poem (duplicated in the last, un-
written line). If you look up the waxwing in the OED, you
will find that it is 'a passerine bird of the genus
Ampelis, esp. A. garrulus, the Bohemian waxwing. Detached
from the chatterers by Monsieur Vieillot.' The poet, a
Bohemian, is detached from the chatterers of the world.
The waxwing (belonging to the king's party) has red-
tipped quills like sealing wax. Another kind of waxwing
is the Cedar Waxwing. Botkin has fled to Cedarn. The
anagram of Cedarn is nacred.

More suggestively (in the popular sense), the anal
canal or 'back door' or 'porte étroite' is linked with a
secret passage leading by green-carpeted stairs to a green
door (which in turn leads to the greenroom of the Onhava
National Theater), discovered by the king and a boyhood bed-
fellow. It is through this secret passage (made for Iris
Acht, a leading actress) that the king makes his escape
from the castle. Elsewhere a 'throne,' in the child's
sense of 'the toilet,' is identified naughtily with the
king. When gluttonous Gradus arrives in Appalachia, he is
suffering from a severe case of diarrhea, induced by a conflict of 'French' fries, consumed in a Broadway restaurant,
with a genuine French ham sandwich, which he had saved from
his Nice-Paris railway trip. The discharge of his bowels
is horribly paralleled with the discharge of the automatic
pistol he is carrying; he is the modern automatic man. In
discharging the chamber of his pistol he is exercising
what to him is a 'natural' function; earlier the slight
sensory pleasure he will derive from the act of murder is
compared to the pleasure a man gets from squeezing a
blackhead.

This is no giggling, high-pitched, literary camp. The
repetitions, reflections, misprints, and quirks of Nature
are taken as signs of the presence of a pattern, the stamp

or watermark of a god or an intelligence. There is a
web of sense in creation, old John Shade decides — not
text but texture, the warp and woof of coincidence. He
hopes to find 'some kind of correlated pattern in the
game, / Plexed artistry, and something of the same /
Pleasure in it as they who played it found.' The world
is a sportive work of art, a mosaic, an iridescent tissue.
Appearance and 'reality' are interchangeable; all appearance, however deceptive, is real. Indeed it is just this
faculty of deceptiveness (natural mimicry, trompe l'oeil,
imposture), this power of imitation, that provides the
key to Nature's cipher. Nature has 'the artistic temperament'; the galaxies, if scanned, will be an iambic line.

Kinbote and Shade (and the author) agree in a detes-
tation of symbols, except those of typography and, no
doubt, natural science ('H_2O is a symbol for water').
They are believers in signs, pointers, blazes, notches,
clues, all of which point into a forest of associations,
a forest in which other woodmen have left half-obliterated
traces. All genuine works contain pre-cognitions of other
works or reminiscences of them (and the two are the same),
just as the flying lizard already possessed a parachute,
a fold of skin enabling it to glide through the air.

Shade, as an American, is naturally an agnostic, and
Kinbote, a European, is a vague sort of Christian who
speaks of accepting 'God's presence — a faint phosphorescence at first, a pale light in the dimness of bodily
life, and a dazzling radiance after it.' Or, more conces-
sively, 'Somehow Mind is involved as a main factor in the
making of the universe.' This Mind of Kinbote's seems to
express itself most lucidly in dualities, pairs, twins,
puns, couplets, like the plots of Shakespeare's early
comedies. But this is only to be expected if one recalls
that to make a cutout heart or lacy design for Valentine's
Day all a child needs is a scissors and a folded piece of
paper — the fold makes the pattern, which, unfolded,
appears as a miracle. It is the quaint principle of the
butterfly. Similarly, Renaissance artificers used to make
wondrous 'natural' patterns by bisecting a veined stone,
an agate or a carnelian, as you would bisect an orange.
Another kind of magic is the child's trick of putting a
piece of paper on the cover of a school book and shading
it with a pencil; wonderfully, the stamped title, 'Caesar's
Gallic Wars,' emerges, as though embossed, in white letters.
This, upside down, is the principle of the pheasant's
hieroglyph in the snow or the ripple marks on the sand,
to which we cry 'How beautiful!' There is no doubt that
duplication, stamping, printing (children's transfers), is
one of the chief forms of magic, a magic we also see in

Jack Frost's writing on the window, in jet trails in the
sky — an intelligent spirit seems to have signed them.
But it is not only in symmetry and reproduction that the
magic signature of Mind is discerned, but in the very im-
perfections of Nature's work, which appear as guarantees of
authentic, hand-knit manufacture. That is, in those blemishes and freckles and streakings and moles already mentioned that are the sports of creation, and what is a vice
but a mole?

Nabokov's tenderness for human eccentricity, for the
freak, the 'deviate,' is partly the naturalist's taste for
the curious. But his fond, wry compassion for the lone
black piece on the board goes deeper than classificatory
science or the collector's choplicking. Love is the burden
of 'Pale Fire,' love and loss. Love is felt as a kind of
homesickness, that yearning for union described by Plato,
the pining for the other half of a once-whole body, the
straining of the soul's black horse to unite with the
white. The sense of loss in love, of separation (the
room *beyond*, projected onto the snow, the phantom moves
of the chess knight, that deviate piece, *off* the board's
edge onto ghostly squares), binds mortal men in a common
pattern — the elderly couple watching TV in a lighted
room, and the 'queer' neighbor watching *them* from his
window. But it is most poignant in the outsider: the
homely daughter stood up by her date, the refugee, the
'queen,' the bird smashed on the window pane.

Pity is the password, says Shade, in a philosophical
discussion with Kinbote; for the agnostic poet, there
are only two sins, murder and the deliberate infliction
of pain. In the exuberant high spirits, the wild laughter
of the book, there is a cry of pure pain. The compassion
of Nabokov stops violently short of Gradus, that grey,
degraded being, the shadow of a Shade. The modern, mass-
produced, jet-propelled, newspaper-digesting killer is
described with a futy of intimate hatred; he is Death on
the prowl. Unnatural Death is the natural enemy of the
delicate, gauzy ephemerids who are Nabokov's special love.
Kinbote makes an 'anti-Darwinian' aphorism: 'The killer
is *always* his victim's inferior.'

But except for the discussions between the poet and
his neighbor and Kinbote's theological justification of
suicide, the book is quite free of religion — a remarkable achievement for a work that plays on traditional
associations. How was it possible to avoid the Holy
Rood, the Trinity, the Harrowing of Hell, the Resurrac-
tion, etc.? Among the myriads of references, there seem
to be only two of Christian legend: the oblique one to
St. Peter as gatekeeper of Heaven and the chess-jesting

one to the Black King of the Magi. The book is obstinately, adamantly secular. It flies this fact gallantly like
a flag of difference. The author's attitude toward the
mystery of the universe is closer to the old botanist's
wonder than to the modern physicist's mysticism. His
practical morality, like Kant's, seeks to reconcile the
Enlightenment with universal maxims of conduct held as
axioms. Nabokov's pantheism contains Platonic gleams:
Kinbote's 'phosphorescence' recalls the cave myth. Kinbote reverts to this notion when he concedes in his final
remarks that Shade's poem, for all its deficiencies, has
'echoes and wavelets of fire and pale phosphorescent
hints' of the real Zemblan magic. This madman's estimate
is also the author's apologia for his own work, in relation to the fiery Beyond of the pure imagination —
Plato's Empyrean, the sphere of pure light or fire. But
Plato's Empyrean is finished, a celestial storehouse or
vault of models from which the forms of earthly life are
copied. In Nabokov's view (see Shade's couplet, *'Man's
life as commentary to abstruse / Unfinished poem.* Note
for further use'), the celestial Poem itself is incomplete.

I have not been able to find, in Shakespeare or anywhere else, the source of 'pale fire.' In the commentary
there is an account of the poet burning his rejected
drafts in 'the pale fire of the incinerator.' An amusing
sidelight on the question may be provided by the word
ingle, used by Kinbote to mean a catamite or boy favorite,
but which also means blaze, from the Gaelic word for fire.
A Helena Rubinstein product is called Pale Fire. I think
too of the pale fire of opals and of Wordsworth, one of
the patron saints of the grotesquely named Wordsmith
College: 'Life like a dome of many-colored glass / Stains
the pale radiance of eternity.' Whether the visible world
is a prismatic reflection of eternity or vice versa is
perhaps immaterial, like the question of which came first,
the chicken or the egg. In the game of signaling back and
forth with mirrors, which may be man's relation with the
cosmos, there is perhaps no before or after, only distance
— separation — and, across it, the agitated flashing
of the semaphore.

In any case, this centaur-work of Nabokov's, half poem,
half prose, this merman of the deep, is a creation of perfect beauty, symmetry, strangeness, originality, and moral
truth. Pretending to be a curio, it cannot disguise the
fact that it is one of the very great works of art of this
century, the modern novel that everyone thought dead and
that was only playing possum.

30.   DWIGHT MACDONALD IN 'PARTISAN REVIEW'

Summer 1962, 437-42

Dwight Macdonald (born 1906) is an American author, journalist and anthologist.

Except possibly for [Herman Wouk's] 'Youngblood Hawke,' this is the most unreadable novel I've attempted this season. Mr. Nabokov's impenetrability is a negative print of Mr. Wouk's; the latter is not clever enough, but the former is too clever by half. This British locution is, of course, not only philistine but also false: one cannot be too clever any more than one can be too rich or too virtuous, and one of the few racial defects of the English is — or used to be until recent years, when brains have become fashionable everywhere, even in London — that they suspect cleverness per se; thus Stanley Baldwin and Neville Chamberlain were trusted (up to 1940) and Winston Churchill was not, and thus Max Beerbohm, who had one of the clearest and most original minds of his period, was never taken seriously. Still, there is a legitimate complaint against cleverness and that is when it becomes disconnected from meaning, when the virtuoso becomes so proficient at his instrument that his delight in showing off its qualities goes beyond the artistic purposes technique is supposed to serve.
   Mr. Nabokov is a stylistic virtuoso who is all the more remarkable because English is not his native tongue. He is often compared to Conrad, but the comparison is unfair to both writers: to Nabokov because he can sound a greater range of notes; to Conrad because the few he did sound were major. Nabokov is a minor writer, by which I intend no insult; so is Herrick compared to Donne, Austen to Dickens, Gogol to Tolstoy, Frost to Yeats or Eliot. It's a matter of scope rather than quality, and while a writer who successfully tackles large themes is more important than one whose ambitions are more restricted — otherwise there would be no point in the major-minor distinction — a good minor writer is much to be preferred to such writers as Wells, Galsworthy, Bennett and — coming down an octave or two — Mrs. Humphry Ward, to name some failed major writers of a conveniently distant time and place. It is our romantic prejudice in favor of the extensive, indeed of the infinite, with its concomitant nonsense about

'genius,' that leads us to over-value the big push....
There is no need, then, to commiserate Mr. Nabokov
because his successful works to date fall into the minor
category. (Muriel Spark is another modern instance of
the minor key being beautifully played.) He has written
one small masterpiece, 'Lolita,' which combines comedy —
high and low — social satire, feeling, and an exuberance
of mood and language that has rarely been displayed in our
literature since the Elizabethans and Laurence Sterne. He
has also written three other excellent works: the stories
about Mr. Pnin; the little book on Gogol, which is the
best introduction to that marvelous writer I know, since
it is as idiosyncratic as its subject and in much the same
way; and his memoir of his early life, 'Conclusive Evidence,' shimmering with nostalgia and wit.
The reviews I've seen of 'Pale Fire' have been cautious-
ly unfavorable, the caution being due to Mr. Nabokov's
literary reputation — and also to the fact his last book
was a best-seller. They give the misleading impression
that, despite reservations, the book is fun to read, full
of 'Quips and cranks and wanton wiles / Nods and becks and
wreathed smiles.' But it isn't fun. In fact, it is precisely its pervasive archness and whimsicality that puts
one off. Nagged on by professional duty, I did stagger
on to the end, like a sober man trudging through the con-
fetti and festoons of an interminable mardi gras. It
seemed to me high-class doodling like 'Invitation to a
Beheading' and one or two other of Mr. Nabokov's earlier
books, as boring as any exhibition of virtuosity disconnected from feeling and thought — Mr. Cloyne justly com-
plains of the author's 'self-imposed limitations' in both
these departments. I also sensed a perverse bravado, as
if the author, with a superior smile, is saying to the
large public that read 'Lolita': 'So you think I'm a manufacturer of best-sellers? Try *this* on your pianola!' I
must confess I find this attitude, if not its product,
attractive.
'Pale Fire' is in four unequal parts: a poem with that
title supposed to have been written by John Francis Shade,
an eminent and elderly poet who is in residence at an
American university not unlike Cornell, where Mr. Nabokov
taught for some years — the only alive parts of the book
are the satirical glimpses of American academic life —
and a foreword, commentary and index by Charles Kinbote,
a colleague at the same institution....
The raison d'être of the book is the commentary....
The skill with which the author, speaking always through
Kinbote, manages to let these cats out of his capacious
bag without ever damaging the structure of Kinbote's

paranoiac fantasy, this must be admired. But, not I think,
applauded. For the technical exertions he expends on the
project are so obtrusive as to destroy any esthetic pleasure on the reader's part. His chief device, for instance,
is a parody of academic method: Dr. Kinbote's line-by-
line commentary, which is more than five times as long as
the poem, uses the most far-fetched interpretations to
wrench everything into a Zemblan context. High jinks —
but how elaborate can a joke be? Two hundred and twenty-
eight pages is just too much. I am no foe of parody, but
this parody seemed to me almost as boring as its object;
one soon begins to suspect that the parodist has more in
common with the parodee than he will admit, or perhaps
than he is aware of. He, too, enjoys the game and so
what he has produced, in this garrulous commentary ('The
wedding guest here beat his breast / For he heard the
loud bassoon'), is more pastiche than parody. His ingenuity is as much misplaced as that of the Kinbotean pedants
he thinks he is satirizing. He has looked too long into
the abyss and, as Nietzsche warned, the abyss is now looking into *him*....

I was just finishing this review when Mary McCarthy's
lengthy celebration of 'Pale Fire' appeared in the June 4
'New Republic.' I respect greatly her critical acumen,
but in this case I am unable to explain her enthusiasm
except by the hypothesis that she enjoys solving double
crostics more than I do, and in fact that she thinks they
are a form of literature. Her review is five pages long
and is practically all devoted to scholastic detective-
work of the most elaborate kind. Literary criticism —
that is, evaluation — is confined to the final paragraph,
which seems stuck on as if she realized it was necessary
to justify, however briefly, the preceding four and
fourteen-fifteenths pages of exegesis:

> In any case, this centaur-work of Nabokov's, half
> poem, half prose, this merman of the deep, is a crea-
> tion of perfect beauty, symmetry, strangeness, origi-
> nality, and moral truth. Pretending to be a curio, it
> cannot disguise the fact that it is one of the very
> great works of art of this century, the modern novel
> that every one thought dead and that was only playing
> possum.

This seems to me unconvincing. Without quibbling about
'half poem, half prose' when the proportions are rather
one to five — that merman has scales right up to his
neck — I am unable to find either in the book or in Miss
McCarthy's review the referents for her sweeping value

judgments: 'creation of perfect beauty, symmetry, strangeness, originality, and moral truth ... one of the very great
works of art of this century.' Her exegetical effort is a
formidable one — though it is disturbing to find her attri-
buting to Wordsworth the well-known tag from Shelley's
Adonais: 'Life like a dome of many-colored glass / Stains
the white radiance of eternity,' — and also to find her,
as a letter in the 'New Republic' notes, changing 'white'
to 'pale' — she has been speculating on the book's title.
Miss McCarthy couldn't find 'pale fire' in Shakespeare,
though Shade's poem indicates it's there, nor could I. But
Mr. Nabokov in an interview says it is from 'Timon of
Athens,' and so it is; in Act IV, Scene 3: 'The sun's a
thief, and with his great attraction / Robs the vast sea;
the moon's an arrant thief / And her pale fire she snatches
from the sun.' The reference to Kinbote's academic rape
of Shade's poem is, as we say, unmistakable. (The exegetical itch is catching.) But explaining a work of art
is one thing and critically evaluating it is another. I'm
afraid that like the book, Miss McCarthy's review seems to
me an exercise in misplaced ingenuity. I finished it with
the uneasy feeling that she, like Mr. Nabokov, had fallen
into the pit that the pedantic Dr. Kinbote had digged.

31. GEORGE STEINER IN 'REPORTER'

7 July 1962, 42, 44-5

George Steiner (born 1929) has taught at Cambridge and in
the USA, and is now Professor of English and Comparative
Literature at the University of Geneva. His books include
'The Death of Tragedy', 'Language and Silence', 'Extra-
territorial' and 'After Babel'.

...What, then, can one say of this cumbersome *jeu d'esprit*?
There are in it bits of dazzling cleverness. The planes
of narrative conspire against each other cunningly. Are
we to believe what Kinbote says of the poem or of his nervous, brief intimacy with John Shade? Is he, actually,
the hunted ruler of Zembla or, as he suggests in a chic
closing twist, merely a lunatic pursued by another lunatic
'who intends to kill an imaginary king'? The poem itself

has passages of stylish grace, and in the prose annota-
tions there are pages only Nabokov could have written.
Even where he enumerates a list of oddments, the effect
is one of precious but witty sensuality....

At the secret core of the book, moreover, reside a
grief and a protest of utter sincerity. Like most of what
is genuine in Nabokov's achievement, 'Pale Fire' is a
lament for language lost. In the age of the refugee,
many have been exiled from their native tongue. Driven
from Russian to French and from French to English, Nabokov
has produced striking work in all three languages. That
is in itself a miracle. But at the same time, he has sustained the proud, bitter assertion that all of his English
writing, however inventive and accurate, is mere journey-
man's labor compared to what he feels himself capable of
achieving in Russian. The challenge which has mattered to
him, and which has kept the condition of banishment acrid,
is that of Pasternak.

At various points in 'Pale Fire' the note of wry
anguish breaks through:

He suffocates and conjures in two tongues
The nebulae dilating in his lungs.

Which Kinbote annotates by listing a series of paired
languages: 'English and Zemblan, English and Russian,
English and Lettish ... English and Russian, American and
European.' Yet if anyone has made of deprivation a virtue, it is Nabokov.

But neither the acrobatics of a passionate comber of
dictionaries nor the occasional stroke of deep, private
candor can make 'Pale Fire' glow. The fable of vice in
'Lolita' was made endurable, and even moving, by ironic
verve. The pederasty of Dr. Kinbote is rendered with
heavy, vulgar jocosity. His idylls (actual or fancied)
with tight-trousered little boys and green undergraduates
sound like senile parodies of the sinister wit of the late
Humbert Humbert. At times the crudity and lack of imaginative resource are appalling. I toy with the thought
of the scorching contempt D.H. Lawrence would have poured
on the avuncular nastiness of page ... (No, find it for
yourself.)

The book is a pedantic witticism spun out at great
length and solemnity. More than he is aware, Nabokov has
fallen victim to the arcane, cobwebbed self-indulgence of
the academic milieu he so deftly mocks. The muses of
academe may be gray spinsters, but they take sly vengeance
on their detractors. Too much of 'Pale Fire' is *ennuyeux,
langweilig* — a bore.

32.   NIGEL DENNIS IN 'SUNDAY TELEGRAPH'

11 November 1962, 6

Nigel Dennis (born 1912) is an English novelist; his books
include 'Cards of Identity' (1955).

The excellent comedy of this absurd book lies mostly in
the King's madcap struggle to distort the meaning of
words — to 'plant' on an innocent poem a 'translation'
that is entirely outrageous. And by the time the King has
finished his impassioned work, he has created still another
world — a world of pure fantasy put together out of such
things as root-endings, snatches of Danish, echoes of
Proust, glimpses of Nice, hints from 'Hamlet,' and close
observation of butterflies.

'Reality,' says King Charles in a sober moment, 'is
neither the subject nor the object of true art, which
creates its own special reality having nothing to do with
the average "reality" perceived by the communal eye.'

This remark indicates exactly what Mr. Nabokov has done.
'Pale Fire' enjoys the 'special reality' of all absurd
fiction, but this 'special reality' also does a practical
job. It shows what the world looks like when it is brilliantly reflected in a clear but cracked eye. It is the
Bedlamite's retort to the solid citizen who has come to
stare at him.

This means that Mr. Nabokov is not just blowing windy
zephyrs into empty air. He has many passionate hatreds
and delights — such as a loathing of the 'grey men' who
forced him into exile and a profound affection for all
that is natural, unconstrained and exhilarating. His
cracked and bouncing king embodies these passions. He
is an example to us all.

Much of 'Pale Fire' is not only delightful but entirely
comprehensible. The poem with which it opens is a *real*
poem, well written and touching. The poet and his practical, protective wife are absolutely substantial characters, as are the professors and local dignitaries of the
university town in which the book is set.

The very pleasure of the novel rests on the fact that
everything in it is absolutely normal — everything except
the squinting, royal eye that plays on it day and night
through a chink in the curtain.

And it is clear that this eye, along with the whole
plot that it detects, is only the eye of a player king.

Mr. Nabokov's Charles II is like Pirandello's Henry IV —
a madman's vision of himself.

Still, in the end, one must admit that 'Pale Fire' is
not likely to be popular.   It is too full of strange
words, rather too over-written, and hard to get the hang
of.   Many readers will object to the very idea of reading
two copies — one open at the poem, the other at the commentary — and having to have Chambers's Dictionary (the
Pocket Oxford is useless) lying heavily on their laps in
readiness.

33.   ANTHONY BURGESS IN 'YORKSHIRE POST'

15 November 1962, 4

The smut-hogs who honked through the pages of 'Lolita'
after lubricious truffles were, of course, ill-equipped
to raise their raisin eyes and gasmask snouts to take in
the greenery, flowers and butterflies that make that most
delectable novel the literary idyll it is.

Humbert Humbert was crazy for nymphets, but Vladimir
Nabokov is crazy only for literature.   His 'love affair
with the English language' achieves a prolonged consum-
mation in 'Pale Fire'.

George Herbert wrote poems in the shape of wings and
hour-glasses;   Nabokov has written a novel in the shape of
a poem that is flanked by a foreword, a phalanx of notes,
and an index.   One of the wittiest and most fragrant
chunks of writing we have met in 20 years masquerades as
an *apparatus criticus*.

What a wonderful joke, but how *recherché*, how rarefied,
how far removed from the sty and stinking mash of the sex-
pigs....

Some of the satire is uproarious: Nabokov is primarily
a great humorist.   But the real joy of the book is the
joy the author takes in the manipulation of language, the
deliberate naughty perverting of literature, the thrown-
away build-up of Kinbote's eccentric personality, the
modern America that is always, like some loved furry beast
with odd habits, lurking in the Nabokovian background.

Finally, we are reminded that the artist's art is
enough for him;   that subject-matter is as finally irre-
levant to the aesthetic experience as the grit in the
oyster.

34. FRANK KERMODE IN 'NEW STATESMAN'

9 November 1962, 671-2

The age is grown so picked that the toe of the critic
comes so near the heel of the artist, he galls his kibe;
Mary McCarthy's authoritative exegesis of 'Pale Fire'
has been available for awed inspection since September,
whereas the novel itself is only now offered to the public. Although it is still 'unlike any novel you have ever
read', as the publishers say, it does remind one occasionally of Miss McCarthy's article, and one especially
remembers, as one obediently reads back and forth through
the book, her final assertion that it is 'one of the
very great works of art of this century'. This thesis
has been severely blown upon by Dwight Macdonald, who
thinks Miss McCarthy has been caught in a tiresome critic-
trap. One doesn't read novels primarily in order to find
out whose side one's on, but I am clear that Miss McCarthy,
who boldly neglects all her own forcibly expressed doc-
trines on fiction when she writes on 'Pale Fire', is
largely right about detailed interpretation and largely
wrong about the value of the whole work.

'Pale Fire' is got up as an edition of an autobiographical poem by a distinguished old sub-Frostian called
Shade — on the evidence provided, a somewhat uneven per-
former. The man who is editing the poem, in the teeth
of Shade's widow and his friends, is a refugee from Zembla
called Kinbote, or, by other people, Botkin. This crazed
homosexual believes that Shade had really wanted to include in his poem a full account of Zembla, and especially
of the revolution which resulted in the flight of the King,
who is none other than Kinbote himself. The commentary
explains how this Ruritanian romance got submerged in
Shade's poem, and how the assassin dispatched from Zembla
to liquidate Kinbote accidentally killed Shade instead,
just as he was entrusting his poem to the hands of his
Zemblan friend. Hints are dropped to give us the true
story: the murderer is really an escaped criminal lunatic who seeks revenge on the judge who committed him, and
whose house Kinbote has rented; he shoots Shade in mistake for the judge.

This, as Miss McCarthy observes, is only the start of
it. 'Pale Fire' is certainly one of the most complex
novels ever written. Kinbote builds up his fantasy out
of stray bits of associative material. He projects the
events of the campus on to Zembla, the fictive land, the

country of semblance. He suffers, you are allowed to
think, from the sort of verbal disorientation which is
symptomatic of some forms of insanity (an idea used by
Musil for his Clarisse). Thus he deals in all manner of
occult associations, private meanings which shape his
fantasy-world; and these are not merely verbal but also
enter into astrology and colour symbolism. The merest
hint in Shade's poem sets off a train of Zemblanisms, and
what may be inverted is inverted, like a mirror-image and
like Kinbote's name and sexuality. The private and mad
character of his activity is suggested by his failure
to perceive obvious allusions in Shade's poem — he cannot
even understand the title, because his copy of 'Timon of
Athens' is a Zemblan translation.

There is here a fleeting resemblance to Golding's
method in 'Pincher Martin'; but the tone and purpose is
very different. Nabokov, having researched all these
occult interrelations, hands them over to poor old crazy
Botkin to make a world of, but leaves enough Nabokovian
traces on the text to assure us that he's there, sane
and interested. And the big question isn't whether you
can spot all these weird multiple associations, but why
Nabokov should have wanted to make them up — he says he
loathes 'symbolic' novels — and present them to his madman.

To answer it, one would need to look at Nabokov's
whole output, which includes a large element of what
Dwight Macdonald calls 'high-class doodling'. This,
abating the pejorative implication, would indeed do to
describe his whole method. His attention all goes to
the formal aspects of the work; he is fascinated by the
medium. To describe the relation of his fictions to
reality would be an impossible assignment; and this is
one of the points of 'Pale Fire'. In a novel, the facts
need not be true, but their interrelations must be; and
the novelist's world stands in relation to common reality
as Kinbote's commentary stands to Shade's poem. Both are
out of focus, both deliver versions of reality different
from the brute facts. Hence Kinbote's homosexuality, which
is a metaphor for the artist's minority view of a bad
world, of 'our cynical age of frantic heterosexualism'. If
one dared risk a guess at correlative idiosyncrasies in
Nabokov himself, one would have to point to his intellectual disgust with Freudianism or, remembering that he
is a member of the Russian émigré minority, his loathing
of Marxism.

But the main reason why Kinbote serves Nabokov's purpose is that he is obsessed, intoxicated by his text,
exactly, and with the same disinterest, as Humbert Humbert

was obsessed by his girl. Nabokov's novels are usually
concerned with elevated, amoral states of mind comparable
no doubt to that of the author in creating them. One
consequence is that they have the kind of contempt for
realism demonstrated, in the degree of mania, by Kinbote.
On occasion Kinbote describes some royal Zemblan portraits in which the painter, master of *trompe-l'oeil*, has
emphasized his skill by sometimes inserting pieces of
wool, gold or velvet, instead of painting them. This,
says Kinbote, has 'something ignoble about it', and dis-
closes

> the basic fact that 'reality' is neither the subject
> nor the object of true art, which creates its own
> special reality having nothing to do with the average
> 'reality' perceived by the communal eye.

Incidentally, this trick deceives the Russian experts
who tear the palace apart looking for the crown jewels.
No Soviet realism for Nabokov; he is a formalist. And
he repeatedly draws attention to the artifice which constitutes his reality higher than the communal 'reality'.
He has always done so, and Kinbote's whole fantasy is
merely a bold development of this prejudice. His Zemblan
fantasies are a metaphor for the world of fiction.

'Pale Fire', however, includes not only Kinbote's
fantasy but a version of the communal reality as well:
Shade's wife and tragic daughter, Botkin's campus enemies,
the poem which is a rival, saner version of the real.
Thus the author has to show us not only that Kinbote's
activity is the model of his own, but that Kinbote is
justly to be called mad. There ensue many delicate acts
of dissociation, little authorial plots against Kinbote.
For example, he is given certain mannerisms of style
which reflect his sexual interests in a dismally coy
light:

> When stripped and shiny in the mist of the bath house,
> his bold virilia contrasted harshly with his girlish
> grace. He was a regular faunlet.

When Nabokov makes Kinbote speak like this, or otherwise
betrays him, we remember Humbert slipping unwillingly
into compassion when Lolita comes, defeated, to his motel
bedroom.

Yet none of this affects the basic validity of the
metaphor; Kinbote's obsession represents what Nabokov
calls 'aesthetic bliss'.

For me a work of fiction exists only insofar as it
affords me what I shall bluntly call aesthetic bliss,
that is a sense of being somehow, somewhere, connected
with other states of being where art (curiosity, tenderness, kindness, ecstasy) is the norm.

This is the state of being enjoyed by Humbert and Kinbote;
it sets them against the world which prefers men like
machines, supports commonplace dictators like Paduk in
'Bend Sinister', or disgustingly sexless, unextravagant,
mechanical men like Gradus, Kinbote's imaginary assassin,
who is studied throughout the work with fascinated revul-
sion. Yet 'Pale Fire' is, as I've said, technically more
ambitious than 'Lolita', because it renders not merely
isolated bliss but the communal, blissless, 'reality'.
And the occult relations explored by Miss McCarthy reflect
the complicated ties between reality and 'reality', the
artist's vision and the mere facts.
  One instance of this is worth mentioning. Shade is
a Pope scholar, and there are several allusions to 'The
Essay on Man'; this is not a wanton choice of Nabokov's
— though he might he held to have used it wantonly —
because he saw in it a relevant approach to aesthetic
bliss. Shade, meditating an absurd mistake which had
seemed to bring together two dreams of after-life but
depended entirely on a fountain/mountain misprint in a
written report, observes that such near-coincidence is
in a way stronger evidence of 'correlated pattern in the
game' than perfect similarity. 'All Chance, Direction which
thou canst not see' is the line at the back of his mind.
The game metaphor is continued; he thinks of the players,

                          aloof and mute,
    Playing a game of worlds,
                          promoting pawns
    To ivory unicorns and ebon fauns;
    Kindling a long life here, extinguishing
    A short one there; killing a
                          Balkan king...
                          Co-ordinating these
    Events and objects with remote events
    And vanished objects. Making ornaments
    Of accidents and possibilities.

Here Shade is remembering part of Pope's Second Epistle,
and perhaps more extreme statements of an 18th-century
position we know best from Johnson's assault on Jenyns:
disease, madness, sorrow, may be part of some game played
by higher creatures than men. And Nabokov is remembering

that the novelist can, after all, amuse himself by making
a man tumble over in an epilepsy, run mad, or be confounded
by fantastic coincidence. His is the bliss of co-ordi-
nating events and objects with remote events and vanished
objects; he can sit, if he wants to, like the saints
enjoying the torments of the damned.

'Pale Fire' reproduces this divine game and offers
us the pleasures of process as well as of product. But
it is only a kibitzer's pleasure. Nabokov's relationship
with his world is very exclusive; his is the creative
logos, we are, at best, angels privileged to stand by and
applaud. As to those readers who are enslaved to the
communal 'reality', they can expect nothing at all. As
a class, they may be identified as those who thought
'Lolita' was about, not aesthetic bliss, but nympheto-
lepsy. For all such readers the author, engrossed in
the sublime images he has made of his own delight, feels
nothing; or, if anything, contempt.

'The Gift'

1963

Originally written in Russian as 'Dar'; serialized (with
the omission of Chapter 4) in 'Sovremennye Zapiski' (Paris),
1937-8; Russian version published complete in New York,
1952. Translated by Michael Scammell, Dmitri Nabokov and
Vladimir Nabokov and published in New York and London,
1963.

35. STEPHEN SPENDER IN 'NEW YORK TIMES BOOK REVIEW'

26 May 1963, 4-5

Stephen Spender (born 1909), English poet and critic,
has been co-editor of 'Horizon' and 'Encounter'.

This thickly woven, immensely rewarding novel.... This
English version ... has those qualities of freshness
combined with highly original and detailed observation
that make the best Russian books in English seem not so
much translations as a special branch of English literature with a peculiarly strong flavour. For many readers
this novel will be put on their bookshelves beside the
stories of Tolstoy and Chekhov....
    'The Gift' ... is essentially a novel about imaginative
truth: the truth of fiction, and beyond this, the truth
of poetry. What it most reminds me of is a work for
which — I suspect — Nabokov would have little sympathy,
Rilke's 'Notebooks of Malte Laurids Brigge', another novel

woven of reminiscences, dreams, history and introspection.
It also challenges comparison with Joyce's 'Portrait of
the Artist as a Young Man', similarly about a young man's
consciousness of his gift. Nabokov has more irony, humour,
richness of enjoyment, love of real flesh and blood than
Rilke; but in merging the actual with the imagined, he
makes the question of what is real, what unreal, fundamentally an aesthetic one, whereas Joyce, with his Jesuit
philosophic training, avoided this identification of different kinds of truth. In 'The Gift', Nabokov steers
clear of the ghastly spiritual self-indulgence of Rilke,
but he does not altogether avoid whimsy.

Nabokov is a writer of genius who is digressive, wayward and an imperfect artist. His books, though written
with immense care, do not seem architecturally planned.
What one values in 'The Gift' are passages of great power
sustained over many pages — the conversation between the
poets, the account of Fyodor's explorer-father, the memories of a Russian childhood and the descriptions of life
in the German capital which may be set beside those of
Isherwood in his Berlin stories.

36.   DONALD DAVIE IN 'MANCHESTER GUARDIAN'

8 November 1963, 8

Donald Davie (born 1922), English poet and critic, has
taught at the universities of Dublin, Cambridge and Essex
and at Stanford University. His books include 'Purity
of Diction in English Verse' (1952), 'Articulate Energy'
(1957), and studies of Scott, Hardy and Pound. His 'Collected Poems' appeared in 1972.

...'The Gift' seems to me not just brilliant (Nabokov is
always that), but also profound and persuasive, the only
émigré novel to stand beside 'Doctor Zhivago'. (In their
militant aestheticism the two books have much in common.)
As in 'Lolita', Nabokov sets our teeth on edge — but
deliberately, to make a point that could be made so forcibly in no other way. The resolution he effects in his
last chapter is the acceptance by the hero of the Imagist's
world which impinges on the senses, for the case against

the humanitarians is that characteristically, for all
their materialism, they are blind to this world. But
the resolution is also the acceptance, by the Russian
writer, of the place where he finds himself, Berlin.
Russian literature can and will be continued — but it
may be written in other languages than Russian. Nabokov
speaks of 'The Gift' as 'the last novel I wrote, or ever
shall write, in Russian'; and that too is part of what
the novel movingly says about itself.

37. DONALD MALCOLM IN 'NEW YORKER'

25 April 1964, 198, 202-4

Admirers of Vladimir Nabokov are likely to find a reading of 'The Gift' at once rewarding and disconcerting.
Although it is the most recent of his novels to be published in English, the book actually was written in the
middle nineteen-thirties, and in Russian. The translation, we are told in the foreword, has been 'carefully
revised' by the author, and while a monolingual reader
cannot determine the extent of the verbal adjustments, he
may be tempted to guess that they have been considerable.
The ear repeatedly detects the accomplished, the assured,
the very individual English voice of the contemporary Mr.
Nabokov; at the same time, one's literary sense is perpetually reminded that the substance of 'The Gift' belongs
to an earlier period in the author's career. To the susceptible reader, this subtle discrepancy between matter
and tone produces an odd feeling of dislocation in time.
It is almost as if Mr. Nabokov were conducting us upon
a retrospective tour of his literary progress, hustling
us pastward at several hundred words a minute, and pointing out the sources of later achievements, the germs of
subsequent themes. We come upon passages that contain,
all unknowing, whole futures in Nabokovian art. On one
page we discover an episode that is destined to expand
into a component of 'Speak, Memory,' on another we greet
an infant revolver that will commit major execution in
'Lolita,' and on another we discern a suggestion of the
scheme for 'Pale Fire.'
    'The Gift' itself might be described as a prolonged
meditation upon the psychology of art....

[The novel] inflicts, at last, the boredom of surfeit.
In so doing, it obliges one to recognize the fact that
a strong and highly personal literary gift is apt to present itself not as a glib talent to be exploited but as
a difficult literary problem to be solved.   In the instance
of Fyodor Godunov-Cherdyntsev (and of Vladimir Nabokov),
the afflictive gift is an almost preternatural acuity of
the senses — chiefly of vision — coupled with the power
to render each sensation dazzlingly manifest in words.
'A crow will settle on a boulder, settle and straighten
a wing that has folded wrong.' Mr. Nabokov brings down
his crow with a single shot and fixes him forever. But
when each neighboring sentence similarly preserves in
its amber a row of telegraph poles, the slant of a steer-
ing wheel, dust, stillness, a skylark, and a hay wagon,
and when each succeeding paragraph further compounds the
profusion of separate visions, then the reader is likely
to run out of mental accommodations for them all.   The
problem, essentially, is one of proportion and scale.
'The Gift' resembles nothing so much as a mosaic whose
every tile is itself a perfect cameo. There simply is no
proper distance from which to view it. If one relishes
each fragment, the larger patterns are lost. If one
attempts to grasp the picture in its entirety, then one
finds its manifold glimmering components a great hindrance
to the larger vision.

With only 'The Gift' to judge by, a friendly reviewer
might be tempted to urge Mr. Nabokov toward a style of
broader strokes and coarser texture, as being more suited
to the amplitudes of the novel. Such advice, however,
would merely go to demonstrate that writers seldom can
derive much benefit from their critics and ought never to
attend to them. By obstinately pursuing his gift to the
top of his bent, Mr. Nabokov has perfected a variety of
means for turning a troublesome strength to effective
account. 'Lolita,' for example, easily surpasses 'The
Gift' in its wealth of preserved glimpses, and yet
'Lolita' is a triumph of coherent art. In great measure,
this happy difference is owing to the singular power of
this novel's crucial relationship, which — involving,
as it does, the grotesque passion of a grown man for a
child — fairly impels every fragment into alignment.
For Humbert and Lolita exert an influence on their fictional surroundings that borders on the magnetic. At
their mere approach, motels and playgrounds, New England
towns and Western expanses all seem to pivot slightly
and expose an unexpected surface to our scrutiny. Just
as every glimpse of normal American life serves to empha-
size the outrageousness of their affinity, so does that

bizarre affinity impose a new perspective on what passes,
among us, for normality. There is a strength of connection in these reciprocities of meaning which serves to
bond the smallest observation firmly to the body of the
work. Such themes as that of 'Lolita' are not to be found
every day, however, and in 'Pale Fire' Mr. Nabokov strikes
off a more formal solution to the problem of fitting a
multitude of vivid miniatures into a single composition.
Here he frankly offers the reader an intricate puzzle
for solution and thereby induces him to sift and sort, to
juggle and fit each vivid fragment into its proper place,
in order to view the final portrait whole. The brief,
bright visions of 'Pale Fire,' which are embedded in the
scholarly and totally insane notes of the narrator, serve
the purpose that is more coarsely served in the ordinary
detective story by hidden clues and extravagant decep-
tions. Once the reader's interest is engaged by them, he
is willing to riffle pages forward and back, pursue connections, and generally expend the intellectual effort
necessary to solve the mystery and to bind the disparate
elements into literary unity. For those readers who de-
cline to make the mental effort, it remains — if one
may judge by reviews of the novel — a mere aggravating
jumble of components.

It is worth observing that the protagonists of both
these later works are monsters, one being a nympholept
and the other a melancholy, mad old pederast. The value
of narrator-monsters to a writer of Mr. Nabokov's special
gift is evident. They provide a rationale for the longest
stroke of a sportive pen, and in this they enjoy a paradoxical advantage over the poet-narrator of 'The Gift.'
When Godunov-Cherdyntsev puts his sensibility to the
stretch and enlivens his narrative with dialogues that
eventually prove to be entirely imaginary, he is more than
somewhat irritating. One can appreciate his determination
to give words dominion over experience, and yet, at the
pinch, one must resent the liberties he thereby takes with
his reader. He has, one feels, only a sort of *professional*
interest in promoting such excursions. No such resentment
attaches to the verbal extravagances and acrobatics of
Nabokov's madmen, for these reflect an inner, a psychological necessity that is their justification and strength.

'The Defence'

1964

Originally written in Russian as 'Zashchita Luzhina';
serialized in 'Sovremennye Zapiski' (Paris), 1929-30; published in volume form in Berlin, 1930. Translated by
Michael Scammell and Vladimir Nabokov and published in
New York and London, 1964.

38. JOHN UPDIKE IN 'NEW REPUBLIC'

26 September 1964, 15-18

John Updike (born 1932), American author, has published
novels, short stories and poems.

One hesitates to call him an 'American writer'; the
phrase fetches to mind Normal Mailer and James Jones
and other homegrown cabbages loyally mistaken for roses.
Say, rather, that Vladimir Nabokov distinctly seems to be
the best writer of English prose at present holding American citizenship, the only writer, with the possible exception of the long-silent Thornton Wilder, whose books, considered as a whole, give the happy impression of an *oeuvre*,
of a continuous task carried forward seriously, of a solid
personality, of a plenitude of gifts exploited knowingly.
His works are an edifice whose every corner rewards inspection. Each book, including the super-slim 'Poems'
and the uproariously pedantic and copious commentaries to
his translation of 'Eugene Onegin', yields delight and

presents to the aesthetic sense the peculiar hardness of
a finished, fully meant thing. His sentences are beautiful out of context and doubly beautiful in it. He writes
prose the only way it should be written — that is,
ecstatically. In the intensity of its intelligence and
reflective irony, his fiction is unique in this decade
and scarcely precedented in American literature. Melville
and James do not, oddly, offer themselves for comparison.
Yet our literature, that scraggly association of hermits,
cranks, and exiles, is strange enough to include this
arrogant immigrant; as an expatriate Nabokov is squarely
in the native tradition. Very curiously, his *oeuvre* is
growing at both ends. At one end, the end pointed toward
the future, are the works composed in English, beginning
with the gentlest of his novels, 'The Real Life of Sebastian Knight', and terminating, for the time being, in
his — the word must be — monumental translation of
'Onegin,' a physically gorgeous, sumptuously erudite
gift from one language to another; it is pleasant to
think of Nabokov laboring in the libraries of his adopted
land, the libraries fondly described in 'Pnin,' laboring
with Janus-faced patriotism on the filigreed guy-wires
and piled buttresses of this bridge whereby the genius
of Pushkin is to cross after him into America. The translation itself, so laconic compared to the footnotes, with
its breathtaking gaps, pages long, of omitted stanzas
whose lines are eerily numbered as if they were there,
ranks with Horace Gregory's Catullus and Richmond Latti-
more's 'Iliad' as superb, quirky, and definitive: a permanent contribution to the demi-art of 'Englishing' and a
final refutation, let's hope, of the fallacy of equivalent
rhyme. In retrospect, Nabokov's more recent novels —
obviously 'Pale Fire' but there are also Humbert Humbert's
mysterious 'scholarly exertions' on a 'manual of French
literature for English-speaking students' — transparently
reveal glimpses of the Pushkinian travail begun in 1950.
 At the other end (an end, as in earthworms, not immediately distinguishable), Nabokov's *oeuvre* is growing
backwards, into the past, as English versions appear of
those novels he wrote in Russian, for a post-Revolutionary
émigré audience concentrated in Paris and Berlin, during
his twenty years of European residence (1919-1940), under
the pen name of 'V. Sirin.' 'The Defence,' originally
'Zashchita Luzhina,' is the latest of these to be translated. In the chronology of his eight Russian novels,
'The Luzhin Defence' (this literal title was used by the
'New Yorker' and seems better, in clearly suggesting a
chess ploy, though the ghosts of 'illusion' and 'losin''
fluttering around the proper name perhaps were worth exor-

cising) comes third, after two untranslated ones and just
before 'Laughter in the Dark.' It is thus the earliest
Nabokov work now available in English. An author's foreword states that it was written in 1929 — that is, when
Nabokov was thirty, which is the age of Luzhin, an ex-
chess prodigy and international grandmaster. Like his
hero, the author seems older; few Americans so young
could write a novel wherein the autobiographical elements
are so cunningly rearranged and transmuted by a fictional
design, and the emotional content so obedient to such
cruelly ingenious commands, and the characterization so
little colored by indignation or the shock of discovery.
On this last point, it needs to be said — so much has
been pointlessly said about Nabokov's 'virtuosity,' as if
he is a verbal magician working with stuffed rabbits and
hats nobody could wear — that Nabokov's characters live.
They 'read' as art students say; their frames are loaded
with bright color and twisted to fit abstract schemes but
remain anatomically credible. The humanity that has come
within Nabokov's rather narrow field of vision has been
illuminated by a guarded but genuine compassion. Two
characters occur to me, randomly and vividly: Charlotte
Haze of 'Lolita,' with her blatant bourgeois Bohemianism,
her cigarettes, her Mexical doodads, her touchingly clumsy
sexuality, her utterly savage and believable war with her
daughter; and Albinus Kretschmar of 'Laughter in the
Dark,' with his doll-like dignity, his bestial softness,
his hobbies, his family feelings, his craven romanticism,
his quaint competence. An American housewife and a German
businessman, both observed, certainly, from well on the
outside, yet animated from well within. How much more,
then, can Nabokov do with characters who are Russian, and
whose concerns circle close to his own aloof passions!

His foreword, shameless and disdainful in his usual
first-person style, specifies, for 'hack reviewers' and
'persons who move their lips when reading,' the forked
appeal of 'this attractive novel' — the intricate immanence in plot and imagery of chess as a prevailing metaphor, and the weird lovableness of the virtually inert
hero. 'Of all my Russian books, "The Defence" contains
and diffuses the greatest "warmth" — which may seem
odd seeing how supremely abstract chess is supposed to
be. In point of fact, Luzhin has been found lovable even
by those who understand nothing about chess and/or detest
all my other books. He is uncouth, unwashed, uncomely —
but as my gentle young lady (a dear girl in her own right)
so quickly notices, there is something in him that transcends ... the coarseness of his gray flesh and the sterility
of his recondite genius.'

What makes characters endearing does not admit of such
analysis: I would divide Luzhin's charm into (a) the
delineation of his childhood (b) the evocation of his
chess prowess. As to (a), Nabokov has always warmed to
the subject of children, precocious children — David Krug,
Victor Wind, the all-seeing 'I' of 'Conclusive Evidence,'
and, most precocious and achingly childlike of all, Dolores
Haze. The four chapters devoted to little Luzhin are pure
gold, a fascinating extraction of the thread of genius
from the tangle of a lonely boy's existence. The child's
ominous lethargy: his father's brooding ambitiousness for
him; the hints of talent in his heredity; the first
gropings, through mathematical and jigsaw puzzles, of his
peculiar aptitude toward the light; the bizarre introduction, at the hands of a nameless violinist who tinges
the game forever with a somehow cursed musicality, to the
bare pieces; his instruction in the rules, ironically
counterpointed against an amorous intrigue of which he is
oblivious; his rapid climb through a hierarchy of adult
opponents — all this is witty, tender, delicate, resonant.
By abruptly switching to Luzhin as a chess-sodden adult,
Nabokov islands the childhood, frames its naive brightness so that, superimposed upon the grown figure, it
operates as a kind of heart, as an abruptly doused light
reddens the subsequent darkness.

As to (b), Nabokov has never shied from characters
who excel. In 'Pale Fire' he presumed to give us a long
poem by an American poet second only to Frost; Adam Krug
in 'Bend Sinister' is the leading intellectual of his
nation; no doubt is left that Fyodor Godunov-Cherdyntsev
of 'The Gift' is truly gifted. Luzhin's 'recondite
genius' is delineated as if by one who knows....

However, I am not sure it perfectly works, this chess
puzzle pieced out with human characters. In the last
third of the book, the author's youth may begin to show;
émigré parties, arranged by Mrs. Luzhin, are introduced
for no apparent better reason than that Nabokov was going
to such parties at this time. A 'mercilessly stupid'
Leningrad visitor pops up irrelevantly, as a naked index
of editorial distaste for the Soviet regime. It is as if
pawns were proliferating to plug a leaky problem. The
reintroduction of Valentinov, though well-prepared, does
not function smoothly; if the plot were scored like a game,
this move would receive a (?). One becomes conscious of
rather aimless intricacies: the chronic mention of a one-
armed schoolmate (Nabokov's teasing of cripples, not the
most sympathetic of his fads, deserves a monograph to itself), and the somewhat mannered withholding of the hero's
first name and patronymic until the last sentences, which

then link up with the first. In short, the novel loses
inevitability as it needs it most. Suicide, being one
experience no writer or reader has undergone, requires
extra credentials to pass into belief. I can believe in
the suicides of Anna Karenina and Emma Bovary as terrible
but just — in the sense of fitting — events within the
worlds the authors have evolved. I am even more willing
to believe in Kirillov's suicide in 'The Possessed' as
the outcome of a philosophic-psychotic mental state explored with frightening empathy. But I am unable to feel
Luzhin's descent into an eternity of 'dark and pale
squares' as anything but the foreordained outcome of a
scheme that, however pretty, is less weighty than the
human fictions it has conjured up.

Early in 'The Defence' Nabokov describes an obtuse chess
spectator who, exasperated by what seems to him a premature
concession, itches to pick up the pieces and play the game
out. So too, I cannot see why, now that Luzhin is equipped
with a willing if not enthusiastic female caretaker and
furthermore a wealthy father-in-law, the grandmaster is
hopelessly blocked from pursuing, this side of madness,
his vocation. He is lovable, this child within a monster,
this 'chess moron,' and we *want* him to go on, to finish
his classic game with Turati, and, win or lose, to play
other games, to warm and dazzle the exquisite twilit
world of his preoccupation with the 'limpidity and lightness' of his thought. He seems blocked by something outside the novel, perhaps by the lepidopterist's habit of
killing what it loves; how remarkably few, after all, of
Nabokov's characters do evade the mounting pin. But in
asking (irrationally, he has been dead for over thirty
years) that Luzhin survive and be fruitful, we are asking
no more than his creator, no pet of fate, has asked of himself and has, to his great honor, done.

39. NIGEL DENNIS IN 'NEW YORK TIMES BOOK REVIEW'

27 September 1964, 4

The theme is a wonderful one ... an intellectual theme ...
and just the sort that should suit Mr Nabokov's particular
talent for inventing striking 'combinations' and studying
the minds of men who are obsessed with these to the point
of derangement. Yet it is a very difficult theme to treat.

What goes on in a character's mind cannot just be plunked
on the page and left there, rotating in inky circles. It
must somehow be dramatised; the elaborate mental movements must be released from the brain and transposed into
incidents and actions. Mr Nabokov showed exactly how this
should be done in 'Pale Fire': after reading that novel,
one does not forget how dramatically it was shaped and how
admirably the intellectual puzzles and complicated delu-
sions were made essential parts both of the lively narrative and the principal character.

This art is not present in 'The Defence'. Were Mr
Nabokov to write the book today, there is no doubt at all
that he would know how to turn a chess-brained nut into a
rare and interesting person. But thirty-five years is a
long time — and 'The Defence' shows all of its author's
weaknesses and few of his powers.

40. STUART HAMPSHIRE IN 'NEW STATESMAN'

6 November 1964, 702-3

Sir Stuart Hampshire (born 1914) is Warden of Wadham
College, Oxford. He has published widely on philosophy.

In many periods in the past, to write books for a living,
and to entertain the public, have seemed ignoble necessi-
ties, unworthy of a gentleman: particularly so if the
books were of the kind that disclose the emotions of private life, about which one might perhaps talk to friends
in one's own house. There could be thought to be some
element of vulgarity, the vulgarity of the showman on the
road, in the very act of publication. The public comes to
stare and demands to be pleased; and in spite of a restless talent, one might not wish to be counted among the
performers, the greenroom crowd, who submit themselves to
these intrusions. The doctrine of art as a special calling, and of the artist as a new kind of aristocrat or
dandy, helped in the last century to soothe the irritable
and fastidious temperament of those who would not be seen
standing with their wares in the marketplace. At least
the sweating and earnest public might be teased a little,
and made to pay, in the ridicule of misunderstanding, for

their clumsy attentions. It is often remarked that most
of the greater European writers of the last 50 years have
preserved or assumed aristocratic attitudes, and have
defied the revolt of the masses.

Among fastidious and irritable men of letters Mr
Nabokov is an extreme case. His disdain of publicity
and applause, even of the trade, or profession, of being
a writer, makes itself felt in a different way in each of
his novels, as if scribbling was an indignity, a loss of
his proper independence. So he mocks his inquiring reader
and sets his booby-traps with a peculiarly bitter relish.
'The Defence' is the translation of a novel first published in 1930, and it has a proud preface warning his
readers and critics in advance against their sentimental
errors and earnest misunderstandings. The novel itself
is a harsh essay in misanthropy and disappointment. The
story is too monotonously black; taken as a whole, the
novel may seem rather an exercise in proving a point.
When compared with 'The Gift', it is constricted, too
little suggestive and too controlled. But I would still
find it difficult to understand how anybody could begin to
read it and not continue with excitement to the end —
unless he threw it away in a humanitarian rage.

Many of the now celebrated Nabokov qualities are present: the building of a story, here the story of a chessmaster, to its violent climax with the greatest possible
intensity; the swooping in and out between minds that
are swollen with obsession and maniacally concentrated
and minds that are cold, removed, ironical and indifferent — the minds of men and women who have virtually
died long ago, in the revolution, and who now in exile are
only playing at being alive; the sharpness of an obsessed
vision; the sudden poetical and painful descriptions of
a lost Russia, a lost home, and of the atmospheres of
childhood minutely remembered.

Mr Nabokov achieves the reverse of a poetical haze in
description; he makes objects unnaturally distinct, as
if seen from very close to; he pecks at nature, like a
peacock, and picks up strange objects in his prose like
an amateur collector who hoards. He turns the pathetic
fallacy upside down: so far is he from spreading human
sentiments onto natural objects that he makes one see
details of the surface of a person and of his surroundings,
the distinguishing jerk of his movements, the litter of
his rented room, with equal objectivity. Each character
is a distinct species in his cage in the zoo, displaced
and in captivity. The common human sentiments are ignored,
and contact between persons, as between creatures of distinct species, consists always of misunderstandings. The

principle is not 'only connect' but rather 'only distinguish: find the outline, or the point of difference,
and sharpen it.' Any merging of distinct things and persons is made to seem a disgusting promiscuity.

Separateness is caricatured in 'The Defence'. The
father is well-meaning, 'human', and therefore weak,
sentimental: an insipid popular writer, a gentle monster
of formlessness and of soft, stray good intentions. The
son is a genius of formal intellect, a chessmaster, 'inhuman', enclosed: for him the world is covered with black
and white squares and patterned with abstract possibilities.
Father and son cannot come together, and therefore there
can be no art or civilised life in their home. For the
son there is only exile in hotels, among pushing, gaping
aliens, dimly heard, who pay to watch the performance.
They are the public which battens on genius, an irrele-
vance to the creative mind, scarcely noticed. The hero
must juggle with abstract patterns, which are like music,
but are not music. The patterns of chess express nothing
but the power relations between the pieces. They do not
betray feeling.

The only sound that might penetrate his defence against
feeling is the voice coming from a Russian family, which
preserves, in exile, a Russian house, with its sounds and
smells, the ikon, the provincial snobbery, a Chekhov interior of garrulity and of endless complaint, of slippered,
shuffling idleness, of sudden scenes and deep affections,
of slamming doors and idealistic daughters. But the voice
of the idealistic daughter cannot penetrate the hero's
defence, and cannot restore him to some sight of reality,
just because hers is the only voice of Russian idealism,
of that peculiar native compassion, represented in Gogol
and Dostoievsky, which loves absurdity and weakness and
looks for the opportunity of self-sacrifice in their defence.
The man who loves form and intellectual order is always a
stranger to her. Since the marriage between compassion
and a sense of order cannot be consummated, the Russian
genius must destroy himself. The separation of Christian
feeling from the entirely abstract, mathematical intellect
— the two aspects of Russian genius — is final. Nothing
is left.

It is a rigid, hopeless little story, marvellously
executed, with wit and precision and a shining newness
of vocabulary. In the glitter of Mr Nabokov's writing,
no tired thought, no cliché, can find a place. But it is
not a many-sided, moving novel like 'The Gift', which came
later; the theme of the exile, who must find a substitute home in the structure of a new language and must make
a virtue of translation, is not yet fully developed.

Reading 'The Gift', one is made to feel that a Russian
exile is the most poignant and final of all exiles, as if
a Russian, expelled from his landscape to shadowy foreign
cities, must live the remainder of his life as a kind
of perpetual translation. Russian words, and the names
of things learnt in his childhood, are closer to nature
than their English or German equivalents; the spoken
language and the landscape have an affinity, as if one
were a natural symbol of the other. Pushkin's words are
the voice of nature for anyone who has grown up with those
sights and sounds.

In 'Lolita' the American landscape is shown as a
monstrous abstraction, a great gaudy polysyllable, in
which all concrete meanings, all immediacy of touch and
sight, have been lost. One drives for ever along the flat
highways of generality, without a turn or a nuance, without the sight of a hedge or a ditch, towards some commonplace, or common meeting-place, of social equality; and
the lights of an undifferentiating morality, red and
green, stop and go, herd the traffic, which can no longer
respond to anything but these bare imperatives. This
raw landscape of mechanical cunning, neither country nor
city, generates its own poetry and its own eroticism —
that of a satyr in pursuit through a thicket of telephone
wires and neon lights. In 'Lolita' Mr Nabokov found the
matching style for his great, sprawling subject, and in
representing that impossible meeting between the old and
the new achieved a full concentration of effect.

In these earlier books, now translated with his aid,
he is seen just beginning to form his new kind of international novel, in which the play with language, and with
the game of translation, recalls a broken past, the childhood of a displaced person, now scattered in fragments in
a mind which builds a private world of obsession in order
to survive among the barbarians. 'The Defence' has a
terrible description of the son leaving home to be left
speechless and numb among the cruel oafs outside. Mr
Nabokov seems not to be interested here in the ordinary
aliens. His virtuosity in describing the mind of a chess-
player remains only virtuosity, and the depth and poetry
beneath the glitter of 'The Gift' and of 'Lolita' are
still a long way ahead.

41.   MALCOLM BRADBURY IN 'SPECTATOR'

13 November 1964, 644

Characteristically, we may not know in this book whether
the moments of special revelation that Luzhin seems to
reach are genuinely invested with meaning, or whether
they are simply delusion.   Nabokov's fictional procedure
is to jest with the numinous;   in a sense his novels are
romantic joke-books — he regards fiction as play.

If this makes Nabokov sound trivial, if, for instance,
Mary McCarthy's 'Encounter' comments on 'Pale Fire' make
the book sound a childish performance, then an injustice
is being done.   I take it that Nabokov's work belongs to
one of the essential fictional traditions, that which
regards the novel as verbal construct, in hazardous relation to life, and exploits the comedy implicit in that
relationship.   And I take it, too, that 'The Defence' is
not only about the deprivation of order and meaning, but
the aesthetic sources in which meaning and order can be,
however dangerously, recovered.   In any case, as Nabokov
points out, this is 'an attractive novel,' with likeable
personages and pleasing relations between them.   It is
more;   it has in embryo many of the devices used much
more showily — and more finely — in later novels;   but
it will satisfy readily at the level of story as well.

42.   STEPHEN WALL IN 'LISTENER'

19 November 1964, 806

Stephen Wall is a Fellow of Keble College, Oxford, and an
editor of 'Essays in Criticism'.

The gradual emergence of Nabokov's Russian novels — 'The
Defence' first appeared in 1930 and is now translated by
Michael Scammell and the author — is an awesome process.
It is strange to think of these remarkable works lying
dormant, as far as the English reader is concerned at any
rate, until released by the celebrity of 'Lolita'.   'The

Defence' is about Luzhin, a chess grand master: his
childhood when he discovers his genius for the game;
his 'seedy manhood', travelling from tournament to
tournament; his tragic end. Increasingly the chess-
board — or rather the luminous ideal world of relations
which is crudely acted out on the chess-board — becomes the only reality for him. Personal relationships,
even with the girl who out of a kind of fascinated pity
marries him, become marginal, shadowy. As often in Nabokov's fiction, the hero's is the only fully investigated
consciousness; the other characters are merely grotesquely
carved buttresses propping him up. They are only redeemed
from futility by being accessory to the main dialogue in
the novel — that between hero and author. Nabokov's attitude to Luzhin is difficult to sum up, but it involves
remote affection and derisive pity. Luzhin's solitary,
almost solipsistic existence, his incomprehension of the
normal, his obsession with the radiantly abstract world of
chess, are intimately conveyed, and yet his sympathy is
distanced by the arrogant intervention of Nabokov's unique
prose (though it is hard to tell how fully this was originally there and how much has been subtly sharpened in
translation), and by the absurdity of Luzhin's family and
associates.

Generally, Nabokov seems to think of life as a far from
golden bowl of clichés, the pitiful banality of which can
only be redressed by the stratagems of art. This attitude might seem insufferably aesthetic if it were not for
the pervasive sense of menace — not lessened by often
appearing in a farcical guise. Here, the chess defence
which the pathetic Luzhin tries to construct against his
opponent becomes a metaphor with larger implications.
The way in which the moves lead implacably to 'devasta-
tion, horror, madness' points far beyond the apparently
sterile world of chess. 'The Defence' is constructed
with Nabokov's usual cunning and ingenuity, but it is
much more humanly engaged than one might think.

43.   P.N. FURBANK IN 'ENCOUNTER'

January 1965, 84, 86

P.N. Furbank (born 1920) has taught at Cambridge and is
now Reader in English at the Open University. His books
include a study of Samuel Butler and the authorized biography of E.M. Forster.

...Nabokov's theme? It is a profound and despairing one —
the theme, as I take it, of 'Lolita' too. It is that the
only alternative to perversity, with its magical and terrible privileges, is banality. Poor Luzhin lives sur-
rounded by banality. He is a victim of his father's banal
Wunderkind fantasies; his wife, admirably loving and
courageous as she is, is another banal sentimentalist,
forcing him into her own novelettish version of life. His
parents-in-law's flat, which so enraptures him with its
'Russian' quality, is utterly bogus. When his wife, hoping he might take an interest in politics, reads emigré
newspapers aloud to him, he does his best to look attentive, all the time indulging forbidden chess-reveries —
and he is right, émigré politics are twaddle, she feels
it herself. The 'life' which she strives so tenderly to
interest him in is not only childish (that would have been
appropriate) but silly too.
     Nabokov is a truly despairing writer. He really does,
I think, see this antithesis between perversity and banality as exhausting the possibilities. And of the two elements in his own art — the jigsaw element, the creative
leap from the part to the whole, and the chess-element,
the perverse, inhuman exhibition of prowess in the invention of puzzles and strategies — he is, in mere despair,
drawn to the second. Hence something characteristic in
all his work. Every now and then he loses his faith in
his actual human material. Suspecting that the jigsaw,
when completed, will turn out to be like any other jigsaw,
a tawdry banality, he forestalls the verdict. With his
teeth set in contempt, he writes a nondescript passage, a
perfect sample of stupid, commonplace novel-writing, to
tell the reader he isn't interested in what's on the face
of the jigsaw-pieces, only in how they fit. There is some
of this contemptuous behaviour in all the novels of his
that I have read, though least in 'Lolita'. It is a
defensive gesture, like the black arrogance of his pre-

faces, in the face of an unsolved problem, and it damages
'The Defence' a bit, especially in the second half. The
novel is not quite a masterpiece; but it is, as Nabokov
is the first to point out, an 'attractive novel' and a
very brilliant one.

'Eugene Onegin'

1964

44. CHRISTOPHER RICKS IN 'NEW STATESMAN'

25 December 1964, 995

Christopher Ricks (born 1933) has taught at Oxford and
held a chair at Bristol; he is now Professor of English
at Cambridge. His books include critical studies of
Milton, Tennyson and Keats.

Nabokov's commentary on Pushkin's wonderful 'novel in
verse' is like something from a bygone age. Massively
crotchety, superbly opinionated, humiliatingly erudite —
and about as undeviating as 'Tristram Shandy'. Brilliant
though, and hugely readable. Anybody who is engaged in
editing anything had better look up Nabokov's index — he
really is a mine of out-of-the-way information on life
and literature. Fortunately the aid of the Bollingen
Foundation has allowed the edition to be big enough to
accommodate Nabokov's eccentricities and vendettas without crowding out all that is central. The textual variants are fascinating; the introduction is intricate
but lucid; and the last volume reprints the Russian text.
The 100-page appendix on prosody animates that corpse of
a topic, and seems to me to break important new gound in
its definitions and English instances (wittily chosen).
    There is a mass of information here, too, about poetic
diction, Augustan and Romantic. On the etiquette of
duelling, on the taste of truffles, on Beau Brummell's
dressing-glass, on the soothsayer's belief that a person
cannot help writing the future date of his death in a

slightly different hand from that in which he writes any
other date — on all such matters Nabokov is delightful
and authoritative. His literary swipes are a great deal
less apt, and the style often sinks into that facetious
provocativeness which is always waiting to claim Nabokov.
Cervantes, George Eliot, Mann, Faulkner — can even Nabokov's undoubted powers of sarcasm quite deal with those
four in three lines? A note refers us to 'Fyodor Dostoevski, a much overrated, sentimental, and Gothic novelist of the time'.

The tone of his best notes, and his worst, is one of
patiently patrician calm. The duel which killed Pushkin
was precipitated by the poet's calling Heeckeren 'the
pimp of his bastard' — at which Nabokov's old-world
courtesy asserts itself: 'This last epithet was a perfectly gratuitous insult since Heeckeren was a confirmed
homosexual, a fact well known to our poet.' Yet that
coolness can easily become the condescending heartless-
ness which so attenuates Nabokov's fiction, as in a note
on the duel where Sheremetev was shot through the breast.
'In his ire and agony, the poor fellow flapped and plunged
all over the snow like a large fish.' Should even Nabokov
cast quite so cold an eye? It is astonishing that the
same man can perpetrate that blasé bit of self-indulgence
and yet translate so feelingly the magnificent scene
when Onegin kills his friend Lenski in a duel.

The glory of the commentary, though, is its manifest
evidence that Nabokov has considered the full implications of every word of his translation. Does 'agrestic'
seem too precious an avoidance of 'rustic'? A note justi-
fies it. Does *dulcitude/juventude* fail as a 'stock
rhyme' because it never has been a stock rhyme in English?
Well, yes, and Nabokov's note does not try to brazen this
out, but humbly concedes that here he has fallen short of
perfection. Just occasionally one could have done with
an assurance that the English word was not more liquidly
affected than the Russian. 'Mollitude' turns up a very
great deal, and 'apparition' is used for 'appearing'
('Onegin's apparition at the Larins'') in a way that does
not carry its own conviction.

All the same, the commentary altogether wins the confidence of the reader — Nabokov knows what he is doing.
Archaisms like 'moveless' and 'stirless' are finely used.
Graceless inversions? He is 'braving inversions and obso-
letes' in the paramount interests of literalism. Still,
many of the inversions don't make for distinguished English: 'Eight rubbers have already played whist's heroes';
'him who has felt disturbs the ghost of irrecoverable days'
(especially as the line-break is after 'disturbs').

These are blemishes — but at any rate they are not due
to ignorance or carelessness.

Nabokov ruthlessly displays the folly of his predecessors. Among 'the four "English", "metrical" "translations" ... unfortunately available to students' is that
by Babette Deutsch, now issued as a Penguin Classic. In
the magnificent sequence of Tatiana's dream, the shaggy
bear carries her, in Nabokov's version,

> and straight he goes into the hallway
> and on the threshold lays her down.

Miss Deutsch's lines suggest something quite other:

> And doing with her as he will,
> He lays her down upon the sill.

Nabokov — and one might not have expected it — is a
great deal better at the simple business of telling the
story, surely one of the best of love-stories in its
humour and pathos. His decision was to abandon all attempt at reproducing Pushkin's intricate stanza, or indeed
any stanza. His lines are of the length that the literal
sense demands, and the verse is held together only by the
loosely iambic rhythm. There must have been a strong
temptation to compensate for this sacrifice by a heightened
colouring in diction, but Nabokov seems to have resisted
it. He would presumably honour Beerbohm's 'Statesman of
Olden Time, making without wish for emolument a flat but
faithful version of the Georgics' — provided it really
were faithful.

Where Nabokov is exhilaratingly successful is in his
mastery of sound-patterns, where alliteration and assonance are interwoven with delicacy and emphasis. His
notes are very illuminating on such effects (in Dryden
and Wordsworth as well as Pushkin). Compare Miss Deutsch:

> He sang of parting and repining:
> The mystic, wistful hours of night;
> Of distance, promising delight;
> He sang the rose, romantic flower.

Her internal rhymes are not so much tremulously sentimental (the needed effect) as galumphing. And 'romantic
flower' is not exactly vibrant. Nabokov:

> He sang parting and sadness,
> and a vague something, and the dim
> remoteness, and romantic roses.

'Remoteness' is the pivot, echoing 'sadness' and leading
effortlessly into 'romantic roses'. A highly mannered
style, yes, and Nabokov is at his best when that is the
point. His finest passages are the great winter-scenes,
where the effects of frost, ice and snow are themselves
ones of patterned delicacy. Icy artifice, which elsewhere may be the accusation against Nabokov, is here just
what was needed.

45. RONALD HINGLEY IN 'SPECTATOR'

1 January 1965, 19

Ronald Hingley (born 1920) has taught at London University
School of Slavonic and East European Studies and at Oxford.
His publications on Russian language and literature in-
clude studies of Chekhov and Dostoevsky.

'Eugene Onegin' is the greatest poem in the Russian language and, arguably, the greatest Russian novel as well.
Can it be made accessible to the English-speaking reader
who has no Russian? These two translations (1) suggest
very different answers.
  Miss Deutsch offers the more conventional solution,
by reproducing the metre, length of line and complicated
stanza-structure of the original, which is what Mr. Nabokov calls 'mutilating its meaning for the sake of a
pleasure-measure rhyme.' His own solution is a literal
translation into unrhymed iambic lines of unequal length.
In preserving the letter of Pushkin, Mr. Nabokov is also
nearer to his spirit....
  Mr. Nabokov's work is a curious combination of the
magisterial and the modest. He refers to his translation as a mere 'crib,' and says its 'only purpose is textual fidelity with just as much music as might not inter-
fere with accuracy of sense.' This was just the right
thing to aim at in the very special case of Pushkin,
even if the execution sometimes falls short. It was a
mistake, for example, to attempt to reproduce so faith-
fully Pushkin's stylistic fireworks, and, in particular,
the fusion of casual colloquialisms with more sonorous
samples of poetic diction. This comes off in Pushkin's

Russian, but not in English. Thus, on the colloquial
side, Nabokov's 'Onegin, a good pal of mine,' and 'The odd
chap was already cross' are not among his happier lines.
Nor are those in the 'high style' couplet:

> Tatiana credited the lore
> Of plain-folk ancientry.

In the latter example, as in many other places, I find
myself having to recall Pushkin's Russian in order to
understand Mr. Nabokov's translation into ... I had nearly
said 'my own language,' but perhaps Nabokovese' is a
truer term, especially as he sometimes seems to be coining
his own vocabulary. Or at least his English seems to have
a strong foreign intonation. It has many admirers among
readers of 'Lolita,' and in reading this translation and
commentary I have almost become one of them. Yet somehow I can't quite throb in sympathy....

Mr. Nabokov's vast commentary is an extraordinary
baroque momument. Hard fact is what he goes for, and the
more detailed the better. 'Why Miss Deutsch should think
fit [he thunders] to transform a coleopterous insect into
an orthopterous one [she had called beetles 'crickets']
is incomprehensible.' (She has recoleopterised the line,
incidentally, in this revised version.) This happens to
touch on Nabokov's expertise as an international authority
on entomology, but he seems equally erudite in non-ento-
mological fields as well. Thus his commentary is a mine
of information, much of it fascinating and most of it
having some sort of bearing on the poem.

The discursiveness of the commentary is one of its
delights or irritations, according to your taste. One
certainly never knows what is going to turn up next. For
instance, in a draft version of Chapter Two, Pushkin de-
leted the words 'exegi monumentum,' and this naturally
demands some reference to his well-known lyric, Exegi
monumentum of 1836. But surely three full pages are a
bit much, especially when they include a lengthy comment
on the term 'Alexandrine Column,' used in the lyric, but
not in 'Eugene Onegin' itself. We are even given the
exact dimensions of various columns which have been
termed Alexandrine throughout history, but happen not to
be the specific column that Pushkin had in mind.

Can parts of this work be intended as an elaborate
joke, a commentary to end all commentaries? Can the
author of 'Pnin' perhaps be taking the mickey? The facsimile reproduction in volume four of the 1837 editio
optima of 'Eugene Onegin' (over 300 pages of print so
small that you almost need a magnifying glass to read it)

is an extravagance which would bear out such a suggestion.
It would have been better either to omit the Russian version entirely or to print it legibly.

One could go on and on writing about this fantastic
production and highlighting its more bizarre features, but
I have had many happy hours with it, and it does after
all make a big contribution to the study of Pushkin.
Its very eccentricity means that it fulfils the first
necessity of a Russian work in the eyes of us stolid Anglo-
Saxons, though there is a danger that it may therefore be
overpraised by our indulgent amateurs of things Russian.
And with all its gothic towers, sprawling buttresses,
mazes, flying columns, sprouting follies and secret passages, it remains a great monument of devotion and learning. 'Eugene Onegin' will be full of deeper meaning to
those who work through it.

Note

1 The review deals both with Nabokov's translation and
   with the Penguin edition of Babette Deutsch's translation of Pushkin's poem.

46. ROBERT CONQUEST IN 'POETRY'

June 1965, 236-8

Robert Conquest (born 1917) edited the influential anthology 'New Lines' (1956).

This four-volume presentation of one of the world's most
attractive poems contains much material which will primarily interest the Pushkinist. The sound and penetrating Appendix on prosody deserves a wider readership — if
only because nowadays there is a mass of writing about all
aspects of poetry except the one thing which actually de-
fines it as poetry rather than prose, its technique and
metric. (It might be supplemented by lines 30-38 of
Nabokov's own poem An Evening of Russian Poetry.) The
long Commentary which fills out half this bulky production is full of insights too: for example on 'the

aphoristic style which was Pushkin's intrinsic concession to the eighteenth century'. It is also a regular
rodeo of hobbyhorses. Nabokov scoffs at Virgil, Hudibras,
Swift, Shchedrin, Béranger. He thinks Coleridge's The
Pains of Sleep a great poem. He urges the abolition of
the Cyrillic alphabet. He sneers at other translations.
Odd stuff, but at least individual. As with Yvor Winters
preferring Bridges to Hopkins, agreeing or not we must
respect this more than a thousand acceptances by rote of
current, and probably ephemeral, orthodoxy. Meanwhile, we
can note in passing, from Nabokov's extreme rudeness to
previous translators, that he would hardly expect any hostile criticisms of himself to be too muted.

In an age of 're-creations' — parasites sucking a
little vitality from some great host — it is good to find
Nabokov defining true translation as 'rendering, as closely
as the associative and syntactical capacities of another
language allow, the exact contextual meaning of the original'. He adds that, whatever the ideal situation, it
is impossible to translate a poem like 'Eugene Onegin'
truly with the retention of its rhymes. But here we begin
to get into difficulties. There is, of course, a great
deal to be said for a straight prose translation. Still,
if we miss the versification of the poem we miss a very
great deal indeed — particularly as Pushkin, like Racine
in a different mode, depends a lot on an inevitably felicitous handling of what appear on analysis to be ordinary
phrases and stylized properties.

But let us have prose, if we must. Unfortunately Nabokov does not go the full length. He takes the view that
something can be retained: the iambic rhythm. This turns
out to be pointless, as it results in a totally different
form and style — a blank verse varying from four syllables
to twelve or more. Moreover, he has retained a single
'poetic' device, and one which only falls naturally in a
highly formal verse structure and even then is something
to be cautious with — inversion.

So we get (a fair example):

Having decided to detest
the coquette, boiling Lenski did not wish
to see before the duel Olga.
The sun, his watch he kept consulting...

In fact, the approach produces awkwardness and insipidity.
This is a pity, for Nabokov's own attempts at metrical
paraphrase are rather effective (see vol. 2, page 120).

There is a more essential blemish yet — an unsuitable
vocabulary. Nabokov speaks admirably in the Commentary of

the twin errors of 'impoverishing or enriching the sense'.
He himself has not been able to resist the temptation. We
get 'pacific sites' for a Russian 'peaceful places', and
so on. Worse still, this tendency leads to a liberal
scattering of inappropriately stilted or antiquated words:
buttsome, vernant, strangeling, youthhood, infantine,
joyance, vacillant, halfwise, lightsome, moveless, plangor-
ous, varivoiced, familistic, yearnsome, juventy, monocrati-
cally, prevene, volation. Almost invariably rendering
something quite ordinary in Russian, these may remind
us of Auden's complaint, about an Anglo-Icelandic Dictionary, that it was 'full of non-existent words'. In
fact a few are strictly non-existent (not even in the big
OED): others are 'obsolete, chiefly Scotch', or to be found
only in the OED word-cemetery, not even making the very
tolerant 'Shorter' OED. Even those that do get that far
will mostly be recognized as full of 'ancientry' (another
Nabokov word) — the equivalents of the 'blithesome and
cumberless' which made Hogg's notorious lines such a
laughing-stock.

Moreover, we get 'mollitude' for luxury; 'sauvage' for
dik, wild; 'campestral' for the simple *polevoy*; 'Adrian'
for Adriatic; 'the fairs' for 'the fair ones'; 'ananas'
for pineapple; 'Tsargrad' for Constantinople; 'Eol' for
Aeolus. For *loshadka* Nabokov objects to Oliver Elton's
'old mare', but he himself gives us 'naggy'. There is
inappropriate slang (e.g. 'tosh', first quoted by the OED
from 1872). And so on.

It is sad to knock any attempt to bring Pushkin before
us. There are long passages without these faults. Nevertheless, on the whole this is too much a transposition
into Nabokovese, rather than a translation into English.
It gives the impression of a foreigner who has not quite
learnt the language with the extreme perfection required,
perhaps, only at this extravagant periphery of idiom.
Under control, Nabokov could have given us a good, un-
decorated prose translation — even, with great toil, a
fine verse one. Meanwhile, the reader with no Russian
will probably find one or other of the despised verse ren-
derings (Elton's advisedly) still the best available, with
all the faults that Nabokov rightly points out in them.

47.   EDMUND WILSON IN 'NEW YORK REVIEW OF BOOKS'

15 July 1965, 3-6

Edmund Wilson (1895-1972) was a prolific and versatile author and one of the most influential critics of his generation. He published fiction, poetry, plays and essays as well as such important critical works as 'The Wound and the Bow' (1941). For his correspondence with Nabokov, see p. 33.

This production, though in certain ways valuable, is something of a disappointment; and the reviewer, though a personal friend of Mr Nabokov — for whom he feels a warm affection sometimes chilled by exasperation — and an admirer of much of his work, does not propose to mask his disappointment. Since Mr Nabokov is in the habit of introducing any job of this kind which he undertakes by an announcement that he is unique and incomparable and that everybody else who has attempted it is an oaf and an ignoramus, incompetent as a linguist and scholar, usually with the implication that he is also a low-class person and a ridiculous personality, Nabokov ought not to complain if the reviewer, though trying not to imitate his bad literary manners, does not hesitate to underline his weaknesses.

Mr Nabokov, before the publication of his own translation of 'Eugene Onegin', took up a good deal of space in these pages to denounce a previous translation by Professor Walter Arndt. (1) This article — which sounded like nothing so much as one of Marx's niggling and nagging attacks on someone who had had the temerity to write about economics and to hold different views from Marx's — dwelt especially on what he regarded as Professor Arndt's Germanisms and other infelicities of phrasing, without, apparently,being aware of how vulnerable he himself was. Professor Arndt had attempted the *tour de force* of translating the whole of 'Onegin' into the original iambic tetrameter and rather intricate stanza form. Mr Nabokov decided that this could not be done with any real fidelity to the meaning and undertook to make a 'literal' translation which maintains an iambic base but quite often simply jolts into prose. The results of this have been more disastrous than Arndt's heroic effort. It has produced a bald and awkward language which has nothing in common with Pushkin or with the usual writing of Nabokov. One knows

Mr Nabokov's virtuosity in juggling with the English
language, the prettiness and wit of his verbal inventions.
One knows also the perversity of his tricks to startle or
stick pins in the reader; and one suspects that his perversity here has been exercised in curbing his brilliance;
that — with his sado-masochistic Dostoevskian tendencies
so acutely noted by Sartre (2) — he seeks to torture both
the reader and himself by flattening Pushkin out and denying to his own powers the scope for their full play.

Aside from this desire both to suffer and make suffer —
so important an element in his fiction — the only characteristic Nabokov trait that one recognizes in this uneven
and sometimes banal translation is the addiction to rare
and unfamiliar words, which in view of his declared intention to stick so close to the text that his version may be
used as a [crib], are entirely inappropriate here. It
would be more to the point for the student to look up the
Russian word than to have to have recourse to the OED for
an English word he has never seen and which he will never
have occasion to use. To inflict on the reader such words
is not really to translate at all, for it is not to write
idiomatic and recognizable English. Nabokov's aberrations
in this line are a good deal more objectionable than anything I have found in Arndt. He gives us, for example,
*rememorating, producement, curvate, habitude, rummers,
familistic, gloam, dit, shippon* and *scrab*. All these can
be found in the OED, but they are all entirely dictionary
words, usually labelled 'dialect', 'archaic', or 'obsolete'....

There are also actual errors of English. I had never
seen the word *loaden* before, and I have found, on looking
it up, that it is '*Obs.* exc. *dial.*', and that it is not a
past participle, as Nabokov makes it: the past participle,
it seems, is *loadened*. The past of *dwell* is *dwelt*, not
dwelled;   *dwelled* has long been obsolete. 'Remind one
about me' is hardly English.

If it is a question of picking on Germanisms in Arndt,
it is not difficult to find Russianisms in Nabokov. You
cannot 'listen the sound of the sea' in English; this is
a Russianism: in English you have to listen *to* something....

And then, there is the unnecessarily clumsy style,
which seems deliberately to avoid point and elegance.
'The ache of loss chases Tatiana' (as he chooses to spell
her) — why not 'pursues', which would at least give a
metrical line? 'Well, this now makes sense. Do not be
cross with me, my soul' — 'makes sense' and 'my soul' do
not go together....

The commentary, the appendices, and the scholarly presentation suffer in general from the same faults as Nabokov's translation — that is, mainly from a lack of common
sense — something that is not detrimental to the fantastic
fiction he writes, of which it is, in fact, an essential
element, but which in an erudite work of this kind is a
serious disadvantage. The first requisite for such an
enterprise as Nabokov has here undertaken would have been
to print the Russian text on the opposite page from the
translation; but, instead of this, he gives us a facsimile
of the edition of 1837, which, with the index, takes up
the whole of Volume Four but of which the print is too
small to be read without a magnifying glass. He has elsewhere invariably transliterated the Russian — a procedure
which is confusing and useless....

In a tedious and interminable appendix — or rather, one
that terminates only at the end of ninety-two pages — Nabokov expounds a system of prosody, also invented by himself,
which he claims may be accommodated to both English and
Russian verse....

The commentary, also, to some extent, suffers from being
overdone. It is impossible for Nabokov to mention any poem
without specifying its stanza form, metre, and rhyme scheme
— information which is generally quite useless, since it
can give us no real idea of the poem; and he supplies us
with more information than we need — one sees the lepidopterist here — about the flora and fauna mentioned in
'Onegin', to a degree that we are almost surprised that we
should not be given the zoological data on the bear in
Tatyana's dream....

The Nabokov who bores and fatigues by overaccumulation
contrasts with the authentic Nabokov and with the poet he
is trying to illuminate. It has always seemed to me that
Vladimir Nabokov was one of the Russian writers who, in
technique, had most in common with Pushkin. (I turn with
relief to this aspect of our marvellously accomplished
editor who is perhaps not ideally qualified to be one.)
No poet surpasses Pushkin — not even Dante — for the
speed, point, and neatness of his narrative. How much
ground in how short a space 'Onegin' covers! How compact
and yet easy in every stanza! The fairy tale of the Tsar
Sultan — one of the great triumphs of style in literature — tells a story in its first eighty lines — too
charming to be called 'exposition' — and creates the
whole situation with which the rest of the poem will be
occupied. I first read Pushkin's 'Gypsies' on a short
railroad journey and then, talking about it with a Russian
friend who had not reread it for years, discovered that
she was surprised to learn that it was not a poem of con-

siderable length. Pushkin has moved so quickly that you
feel, in its few pages, that you have spent as much time
with the gypsies as the fugutive hero has and have been
witnessing a fully developed drama. Now, Nabokov himself
can do this. The best of his short stories and novels are
masterpieces of swiftness and wit and beautifully concealed calculation. Every detail is both piquant and
relevant, and everything fits together. Why, then, should
this not be true of his commentary and his two appendices
(for the one on Pushkin's Negro great-grandfather also
makes rather heavy weather of Hannibal's African prove-
nance)? It is as if this sure hand at belles lettres,
once resolved to distinguish himself as a scholar, has
fallen under an oppressive compulsion to prove himself by
piling things up. The truth is that in the 'Onegin' his
brightest moments occur when, as in the passage just
referred to, the author of 'Conclusive Evidence' slips
into a shimmering sentence or performs a sly feat of pres-
tidigitation....

And now for the positive side. The commentary, if one
skips the *longueurs*, does make very pleasant reading, and
it represents an immense amount of labour.... I imagine
that nobody else has explored Pushkin's sources so thoroughly. Mr Nabokov seems really to have done his best to
read everything that Pushkin could possibly have read, and
has shown that he took over from poetry and fiction a good
many current phrases.

Nabokov has also studied exhaustively Pushkin's relations with his Russian predecessors and contemporaries,
and there is a good deal of excellent literary criticism.
I except from this the literary *obiter dicta* which are
partly the result of Nabokov's compulsion to give unnecessary information; he cannot mention a book, however obscure, which has influenced or been mentioned by Pushkin
or which contains something similar to something in 'Onegin' without inserting his opinion of it; and partly the
result of his instinct to take digs at great reputations.
In one paragraph, we are told, for example, that a novel
by Mme. de Staël is 'insipid', one by Nodier 'lurid but
not quite negligible', and that Balzac's 'La Femme de trente
ans' is a 'much overrated vulgar novelette'. Dostoevsky
is identified as 'a much overrated, sentimental, and
Gothic novelist of the time' (what is Gothic about Dostoevsky?); Balzac and Sainte-Beuve as 'popular but essentially mediocre writers'. 'Le Rouge et le noir', also,
is 'much overrated', and Stendhal has a 'paltry style'
(Stendhal's unadorned style is as much 'a part of his act'
as Nabokov's Fabergé fanciness). Chaikovsky's 'Eugene
Onegin' is first a 'silly', then a 'slapdash' opera —

though Nabokov has always declared that he does not like music and knows nothing about it, and the fact that Chaikovsky's libretto has no more to do with Pushkin's poem than Gounod's 'Faust' has with Goethe is of no importance whatever. But when Nabokov is not being merely snide and silly but taking his subject seriously, he gives us excellent little essays — on Derzhavin, on Baratynsky, on Zhukovsky, or Karamzin, and a comparison of the character of Onegin with Benjamin Constant's Adolphe....

In one special department of criticism, Mr Nabokov is supremely competent. With all the recent combing of literature for masked symbols and significant images, with all the exegesis of texts in which the critic diagrams ideas, philosophical, theological, and political, which can never have entered the author's head, there has been shown remarkably little sensitivity to the texture and rhythm of writing, to the skill in manipulating language, for the rendering of varied effects. The explanation of such effects, with illustrations from Pope and Milton, used to be part of the apparatus of the 'rhetoric' of old-fashioned grammars; but they have lately been so much neglected — really so little understood, as one can see from the current non-versified 'poems' which yet do not have the virtues of well-managed prose — that Edith Sitwell has been foolishly ridiculed for devoting attention to the subject. Mr Nabokov — although, for the purpose of his 'literal' translation of Pushkin, he has condemned himself to wear a hair shirt — has this sensitivity highly developed. He is himself adept at such effects, and is enormously appreciative of his poet's skill in assonance, alliteration, enjambement, changing the tempo by speeding or retarding, and all sorts of other subtle devices for fitting the language to the matter. Nabokov's discussion of such achievements seems to me the department of his commentary which is most valuable to the student of Pushkin or to the student of any kind of poetry....

This 'Onegin', it is important to mention, has, aside from its intrinsic merits, a special interest as a part of Nabokov's whole *oeuvre*. The principal theme of his work — from his early novel in Russian 'Mashenka' ['Mary'] to the English 'Pnin', 'Lolita', and 'Pale Fire' — is the situation, comic and pathetic, full of embarrassment and misunderstanding, of the exile who cannot return, and one aspect of this is the case of the man who, like Nabokov, is torn between the culture he has left behind and that to which he is trying to adapt himself. Nabokov, the product in Russia of an English-speaking household, the son of an Anglophile father who led the struggle, as the leader of the 'Kadet' party, for a constitutional monarchy in Russia,

Nabokov, with his Cambridge education and his extraordinary command of English, had already, in his first English book, 'The Real Life of Sebastian Knight', which still seems to me one of his best, written a parable of the hide-and-seek of his Russian and English personalities. And there is a drama in his 'Eugene Onegin' which is not Onegin's drama. It is the drama of Nabokov himself attempting to correlate his English and his Russian sides. As in 'The Real Life of Sebastian Knight', they continue to elude one another. When he tries to invent a prosody in which both languages will be at home, English poetry will not submit to it; when he tries to translate 'Onegin' 'literally', what he writes is not always really English. On the other hand, he sometimes betrays — in his ignorance or misapprehension of certain matters — that he is not quite at home with Russia. Yet Nabokov's work, here as elsewhere, has been serving a useful function of interpretation, cross-fertilization. In spite of his queer prejudices, which few people share — such as his utter contempt for Dostoevsky — his sense of beauty and his literary proficiency, his energy which never seems to tire, have made him a cultural live wire which vibrates between us and that Russian past which still provides for the Russian present a vitality that can sometimes inspire it and redeem it from mediocrity....

Notes

1 Vladimir Nabokov, On Translating Pushkin: Pounding the Clavichord, 'New York Review of Books', 30 April 1964, 14-16.
2 See p. 65.

48. HENRY GIFFORD IN 'TIMES LITERARY SUPPLEMENT'

7 January 1977, 12

Henry Gifford (born 1913) was formerly Professor of English at Bristol University. His books include 'The Novel in Russia' (1964) and studies of Tolstoy and Pasternak.

Nabokov's translation is to be saluted for its integrity.
It has columns of support troops, armed to the teeth in
the notes of the commentary. It can be called a monument
to its author's scholarship and a splendid proof of his
devotion to Pushkin. Nobody seeking to understand Pushkin
will avert his eyes from these four volumes. And the
whole enterprise is a central one for Nabokov. As a
feat of scholarship, and accurate arrangement — I have
noted only one misprint, the omission of *cum* from the
Latin quotation in Volume 3, page 69 — it is stupendous.
    But the translation, though tonic, does not satisfy.
He says with undue modesty that he intends merely to provide a crib. 'Pushkin has likened translators to horses
changed at the posthouses of civilization. The greatest
reward I can think of is that students may use my work
as a pony.' The ideal use for it will be when the translation is flanked by Pushkin's text on the one hand, and
the commentary on the other. That makes a very rewarding
exercise. Still, one would like to say that the crib
stands on its own, that it is what Johnson would have
called a noble version. This it fails to be, partly because the method Nabokov has adopted is too crippling in
its demands, and partly because of the translator's eccentricity. The work is at once austere and wilful,
fascinating and unacceptable. The tuning, alas, is imperfect, and the language alternatively animated and numb.
It would be hard to guess from these contrived pages that
Pushkin wrote verse that is frequently compared with
Mozart's music, and that he was a poet whose truth re-
sided very much in elegance, harmony, clarity, and the
best ordering of words.

49. CLIVE JAMES IN 'NEW STATESMAN'

8 July 1977, 54-5

Clive James (born 1939), writer, journalist and broad-
caster, has been on the staff of the 'Observer' since
1972.

In the week of his death, it is instructive to remember
that Nabokov's translation of 'Eugene Onegin' was a

project dear to his heart. Expert opinions of the recent
second edition were not much more favourable than they
were for the first, mainly because the translator had
not done enough to eliminate what were earlier judged
to be eccentricities of diction, while the commentary
obstinately remained unmodified in all its idiosyncrasies.
There is undoubtedly a sense in which the whole enterprise
is a great folly. But even those Russianists who have been
most inclined to question Nabokov's success in transmit-
ting the essence of Pushkin are usually willing to concede
that this cranky monument of scholarship might at least
come in useful to the beginner.... I should say at the
outset that in several respects Nabokov's Folly serves the
turn. It is a work to be valued, although even the tyro
is bound to find it silly as well as brilliant.

The ideal crib, of course, should merely be the servant
of the original. But Nabokov was incapable of being anybody's servant, even his admired Pushkin's: in paying
homage to his giant predecessor he did his best to keep
his own ego in the background, but ever and anon it
shouldered its way forward. Nabokov's theory of translation was based on 'humble fidelity' to the original, yet
try as he might to give us nothing more pretentious than
a word-for-word equivalent, he still managed to make Pushkin sound like Nabokov.

Nor is the commentary free from quirks. In fact it
is largely made up of them. He has set out to be more
scholarly than the scholars; it is doubtful whether anybody else inside or outside Russia knows as much about
Pushkin; but you don't have to know a thousandth as much
to realise that Nabokov is no more *reasonable* on this subject than on any other....

Nabokov has no call to despise those less informed
translators who have had the temerity to cast their versions in rhyme. His unrhyming version sounds at least as
weird as the very worst of theirs. But as a crib it is the
best available, especially in this second edition, where
each line matches a line in the original — even, in many
cases, to the extent of reproducing the word order. Worse
than useless for the reader without Russian, for the learner
Nabokov's translation would be just the ticket, if only the
commentary were better balanced. But Nabokov's ambitions
as a scholar are thwarted by his creativity. He starts
shaping the facts before he has fully submitted himself to
them. He is immensely knowing, but knowingness is not the
same as knowledge.

'The Eye'

1965

Originally written in Russian as 'Soglyadataj'; serialized
in 'Sovremennye Zapiski' (Paris), 1930. Translated by
Dmitri and Vladimir Nabokov; serialized in 'Playboy',
January-March 1965, and published in New York, 1965, and
London, 1966.

50. STEPHEN KOCH IN 'NATION'

17 January 1966, 81-2

Stephen Koch teaches English at the State University of
New York at Stony Brook.

There aren't many surprises in 'The Eye' ... beyond the
mild jolt of reading it as if it were new, now that its
freshness and promise have been so thoroughly fulfilled.
Though obviously germinal Nabokov, its faults are not
those of the master but of the novice, and for that
reason it hardly seems like Nabokov at all. 'The Eye' —
proud, elegant, unapologetic — forced one principally to
appreciate the tenacious ingenuity with which Nabokov has
developed his rather limited idea of fiction.
     Thus far, 'Lolita' and 'Pale Fire' remain the most
extraordinary books Nabokov has written, and with the
exception of his Gogolesque study in surrealistic terror
and comedy, 'Invitation to a Beheading' (translated in
1959), they humiliatingly outdistance his other works.

Nabokov is one of the few modern authors whose novels
are all facets of an *oeuvre*, an extended literary project.   But I doubt that he will be remembered for this
project.   Despite his great verbal gifts, his merely
conventionally excellent works immediately reveal their
trivial, antiquated forms.   Finally, Nabokov's is a virtuoso, rather than original, genius.   His greatness lies
in certain spectacular manipulations of conventional,
even reactionary, ideas.

All Nabokov's work is gripped by a tension between
modernity and nostalgia;   this seeker of the timeless
must be located historically.   In a now famous review of
Nathalie Sarraute's 'Portrait d'un inconnu,' (1) Sartre
named as a modern phenomenon a certain formal self-consciousness in Nabokov, Waugh and Sarraute herself, which
adopts a wholly negative attitude toward such hoary, time-
tested fictional concerns as psychology, the force of
social convention, moral or thematic truth, and the like.
Demoted from their eminence as the novel's subject, these
became its techniques or, better, its devices, while the
subject becomes fiction itself.   Sartre is at least partly
right.   Nabokov's recurrent theme *is* self-consciousness,
and not the homely process of self-examination so much
as sensitivity to the implications of the narrative act —
an awareness of what it means to re-create the world.   The
novel as art (understood as poetry, love, immortality,
self-discovery) becomes the theme of the novel.   It reflects on itself.

But formal self-awareness is nothing new, even in the
novel, though the naturalistic tradition makes aesthetic
naiveté seem, to some, a virtue.   An entirely different
problem complicates Nabokov's relation to his own time.

Nabokov has found in his own life the model for a
literary convention — an extremely *conventional* convention, at that — which governs all his activity.   From
his beginnings as a young Russian émigré, he has indulged
the rigidly formulated, 19th-century romantic nostalgia
that sees the poet as one at war with reality and his own
time, who lives in exile, who speaks in a tongue too
beautiful and too much his own for others to understand.
This idea, lying at the heart of the 19th-century's pathos,
is Nabokov's pretext for both his extraordinary wit and
his 'poetry' — those ingenious moments of lyric ecstasy
in his books which we are to take as absolutely authentic
transcendence.   For Nabokov himself, this convention and
fact have bisected each other with such horrible precision
that one might expect his treatment of it to be painfully
solemn.   But strangely enough, he is almost never solemn;
he overplays the formula in the name of comedy (flattening,

for example, American social reality to make it seem even
more intractable and Philistine than it is) while he
undermines the lyric tendency with perversion, vulgarity,
simple-mindedness. Though he still dreams of its over-
reaching ecstasy (and seems to attain it) Nabokov has
shifted the romantic agony into the realm of wit.

Nabokov's major devices: his style; his propensity for
allusion and metaphor; his inevitable bifurcation of the
narrator are all devices for ambivalence. Even in 'The
Eye,' where they are behind not wit but a polished and
extended joke, such devices are meant to dissolve the
moralizing solemnity the 'real' is supposed to invoke.
Humiliated by the outraged husband of his mistress, a
fumbling Russian émigré tries to shoot himself, wakes up
in a hospital, and believes himself his own ghost. Within
this ethereal liberation, free to think of himself as an
object, he becomes fascinated by the mystery of another,
flesh-and-blood man who turns out, of course, to be himself....

But all this is Nabokov in theory alone. However conceived, fragmenting the narrator's identity must be upheld
by a style to succeed. In place of a style, 'The Eye'
has a clean, graceful manner which contributes nothing
to the book. The wit of the later works does serve a purpose; it bases itself on the more profound ambivalences
being developed by turning on itself, *becoming aware of
itself* as the work of a poet who, in the name of beauty,
is cheating reality with words.

The attitude toward words is the decisive issue in
Nabokov's art: it underlies his romance, and it underlies
his modernist irony. Nabokov the romantic nostalgist
wants to re-create reality and evoke traditional beauty in
the fumes of language. Nabokov the ironist and wit ('Lolita, light of my life, fire of my loins. My sin, my
soul') uses words to laugh at themselves in recognition
of how questionable this process is. But even drenched
in wit, Nabokov finally insists upon recouping the losses
the poet has suffered under modernism. Thus, Humbert does
finally 'share' an 'immortality' with Dolly: he completes
his creative act by renouncing her and freeing her for
the realm of art — a realm which, even at this late date,
Nabokov wants to exist in *pathetic* relation to facts. An
absolutely standard, creakingly archaic pathos over the
artist as outcast, the beloved as lost, stops the irony
with a tragic overtone.

This entire convention is now so exhausted and suspect
that Nabokov is forced to treat it as the pretext for
wit. Yet, his commitment to it is that of an unflinching
traditionalist. More than anything else, he wants its

ecstasy to be real. The actual conflict in Nabokov is
not between the poet and reality, but between the ironic
novelist and the ecstatic poet. The latter, who is the
hidden genius of all his work, must see his timeless
vision as rendering temporal reality inauthentic. But
the novelist who bases his art on a conflict between imagination and fact can never wholly discredit the durability
of fact. Nabokov resolves this contradiction through a
sly subversion. Reality is undermined with wit, and
poetry triumphs.

Yet, such poetry claims to derive its value from a
novelistic conflict that does not really exist. Nabokov
is perfectly aware of this, and it doesn't trouble him in
the least. True to the most advanced insights into the
substitution of formal manipulations for mimetics, Nabokov
feels no obligation to make his situation felt as life
might be felt. 'Art is free,' he seems to say. 'If my
poetry is there, it's there.' But the thrill of Lolita's
Liebestod or the more abstract aesthetics of 'Pale Fire'
rather resembles the *frisson* of bumping into Napoleon in
a waxworks. It is astoundingly convincing perhaps, but
there is something vulgar in trying to make a lost,
glorious past look so real.

Whereas Nabokov has been unable to resurrect the true
grandeur of his convention, the aspiration to do so undoubtedly saves his work from the flashiness and vulgarity
that repeatedly threatens it. On the other hand, his
wit and the stunning ingenuity of his formal devices
(particularly in 'Pale Fire') easily surpass those of any
other novelist now writing in English. But his literary
virtues gnaw at one another, undermine one another, and
tend to become the vices of gratuitous verbal display and
ersatz transcendence. Nabokov defends his own work on
the basis of a narrow hedonism, the 'aesthetic bliss' his
work provides. But this is not enough for the great and
antiquated form of human nobility he has adopted, which
resolves itself *beyond* hedonism. Somewhere he is aware
of this — perhaps it underlies the truculence of his
public position and the extreme, virtually metaphysical
importance he attaches to his work. The anti-novelist in
him is willing to examine the romantic idea in the light
of cruel irony. But the aristocratic *émigré* who lingers
over Pushkin will not tolerate the slightest suspicion
of its final value. Nabokov's 'bliss' is not self-con-
tained or serene. It is not even elevated. It is intensely hortatory, virulently nostalgic. The greatest traditionalist now writing in English stands on modern literature's shakiest ground.

Note

1 See p. 65.

'Despair'

1966

Originally written in Russian as 'Otchayanie'; serialized
in 'Sovremennye Zapiski' (Paris), 1934; published in
volume form in Berlin, 1936. Translated by Vladimir
Nabokov (London), 1937; retranslated with many revisions
and additions and serialized in this form in 'Playboy',
1965–6; revised version issued in volume form in Britain
and the USA, 1966.

51. VIRGILIA PETERSON IN 'REPORTER'

2 June 1966, 42–4

Virgilia Peterson (1904–66) was an American writer and
critic.

Avant-garde writers on both sides of the Atlantic have
decreed the demise of the old novel. They want the *tabula
rasa* of revolution, to make way for a new kind of novel
to rise to the top. The fact that the wheel has long
since been invented does not satisfy them. They pretend
it does not exist so as to invent it again. They see
nothing paradoxical about a deliberate search for originality. They seem to believe that one has only to look
for a discovery to find it. But while they have been
casting about for new wheels, there has arisen in their
midst a writer who, with any hoop, can write circles
around them all. He did not have to search for originality. He found it — where alone it can be found — inside

himself. In the infinite ramifications of his self-awareness, he is more modern than any of them. No other writer
speaks as surely to the post-Freudian, post-Communist,
post-romantic, post-realistic, post-religious western mind
of today as Vladimir Nabokov.

Nabokov is best known, of course, as the progenitor of
poor Lolita, whose name has become a byword for sultry
adolescence. Readers with long memories may also remember the exiled professor, Pnin, and, more recently, the
young ill-starred chess genius, Luzhin. But if the famous
(or is it infamous?) Lolita had never existed, she would
not have had to be invented to assure Nabokov his place
in contemporary literature. Behind him lies a large and
unique body of work: nine novels written in his native
Russian, of which he has translated six into English, five
novels written in English, four collections of short
stories, a critical biography of Gogol, a memoir of his
boyhood, two volumes of his own poetry, and three volumes
of other poetry translated by him from the Russian. While
it has become fashionable among certain critics to trace
the themes that recur in his work — madness, perverse
pursuit of little girls, treacherous women, homesickness —
to his great predecessors in Russian literature and thereby
to suggest that it is more derivative than original, the
fact remains that his treatment of these themes, his ideas,
his jokes, his characters, and the demons that haunt them
(he is peculiarly the prey and the conjuror of such
hantises), and above all his astonishing virtuosity with
words stamp all his work indelibly with his signature.

The appearance, therefore, of another novel by Nabokov
is an event, even if, as in the case of this newly published book, 'Despair,' it was written as long ago in his
career as 1932 and cannot compare in resonance with the
later novels — to name two of the best, 'The Real Life
of Sebastian Knight' and 'Pale Fire.' As with other books
he wrote originally in Russian, Nabokov has done his own
translation of 'Despair,' revising it to suit as nearly
as possible his present mature temper. In a foreword
that is in part apologia for what he calls the 'bungling
apprentice' that he was three decades ago and in part a
gleeful anticipation of what he is sure will be the
fatuous critical reception of the book, he says that
'Plain readers ... will welcome its plain structure and
pleasing plot...' Only Nabokov himself could have dreamed
up so hilariously improbable a description of the contents
of 'Despair.'

It is true that 'Despair' could be summarized in a
sentence: the story of a murder as told by the murderer.
But to define it thus is, to say the least, an oversimpli-

fication, for the man who is murdered is the alter ego of
the murderer, and therefore, in intent and purpose, it is
the story of a man who murdered himself....

[A plot-summary follows.]

What he did and how, despite inexorable logic, watertight
shrewdness, and genius-like calculation, he discovered —
too late — the one trick his memory had played on him, is
unfolded in a tale as Faustian in its sorcery as any Nabokov has written.

Yet, clearly, 'Despair' is the work of a younger,
colder, harder man than the one revealed in his later
books. Just as Felix is no more than an understudy for
Hermann, so Hermann himself is no more than an understudy
for the Humbert Humbert of 'Lolita' and the Professor
Kinbote of 'Pale Fire,' whose torments, unlike those of
Hermann, elicit the reader's exacerbated pity. In one
of Hermann's reflections on storytelling (reflections
with which his own story is fascinatingly strewn), he
writes that 'the pale organisms of literary heroes feeding under the author's supervision swell gradually with
the reader's lifeblood.' Alas, Hermann's own organism receives no transfusions from the reader. He fails to
swell. He remains no more than one of the inventions of
the most fantastically inventive writer alive today.

52. UNSIGNED REVIEW, 'TIMES LITERARY SUPPLEMENT'

28 July 1966, 655

...This 'plain structure and pleasing plot', as the author
calls it, is very neatly organized — even if its relative
simplicity involves rather leisurely exposition — and the
trumping twists at the end are expertly dealt. But even
though this is all what Mr. Nabokov calls 'great fun' it
is not, as one might expect, the whole story. As is
common in Mr. Nabokov's *pièces noires*, the reader is
tempted to chase after fugitive suggestions of more occult
meanings. These tend, like the butterflies to which this
author is so devoted, to be iridescent, unpredictable in
flight, and fragile enough to be easily broken by clumsy
handling.

Just as 'The Defence' plays with the idea of human
movements which reflect the formal relations of chess
pieces, so here the notion of a double or alter ago (to
be developed in 'The Real Life of Sebastian Knight' and
'Pale Fire') is sustained by the frequent use of the image
of the mirror. The relationship of star to understudy or
stand-in is another variant. Mr. Nabokov mentions the
kind of film (had he seen 'The Student of Prague'?) in
which the split screen technique allows the same actor to
appear simultaneously in two roles, such as twin brothers —
and indeed Hermann at one point pretends to Felix that he
is a film actor. Hermann's imagination is said to 'hanker
after reflections, repetitions, masks', and he even produces, in the (futile) hope of placating the Soviet authorities, a little allegory of his resemblance to Felix in
Marxist terms — a characteristically Nabokovian parody
of dialectical 'correctness'. There is too a curious
passage where Hermann finds his conjugal pleasure enhanced
by dissociation: one self performs while the other seems
to watch. (This is presumably the scene which the publishers rather absurdly say 'could not have been published'
before 'Lolita' broke up 'rigid puritan standards'.)
However, by the end of the book Hermann cannot bear
mirrors, and this fear of his own reflection seems to be
related to the miscarrying of his crime. He more than once
claims his whole murderous design as a work of art, and
bolsters up the case by mocking references to novelists of
crime — Conan Doyle, Dostoevsky, &c. The wrong construction put on his crime by blundering police is likened
to the obtuse missings of the point critics fall into when
faced with the new works of genius. Hermann keeps the
reader continually aware, even if in a fatuously compla-
cent way, of the problems of literary form, and one of the
titles he considers for his book is 'Portrait of the Artist
in a Mirror'. He reflects, perhaps, the baffled vanity
of the artist. It would be interesting to discover how
far this layer of meaning, in which the narrator's story
is made to serve as a model of the artistic process, has
been sharpened in the recent revision.
It must of course be added — if this line of thought
is correct — that Hermann is clearly a monstrous character and can only represent the kind of artist of whom we
are to disapprove. The whole book turns out to be, as it
were, at his expense. Mr. Nabokov is always at his most
exuberant when writing scornfully of human vanity (the
tone of his recent prefaces is ineffably contemptuous),
and his treatment of Hermann is exhilaratingly disdainful.
This relationship between author and hero is the only one
of which, as in other novels of Mr. Nabokov's, we have any

acute sense. However, this aristocratic detachment should
not always be taken at face value. Perhaps — a last
twist of the resemblance theme — Hermann is in the final
analysis a kind of *hypocrite romancier*, the hated reflection in the novelist's own glass, a disturbing double-
ganger distanced and contained.

Mr. Nabokov, however, is never easy to pin down, and
it is wise to heed his refusal to have anything to do with
the vulgarities of 'message' or self-revelation. The
preface to 'Despair' refers to his work as 'a derisive
mirage organized by my agents'. Certainly, in this fascinating novel, he takes a heartless Olympian glee in the
fact that, if a work of art *is* a mirror, then what it
chiefly shows the eager, trusting reader is himself.

53. RONALD HINGLEY IN 'SPECTATOR'

29 July 1966, 152-3

From the large corpus of Vladimir Nabokov's early work
the novel 'Despair' (first published in Russian and English
thirty years ago) has now been rescued and revamped, and
is here presented anew. The bones of the plot are these:
the hero, Hermann, happens to meet a stranger, Felix, who
exactly resembles him; he gulls Felix into exchanging
clothes on a plausible pretext, and them murders him so
that the 'widow' can collect the insurance money. Like
Dostoievsky's 'Crime and Punishment', this is a thriller.
Must it also be taken seriously as a work of literature?
Parts of it earn this title for the graphic potency of
the writing, which always seems at its best when the two
doubles are in contact: at their first meeting in the
outskirts of Prague; at a rendezvous in the town of
Tarnitz and, above all, at the murder scene itself, this
last being a minor masterpiece.

Unfortunately, the novel is marred by ill-judged
attempts to invest it with literary portentousness. In
particular, Hermann, as narrator, is caused to insert
lengthy comments all over the place on his own technique
of narration. Should a chapter be started in this or that
way? How does the story compare with the work of such
bungling predecessors in the genre as Dostoievsky, etc.?
(There are echoes in the plot of 'The Double' as well as
of 'Crime and Punishment'.) Then these digressions them-

selves form the subject of further digressions, in the course of which one very well-chosen phrase occurs: 'These conversations with readers are quite silly.'

Somehow the apostrophisings of the 'gentle reader' contrive to be aggressive and arch at the same time, which does at least make for an original mixture. Nor do they all fall entirely flat; for instance, one, on the existence of God, is very funny indeed. Still, it is distracting to have one's attention taken up by Nabokov's insistence, in effect, on providing a running review of his own book as he goes along. No sooner does he induce a willing suspension of disbelief than he perversely reinstates the disbelief. Admittedly it is part of the function of Hermann's discursive droolings to characterise him as unhinged, but one would have been prepared to concede that point on less evidence than is provided here.

Can it be that Nabokov sees his relationship to his readers as that of sadist to masochist? There are features in his other works and in the preface to the present volume (with its singularly graceless asperity) which bear out such a theory. Another feature of the book is the ever-present whiff of translationese which makes it sound like the work of a rather tougher-minded Constance Garnett. As with Garnett, off-beat English is redeemed in places by felicitous distortions such as no Englishman could have dreamed up unaided by a Russian original. 'Despair' has the makings of a very fine short story indeed and contains some excellent passages. It was well worth republishing, but could have done with some ruthless pruning.

54. WILLIAM COOPER IN 'LISTENER'

11 August 1966, 213

William Cooper (born 1910) is an English novelist; his books include 'Scenes from Provincial Life' (1950).

For the first three quarters of 'Despair', there's so much whim and so little rule that it's nearly impossible to tell where one's going.... [It] begins menacingly with a man meeting his double, and Mr Nabokov seems to invite

one to make an ass of oneself by identifying the novel as
an Allegory About Self, A Psychological Thriller, An Inquiry Into The Nature Of Writing A Novel, or some such
meat for literary persons. In the last quarter it settles
down to a plot by the narrator to murder his double so as
to get the insurance money. The book has its moments of
verbal fun, fantasy, and personal idiosyncrasy.

55. J. MITCHELL MORSE IN 'HUDSON REVIEW'

Autumn 1966, 513-14

J. Mitchell Morse (born 1912) was formerly Professor of
English at Temple University, Philadelphia, Pa.

...Let us end this review with a book that is worth discussing. 'Despair' is early Nabokov (1932 in Russian, 1937
in English), but even early Nabokov is good. The prose is
for the most part rather awkward, but I attribute that to
the narrator, not to the author. Hermann is a very simple
soul who fancies himself a devil of complexity, and he
writes accordingly. He reminds me of Larbaud's A.O.
Barnabooth. I think the bad writing here is deliberately
bad. 'Nor am I quite certain of the exceptionality of the
aforesaid phenomena,' Hermann writes. He is even capable
of writing 'waive aside,' and 'conservativeness.' Nabokov
doesn't make mistakes except on purpose.
     This leads us to believe that not only the style but
everything else is a mockery and a deception, or at least
an effort to deceive....
     Nabokov often seems to be sunk in reflection like
Narcissus; this novel is full of mirror effects of all
kinds, always ingenious but after a while rather tiresome. This is a functional failure in an otherwise clever
novel. On page 213 Hermann deplores the fact that a minor
error can destroy a masterpiece; this denies his earlier
denials that a minor error can affect a masterpiece at
all. But perhaps a more serious error is the fact that
we must take this bad prose on faith. It hardly seems
worthy of Nabokov. On page 195 Hermann reads a newspaper
account of his crime and writes, 'I was unspeakably shocked
by the tone of the thing: it was in fact so improper, so

impossible in regard to me, that for a moment I even thought it might refer to a person bearing the same name as I; for such a tone is used when writing of some half-wit hacking to bits a whole family.' In this novel Nabokov does justice to Hermann but not to himself, I think. He seems not yet to have found the proper Nabokov tone. 'Despair' is an item in literary history.

56. QUENTIN ANDERSON IN 'NEW REPUBLIC'

4 June 1966, 23-8

Quentin Anderson (born 1912) has been Professor of English at Columbia University. His publications include 'The American Henry James' (1957).

Nabokov, describing the work of 'V. Sirin' (his pseudonym as a Russian emigré novelist) in 'Conclusive Evidence,' says, 'the real life of his books flowed in his figures of speech,' and 'his best works are those in which he condemns his people to the solitary confinement of their souls.' 'Despair,' the sixth of the nine novels Nabokov wrote in Russian, is neatly bracketed by these remarks. He wrote it in 1932, and translated it into English in 1936. But the text now published is a revision of the original — the reader who has no Russian, and no copy of the first translation for comparison is persuaded that important changes have been made by the virtuosity of the concise and resonant English of the present version. Single words carry more weight than they did in Nabokov's first two novels in English, and produce effects of start-ling distinctness, effects quite beyond the reach of the accomplished author of 'The Real Life of Sebastian Knight' (1941) and 'Bend Sinister' (1947)....
  Is the book more than a suffocating joke on its central figure and a trip to a mirrored fun house for its reader? It depends on what you think of the language, it depends on 'the figures of speech' and how much you prize them. The very qualities which led Mary McCarthy to say that 'Pale Fire' was 'one of the very great works of art of this century' are here — not, it is true, in the same measure (the book is not so multilayered), but

still they are here. For example, an extraordinary passage in which Hermann finds that the town in which he has
undertaken to meet his double seems to be almost wholly
built out of reminiscences of his own past; he wonders
whether Felix can in fact appear there, or whether his
very conception of Felix is not the product of an appetite for repetition which is growing in him. The play
with resemblances is, of course, very intricate: is
Felix a 'minus I' in the sense that traces on a blotter
are negatives, and can only be read in a mirror? Did
Felix have the obstinacy, the stubborn bad taste (from
Hermann's viewpoint) to read himself as the positive, Hermann as the negative?

All this is consonant with the patterned games played
in certain other Nabokov novels. 'The Eye,' a novella,
and 'The Defence' resemble 'Despair' in that their chief
figures are condemned as is Hermann to spin a world out
of their fatally repetitive inner resources. With some
qualifications, 'Laughter in the Dark' and 'Lolita' belong in this group.

In the light of one common assumption about the novel
it would be denied that these were novels at all. In
them the recording consciousness is jealous, and won't
give up its world to the reader. What we are given is
theme and variations, and denied any sense of cumulation
or growth. We get experience of the order of a child's
memories, experience deprived of temporal dimension.
Each of the rendered moments is like a separate raid on
the continuum of life which brings back an observation
that is rendered with the tang of immediacy and yet serves
an exemplary use in the web Nabokov is weaving. The life
of his work does in fact lie in his figures of speech.
And there is something in it which is wholly inimical to
our gross appetite for stories of growth, development,
sequential change.

> I confess I do not believe in time. I like to fold my
> magic carpet after use, in such a way as to super-
> impose one part of the pattern upon another. Let
> visitors trip. And the highest enjoyment of time-
> lessness — in a landscape selected at random — is
> when I stand among rare butterflies and their food
> plants. This is ecstasy, and behind the ecstasy is
> something else, which is hard to explain. It is like
> a momentary vacuum into which rushes all that I love.
> A sense of oneness with sun and stone. A thrill of
> gratitude to whom it may concern — to the contrapuntal
> genius of human fate or to tender ghosts humoring a
> lucky mortal. ('Conclusive Evidence')

Nabokov's prose medium deserves a name, partly a desig-
nation, partly frankly incantatory, as is Gerard Manley
Hopkins' 'sprung rhythm.' We might call it the 'light
anthropomorphic,' and find a simple and characteristic
instance of it in the sentence, 'Let visitors trip.' In
this medium the interpenetration of humanity by language,
language by humanity is, moment by moment, felt as complete. Its range, its horizontal range, is very wide,
gallery upon glittering gallery of the tricks by which we
betray ourselves in language and language betrays us. But
its scale is single; it can only tell us what we do to
words and they to us; it cannot tell us what men have
done. It appears to deny the possibility of saying *con-
summatum est* of any human action. It works minutely and
reflectively: one little vaudeville of the light anthropomorphic gives way to the next, and so on until the
pattern is complete....

Everything that threatens the games played in the group
of books to which 'Despair' belongs is fiercely attacked
by Nabokov as if art were unsafe as long as anybody was
generalizing about anything in any context. This is
Nabokov's public role, and it is the only public role he
permits his characters to assume. Historical and cultural
judgment, Marx, Freud, politicians and metaphysicians,
Dostoevsky, Balzac, Stendhal, Proust, the novelist who
is described as 'the family doctor of Europe' — Thomas
Mann? — anyone who classifies anything except words and
butterflies is scorned. A novelist remarks in 'Laughter
in the Dark,' 'Well, when a literature subsists on Life
and Lives, it means it is dying. And I don't think much
of Freudian novels or novels about the quiet countryside.'
The young writer of 'The Gift' remarks on the unsuitability
of a theme: 'I would have become enmired involuntarily
in a "deep" social-interest novel with a disgusting Freudian reek.' (As one might anticipate, there is quite
another view of Joyce, a figure whom Nabokov says he re-
veres.) John Wain has remarked in these columns that
the scorn of Nabokov's appears to be the scorn conventionally attributed to the artist who is asked to write
to somebody else's ends, or everybody else's ends. I
think it is a symptom of something more than this.

The scornful detachment of the prefaces conceals the
fact that in another group of novels Nabokov's art is —
in his sense — very impure indeed. 'Invitation to a Beheading' and 'Bend Sinister' are novels in which all
reality and value inhere in the central figure, and the
environing world is condemned to act out an imprisoning
fantasy which the hero and the reader see through. These
novels are occasioned by their times, and reflect Nabokov's

response to his sense of the idiocy of Communism and Nazi
Germany. They can hardly be defended on the ground on
which Nabokov habitually asserts the independence of his
art from all ideological and psychological generalities.
The human glory of their central figures is dependent on
convictions about human worth that the reader must bring
to the book, convictions on which Nabokov relies. With
these two novels we may associate two more, 'The Gift'
(1937) and 'The Real Life of Sebastian Knight,' in which
the recording consciousness is that of a writer, and is
quite as authoritative for the reader as are the heroes
of the first two novels. I shall come to 'Pnin,' 'Lolita'
and 'Pale Fire' in a moment; these four novels suffice to
make the point that Nabokov has often ignored what he
says in 'Conclusive Evidence': 'in a first-rate work of
fiction the real clash is not between the characters but
between the author and the world.' There is a quite
shameless human glory about Krug in 'Bend Sinister,' about
the figures of the writer's parents in 'The Gift,' about
the hero of 'Invitation to a Beheading' — with these
characters our sympathy is complete. When these persons
are placed beside Hermann, Luzhin of 'The Defence,' the
central figure of 'The Eye,' these latter recede into
the texture of the works in which they appear, seem mere
themes for light anthropomorphic exercises. We are once
more outsiders.

Why shouldn't Nabokov have written in two fictional
modes, giving now one, now the other, the ascendency?
What is important is the critical significance of the
divergence and final confluence of these two kinds in
Nabokov's work. What we may call his naturalism is dominant in Nabokov's recorded memories of his childhood and
youth in 'Conclusive Evidence.' It is a fully peopled
world, rather lush, even sentimental, through which move
the figures of a father and mother (whose splendid worldly
ascendancy is matched by inner grace and strength), a
group of attendant persons, first loves, family retainers
and so on. This interrelatedness, this sense of an ordered life in common with others does not of course recur
in the Nabokov fiction I know. But 'The Gift' offers, in
the persons of the young writer's parents, characters who
survive out of such a time and such a world. These characters are bordered in black, cherished, lonely and doomed,
like Krug and the lepidopterist father of 'The Gift,' who
has, anticipating John Shade of 'Pale Fire,' a relation to
cosmic patterns, 'A sense of oneness with sun and stone.'
This strong sense of a lost sunlit world is the hidden
positive in Nabokov's work; it is what such glinting
constructs as 'Despair' operate to hide. We are justified

in saying that Nabokov's publicly stated aesthetic theory
is equivalent to a historical judgment. He willed time
to a stop. Certain lonely figures in his fiction survive
the actual holocaust and his aesthetic assertion of its
finality. The naturalism survives in his work and re-
emerges (somewhat attenuated) in the sentimental naturalism of 'Pale Fire.' It is as if, having incautiously
trusted to the persistence of the rules of the social
order which had nourished his first nineteen years, he had
determined never again to accept any set of rules from anyone, or write anything which could be subsumed within any
order.

I shall not attempt here to deal with the complex interplay of the patterned as against the naturalist strands
in Nabokov's work. I have suggested that the human
glory of Krug, which is posed against a cruel and mind-
less society, represents a naturalism which gives way to
a more sentimental strain in Nabokov's later work, in
fact in the very next novel, 'Sebastian Knight.' Knight,
unsupported by a sense of the wholeness of a human community of the order we find in 'Conclusive Evidence,'
makes his lonely assertion of the generically human: 'All
things belong to the same order of things, for such is
the oneness of human perception, the oneness of individuality, the oneness of matter, whatever matter may be.
The only real number is one, the rest are mere repetition.'
To reinforce this we may quote Shade's poem in 'Pale Fire':

> And if my private universe scans
> So does the verse of galaxies divine
> Which I suspect is an iambic line.

A longer passage from 'Sebastian Knight,' which, like
Shade's poem, is concerned with a solution to the riddle
of death, may make Nabokov's movement from a naturalism
conditioned by the memory of community to a naturalism
founded on a faith in our kinship with the order of nature
somewhat plainer. Both seem to have been present from
his youth onward, but the ascendancy of the latter grows
as the memory of a society in being recedes.

And the word, the meaning which appears is astounding
in its simplicity: the greatest surprise being perhaps
that in the course of one's earthly existence, with one's
brain encompassed by an iron ring, by the close-fitting
dream of one's own personality — one had not made by
chance that simple mental jerk, which would have set free
imprisoned thought and granted it the great understanding.
Now the puzzle was solved. 'And as the meaning of all
things shone through their shapes, many ideas and events

which had seemed of the utmost importance dwindled not to
insignificance, for nothing could be insignificant now,
but to the same size which other ideas and events, once
denied any importance, now attained.' Thus, such shining
giants of our brain as science, art or religion fell out
of the familiar scheme of their classification, and joining hands, were mixed and joyfully levelled. Thus, a
cherry stone and its tiny shadow which lay on the painted
wood of a tired bench, or a bit of torn paper, or any
other such trifle out of millions and millions of trifles
grew to a wonderful size. Remodelled and re-combined,
the world yielded its sense to the soul as naturally as
both breathed.

The belief that such an awareness of nature might
afford this measure of human fulfillment lies about fifty
years behind us in the European consciousness. It stems
from an age in which science seemed to authorize wider
hopes, rather than pose deeper threats. When we are
thinking of Nabokov as a modernist his grounding in a
sentimental naturalism must be recalled. The hardness,
brightness and echoing intricacy of his patterned fiction
is a culturally determined mode of coping with a world
which denies the 'sense of oneness with sun and stone.'

But I have been speaking as if the Nabokov who willed
time to a stop had in the process suppressed the world
of his childhood, and this is misleading. His delight
in exposing 'the contrapuntal genius of human fate' is
a quite logical extension of that world, or rather the
breakdown of the inter-personal hierarchic order that
world represented. Luzhin, Paduk (the Hitler figure of
'Laughter in the Dark'), Humbert, Hermann, are persons in
whom the child's absorption in his play is prolonged into
adulthood, prisoners rather than makers of patterns.
Humbert keeps wooing the ten-year-old girl of the Biarritz
beach, and our consciousness of this is the source of our
sympathy, which persists together with our awareness that
he has become loathsome. Such figures, like Luzhin, who
also invites our sympathy, nonetheless fail to respond to
the first moral value of the Nabokovian universe, a respect for the singleness of others. The mocking memoir of
Chernyshevski in 'The Gift' brims with venom directed at
a generation which infected us all — infected Lenin himself — with the horrible smarmy presumption that we were
so nearly identical that we could be understood en masse.
Hermann's unforgivable spiritual vulgarity is the hunger
for a resemblance that amounts to identity — something
that can only be attributed to inanimate things, dead
things. And 'Despair' is, like all the internally echoing works, a struggle with the reader; he is being

tested: if he thinks he can assimilate the pattern to his beliefs and expectations he is one more fool who doesn't know the value of singleness.

I have made it plain enough that the works in which everything is subdued to the pattern, while serially brilliant, seem to me as exhaustible in their interest as reported games of chess. The hero of 'Invitation to a Beheading,' while describing himself as incapable of writing says that he has an intuition of the way in which words must be combined, 'what one must do for a commonplace word to come alive and to share its neighbor's sheen, heat, shadow, while reflecting itself in its neighbor and renewing the neighboring word in the process, so that the whole line is live iridescence.' If you find the patterned works delightful it is such effects you delight in. If you are persuaded you are reading a full-fledged novelist you are unaware of the extent of your collaboration. The text under your eye is like a brilliant musical score, but the continuity of the performance is supplied by the reader, who fills in the curve of imagined human action. Of course this is a question of degree. 'Lolita,' up to the death of the mother, has no such limitation. Thereafter it falls, on rereading, into fragments, some of which retain their lustre, like the scene in which Humbert sees his married and pregnant love for the last time, while others have lost it altogether, and in fact share with certain of the American social observations in 'Pale Fire' the *fade* and dissonant quality of the marzipan hot dogs sold in fake Viennese candy shops. 'Pale Fire' is at once more ambitious and less successful than 'Lolita,' because, although there is much to be said for the poem, there is less to be said for the sentimental naturalism which informs it — except as a historical artifact — and the trapped and obsessed figure, Kinbote, unpacked in all his awful flatness and spiritual repetitiousness gives the book the flavor of his sterility. It is possible to be very serious, enormously talented, highly witty, and nonetheless to trivialize what seems a proper outgrowth of Nabokov's career, the attempt to bring to a focus the struggle between the patterned figure, Kinbote, and a last beleaguered human being, John Shade.

But there remains one almost perfect work, 'Pnin.' What I have rather clumsily described as the 'naturalism' is here to be found in the implied character of the narrator, perhaps the most winning of Nabokov's persons, and the book appears to be completely patterned, yet the narrator's scrupulous and tender attention supplies exactly that continuity of human concern that the other patterned works lack. Not that the narrator has an unqualified

role. Indeed his dramatic relation to Pnin is brilliantly
sustained and developed. As he physically approaches Pnin
must recede, because the narrator is precisely that element
within whose ambience Pnin cannot exist. The book is a
delight and a minor classic.

Modernism, the period of Proust, Joyce, Kafka, Eliot,
is over, and the preoccupations of poets and writers of
fiction are now so different that Nabokov has begun to
seem remote. He tries to make language the vessel of our
humanity, and supports in public the contention that art
is its own excuse for being. He gives this contention
away in certain works, and it becomes plain that it is
actually parasitic on the memory of an ordered community.
His assertion of the self-sufficiency of art will come
to seem increasingly unintelligible to a generation unaware
of the hidden premise of his humanism. He will go into a
temporary eclipse. If the world of community were magically to be reborn the influence of the very thing he publicly denies would serve to reinstate him. But the world
in which Beckett, Genet, Burroughs, and the non-novel
flourish is a world in which the politics of the soul is
primary, and verbal adventure has lost its invisible sup-
porting warp of remembered human solidarity. This, I take
it, is the end, so often prematurely announced, of the
romantic movement.

'King, Queen, Knave'

1968

Originally written in Russian as 'Korol, Dama, Valet' and
published in Berlin, 1928; new Russian edition, with
foreword, published in New York, 1969. Translated by
Dmitri and Vladimir Nabokov and published in New York
and London, 1968.

57. GILLIAN TINDALL IN 'NEW STATESMAN'

4 October 1968, 435

Gillian Tindall (born 1938) is an English novelist, journalist and reviewer.

It is a temptation to think of Nabokov's early works
mainly as dress rehearsals for the masterpieces; and so
one must stress that this book is as polished as any that
have followed. Most writers begin with a heart and only
gradually develop anything much like a style: with Nabokov,
the process seems to have been reversed.... As a God without charity the inventor invites us to mock all round....
Only a generation, a couple of languages and a continent
later did he seemingly develop enough heart — or allow
his heart enough place in his works — to mock himself as
well.

58.   DENIS DONOGHUE IN 'LISTENER'

10 October 1968, 480

Denis Donoghue (born 1928) is Professor of Modern English
and American Literature at University College, Dublin.
His books include studies of Swift, Yeats and Emily
Dickinson.

'Of all my novels this bright brute is the gayest,' Mr
Nabokov writes in a new introduction.... The brute is
bright, but not as gay as 'Lolita', as funny as 'Pnin',
as brilliant as 'The Gift'. There are moments in which
it seems to aspire to the condition of 'Kind Hearts and
Coronets', but the debonair effects are not continuous,
effort keeps breaking in. It is common to say that Mr
Nabokov's novels are best understood by taking them as
dream plays, figments, mirror images. Perhaps the present novel should be read as a form of literary criticism,
since the incidents assume the presence of similar incidents in other books, standing between this new fiction
and the begging world. Mr Nabokov's book applies the
force of practical criticism to the analysis of bourgeois
passion. If anything survives the translation into farce,
it may be allowed to pass.

'Ada'

1969

Written in English; published in New York and London,
1969.

59. ALFRED KAZIN IN 'SATURDAY REVIEW'

10 May 1969, 28-30

Alfred Kazin (born 1915) is an American teacher and journalist. His books include studies of F. Scott Fitzgerald
and Theodore Dreiser.

From the beginning, as is usual with Nabokov, one is
aware of allusions that are meant to be snares, puns that
are sometimes alliterative jokes and sometimes crypto-
grammic formulas, 'hidden' meanings that will take you
on exhausting treasure hunts to further jokes, parodies
of other novelists that honor Tolstoy but are insults to
Maupassant. Nabokov loves to play against the reader and
to outwit him, but he also likes to demonstrate his originality in small pedantic matters. Probably no author
since Poe has so often consciously scored over his readers. Yet in his gamesmanship he is never as solemn as
are those few scholars who can uncover most of his tricks,
for Nabokov really enjoys exerting his imagination on im-
probabilities and distortions of perception, inversions
and inventions of language. The babble of many tongues,
the zanily insistent references, the sentences that are

dizzyingly lucid despite their arcane jokes — all warn
the reader that he is being laughed at in small matters
but instructed in large ones. For these doubles and
twinships exist only in space, and trouble most those
who, like Aqua, are mad. Those with the artist's pene-
tration, like Van, know that time transcends space. It
doesn't matter how many successive bodies we inhabit as
we go from childhood to age, how many countries have been
fused by our adventures. Time is the only real element
in which the mind lives, and time is the story that we
alone can write. 'Ada' thus represents a portrait of the
creative process. Time does whatever we like. We seek,
Nabokov hauntingly wrote in 'Speak, Memory,' to know what
there was before we were born and what there will be after
we die. In his view, consciousness is eternal life, and
while we must accept the 'nothing' we can locate before
we were born, we cannot accept a second 'nothing' even if
people call it 'death.' Man cannot conceive of himself
without consciousness, and in this sense 'death' does not
exist. The universe consists of our consciousness and in
our consciousness....

Yet the book, in a sense a thesis novel, gives us the
Lesson According to Nabokov. There are long disquisitions
on the real meaning of time and its dissimulations, and
there are typically farce-like deaths that do not inter-
rupt the action for a moment and remind us that we all
die many times in the course of going on from phase to
phase. But, essentially, the book turns, as the ultimate
of the time sense, on an absolute homesickness for the
fabled and lost estate of childhood, 'Ardis'; on an
ultimate homesickness for the loved one, Ada, as the
name, the name alone, that carries our hero through life.
The book also turns on the commingling of tongues, con-
tinents, nations, cities, inventions, all of which get
blissfully mixed up because in the language-that-is-now-
Vladimir-Nabokov all the separate pieces of his memory
have turned into imagination as the whole. As in 'Gulli-
ver' or 'Tristram Shandy' or 'Alice in Wonderland' (which
Nabokov translated into Russian) one is aware of life
transformed into pure imagination, pure picture, pure
pleasure.

Our Vladimir Vladimirovitch is an extraordinary artist,
in the present situation of the novel absolutely a law
unto himself. 'Ada,' coming as it does after 'Lolita'
and that far more difficult but greater book, 'Pale
Fire,' makes a trilogy that simply has no counterpart just
now for imaginative detail, for range of interest, for
architectural form, for caprice and genius of language.
It is prodigious. As a love story, it is more insistent

and symbolic than believable, but insistency and symbolism are what Nabokov may ascribe most to love. As fiction or invention, it is the most happily loony work since
'Alice.' The little Nabokovs out of whom Nabokov has
made his book fire off so many references that certain
scenes — two take place in bed — suggest a conclave of
pedants released from all earthly ties. The greatest
charm of the book lies in the fact that so many of the
characters are as creative as Nabokov himself. The lovers
are both geniuses. Many mysterious characters are referred
to as if we should know them and would know them, if *we*
were geniuses.

60. MARY ELLMANN IN 'YALE REVIEW'

October 1969, 118-19

The novel is an interplay of young love and old memory,
which produces an illusion of blissful sensuality. In
Van's memory, love retains the intensity, and loses only
the blunders and humiliations, of actual youth. A pretty
idyllic shamelessness seems possible, which in turn makes
possible limpid and perfect, if somewhat perfunctory, copu-
lations. The retrospective imagination dwells less upon
these inarticulate finales than upon all their piquant
preliminaries. The past in 'Ada' is a miscellany of
details (pouting lips and honeyed fingers) which, swim-
ming up separately in the memory, carry with them the
heavy, sweet ambience of lost innuendos, enticements, and
approaches. The disjunction of these details admits the
loss of the whole, even as, nonetheless, each detail defies the loss by its own immanence.

Often then, a lovely nostalgia and, for all the whim-
sies of geography, a lovely *Russian* nostalgia. Something
here continues and revives one's whole literary sense of
that country's romantic White charms — the summery
fields, the white dresses, the odd Chekovian trailings in
and out of the birthday picnic. But 'Ada' is not entirely
a novel of nostalgia. It is a wild attempt at narrative
simultaneity: every scene must recapture its original
quality and at the same time express the current (or *now*)
quality of the Van Veen who remembers the scene. This
twoness accounts, as I have tried to say, for the singular
lightness of its sexuality. But it also accounts for the
novel's singular attitude toward language.

In unforeseeable spurts, words work for the narrator,
fitting the old lost animality as smoothly as a cat's fur.
But more often, he seems to be working for the words.   He
is subject to the same disjunctive sense of words in
the present as of objects in the past, but while all the
returns to the concrete are humid, these excursions into
the abstract are arid.   Old Van remarks, rather smugly,
that 'the sensual was always rimmed by the mental' in the
young Van.   But it's more than a rim now, it's a vise.
(And a vice, as Van would inevitably add.)   The narrator
of 'Ada' cannot settle on a profession: he is half novelist and half word-worrier.   He pecks at syllables in three
languages, poking them apart, jerking them up and down,
like an exotic, hypertonic, and somewhat disoriented bird.

It is all evidently intended to be a perilous, marvellous balance, in the end, of lust and lucubration, a
linguist's love nest.   And, conceivably, it might have
become a remarkable expression of age — of its brief
and yet vivid seances with past passions, its otherwise
analytic concern, crotchety and cackling by turns, with
'interests' or 'subjects.'   Then pleasure might seem involuntarily, necessarily, to diminish in action and to
increase in active verbs.   But any such admission of
slackened life is not made by the narrator.   Old Van is
casual enough about the slackening of libido, but it is
clear that he considers his intelligence just as admirable,
just as *exciting*, as young Van's feelings.   The book exudes
a delight, bordering upon vanity, in its own manic, over-
wrought, and unnatural vocabulary, its inexhaustible translations, allusions, puns, and anagrams.

That teasing of the reader which was sufficient in 'Pale
Fire' is now excessive.   'Ada' contains a knowledge of our
common and terrible hunger for love story, and of its
therefore being possible to charge ten puns for each kiss.
But the book is not all tease.   The standard set is one of
'brilliant coarseness' — the 'throbbing member' (shade of
'La Rose d'Amour') redeemed by the flashing intellect. And
Van says, quite seriously, that the only true honesty of
a writer lies in an 'originality of literary style.'   In
the context of 'Ada,' one realizes that brilliance and
originality are virtues, of course, but rather dry and
brittle virtues.   They depend upon immediate rather than
slow effects, ingenious rather than deep connections,
metaphor rather than symbol — manipulations of words which
are quick, cavorting, and somehow pitiless.   Van and Ada,
teases too, and condescending to all but each other, can
breathe such brilliance, but I miss poor snuffed-out Pnin
and Luzhin.

61.   CAROL JOHNSON IN 'ART INTERNATIONAL'

1969, 42

Carol Johnson (born 1928) teaches at the University of
Victoria (Canada) and has published poetry and criticism.

Nabokov's 'Ada' is a supremely literary product of quite
distinctly limited literary virtue. If this book is to be
enjoyed, it must be enjoyed as a piece of confectionary
archeology, as a joke on the novel (and on the expectations of certain kinds of readers) rather than Litra-
chore, as his heroine might put it. If anyone in our
lamentable century is equipped to fulfill Flaubert's expressed wish of writing a novel 'about nothing', surely
it is Nabokov who with 'Ada' has succeeded in perpetrating
a feat of style (or, more properly, a feat of styles) to
the virtual exclusion of substance, to the extent of 598
pages, in a language not his own. This is not to suggest
that Nabokov is an engineer of prose, he is of course a
connoisseur of prose; this is his gift and yet the gift
is responsible in some respect for his deficiencies as a
novelist. There is no substitute for intelligence. And
intelligence is what one most responds to in Nabokov's
work. Yet neither is there in the art of the novel an
easy substitute for that consciousness, that self-effac-
ing absorption in human behaviour from which the motives
for fiction characteristically derive. The convention of
fiction is to be about people. Nabokov's fictions are
about people only in the most negligently fabricated sense.
He is interested in the behaviour of language, not people,
and — after language — in the thingyness of things. A
remark in his little book on Gogol to the effect that 'his
work, as all great literary achievements, is a phenomenon
of language and not one of ideas' (p.151, Editions Poetry,
London, 1947) has obvious relevance to Nabokov's own work,
and never more obviously than in 'Ada'. The consciousness
of the scrabble addict, the crossword puzzle composer,
the butterfly collector, the aristocrat created 'Ada' and
has constructed therein a diversion, a leisurely wordgame,
but nothing so irreducibly vulgar, so tenaciously middle
class as a novel. For the kinds of recognitions toward
which fiction tends, a writer of Nabokov's sensibility
prefers to distance, to transfer to things by means of
description. He does not dramatize. He does not readily

or convincingly relinquish point of view to his characters.
Like a highly skilled fugitive who desires nevertheless
to be caught, he proliferates clues rather than presents
an action. The aloofness of the exile, the self-absorption
of the displaced person are both relieved and re-lived and
ultimately reinforced in public fantasies that solicit
readers with a kind of contempt.

The private language of happy families with which 'Ada'
is replete is as naturally a mode of exclusion as it is a
mode of inclusion. The reader is invited to detect; he
can never become a sharer. The vanity and trivial-minded-
ness of the Veens, along with the concessions toward 'plot'
in 'Ada', are as much a way of putting the reader in his
place as of satisfying the demands of solipsism. The
humility that does not figure in Nabokov's relations with
his craft or with his readers occurs only, and I think
not insignificantly, in his own autobiography 'Speak,
Memory'. One can achieve suitable deference toward
that which one's deepest experience affirms is truly there.

Nabokov's art is an art of violated expectations: his
and ours. His tactics are uniquely parodistic. If irony
is defensive, a reaction of the cheated, the disillusioned,
representing an ambiguous response, it is demonstrably a
technique of discovery in literature. Parody is perhaps
a more extreme reaction to similar deprivation, but it is
the response of the made up mind. According to Thomas
Mann, a writer for whom Nabokov has little reverence, 'the
love for a form of art, in the historical possibility of
which one can believe no more, will inevitably beget
parody'. (I quote from Erich Heller's 'Thomas Mann, The
Ironic German', p. 253, Meridian books, New York, 1961.)
Not simply the 'form' of the novel but the antecedent
forms of life are for Nabokov no longer commodities in-
ducing rational belief. The rich, humanly availing and
secure world of Nabokov's childhood and youth, disposed
of by history, consigned to memory, furnishes the local
details less for a criticism of life than toward the dis-
crediting of the very tradition of symbolic realism in the
novel. A garbled throwaway version of Tolstoy's opening
sentence in 'Anna Karenina' begins 'Ada or Ardor: A Family
Chronicle' — and its pertinence is immediately disclaimed.

We are repeatedly warned by such tricks that the ensuing narrative neither aims to assuage nostalgia nor to
induce it....

62. MATTHEW HODGART IN 'NEW YORK REVIEW OF BOOKS'

22 May 1969, 3-4

Matthew Hodgart (born 1916) has taught at Cambridge and
Sussex and at various universities in North America; he
is now Professor of English at La Trobe University in
Australia. His books include studies of Johnson and Joyce.

[In its closing paragraphs, the book] provides its own
blurb in hideous parody, and perhaps it would have been
wiser to leave it at that. All Nabokov's books are full
of such built-in anti-reviewer devices, booby-traps that
are not meant to kill or mutilate (Nabokov is not a sadist),
but merely to blow the critic's pants off, leaving him
standing in ludicrous half-nakedness, missing something.
These traps must be detected; some can be avoided by
walking round them gingerly, others must be instantly and
as delicately as possible de-fused. On the other hand,
the books abound in perfectly fair clues, which if followed
up in a straightforward way may lead the reader to a perhaps incomplete but nevertheless satisfactory solution....
    Any sympathetic review of Nabokov begins to look like
Kinbote's demented commentary on Shade; so it needs to be
said simply that despite a proliferation of puns and puzzles
this book contains Nabokov's finest writing. The evocation
of Ardis, especially of the picnics in its woods, is magical,
and the erotic lyricism is of the highest order. It is
quite appropriate that a long extract should have appeared
in 'Playboy,' billed as Nabokov's sexiest work since
'Lolita'; though that is misleading since it is much sex-
ier in a wholly straightforward way. Taking advantage of
current freedoms, Nabokov has written an explicitly sensual
prose-poem of first love, as well as a parody of various vulgar and ludicrous types of pornography. His has achieved
ravishing effects of visual purity, by drawing on his
evidently great knowledge of painting: his is the most
highly trained eye in modern literature. Painting is itself a major theme (the older Veens are art dealers and
collectors, reflections of the great Duveen), and one luminous scene after another is based on the Venetians or the
Impressionists, above all on Renoir; while the grotesque
and demonic aspects of the story are portrayed through the
images of Hieronymous Bosch....

63.   ROBERT ALTER IN 'COMMENTARY'

August 1969, 47-50

Robert Alter (born 1935) is Professor of Hebrew and Comparative Literature at the University of California at Berkeley. His books include 'Fielding and the Nature of the Novel' (1968).

Vladimir Nabokov possesses what is probably the most finely cultivated sense of form of any living writer, and so there is a satisfying justness in the fact that not only his individual works but also the sequence of his books should evince a formal harmony. In his 1956 afterword to 'Lolita,' Nabokov warned that any assessment of his writing was bound to be out of focus without an awareness of his Russian work; since then, the translation or re-issue in English of seven of his nine Russian novels has in fact demonstrated that 'Lolita,' far from being a brilliant sport, was merely the most radiant and engaging in a line of books that for three decades had explored the paradoxical intertwinings of imagination and reality, the artist and his world, through athletically allusive, involuted, and parodistic fictional forms. These same concerns were then given even more original and intricate formal expression in 'Pale Fire,' while a new central emphasis in 'Lolita' on the quest for a paradisiac past (Humbert Humbert's golden 'princedom by the sea') appeared in oblique refraction through Kinbote's longing for his lost kingdom. Now, in his seventieth year, at an age when most novelists one can think of are already gone sadly to seed, Nabokov has produced a major work that in a purely formal sense culminates most of what he has attempted in over forty years of active writing. 'Ada' is the fullest realization of the program for the novel articulated in 1941 in Nabokov's first English book, 'The Real Life of Sebastian Knight'; as Sebastian Knight aspired to do, the author of 'Ada' 'use[s] parody as a kind of springboard for leaping into the highest region of serious emotion,' and thus succeeds in illuminating in new depth and breadth the relation between art, reality, and the evanescent ever-never presence of time past.

Because parody is intrinsic to Nabokov's method, and because he more often parodies plot, situation, and motif than style and narrative technique, a plot-summary of any

of his novels is bound to be thoroughly misleading.   (To
mislead the unsuspecting, of course, is precisely what
Nabokov intends: thus, the four concluding paragraphs
of 'Ada' are a pitchman's synopsis of the book, the prose
of the novel followed by what the narrator, tongue in
cheek, calls 'the poetry of its blurb.')   'Ada,' which is
surely one of the sunniest works of fiction written in
this century, sounds, to judge by the initial outlines of
its plot, like a dark drama of fatal, incestuous passion.
Van Veen, the retrospective nonagenarian narrator, has an
ecstatic affair at the age of fourteen with twelve-year-
old Ada, ostensibly his cousin, later discovered to be his
sister.   The two are irresistibly drawn to each other by
their inner nature but are separated by social taboo and
the course of outward events.   In the two decades from
early adolescence to mature adulthood, the lovers enjoy
four fleeting periods of illicit ardor together, but each
time the subsequent separation is longer, and while Van
seeks the simulacrum of his Ada in a thousand whores and
mistresses, both he and she are physically thickened and
coarsened by the passing years, until at last they come
together ·in late middle age, all passion not spent but
certainly muted.   In the background, moreover, of their
partings and joinings, as the third, unequal angle of a
thoroughly incestuous triangle, is the pathetic figure of
Lucette, their mutual half-sister, who loves Van relent-
lessly body and soul, loves Ada, periodically, in a more
strictly bodily sense, and finally destroys herself when
she is rejected by Van.

All this may sound like rather lurid stuff, especially
when one adds that there is a much higher degree of des-
criptive specification about sexual matters here than
anywhere else in Nabokov's fiction.   The actual tenor of
the novel, of course, is precisely the opposite of what
this summary suggests.   On a stylistic level, the seeming
paradox is easy enough to explain: Nabokov's intricately
wrought, elaborately figurative style, with its painterly
effects and its perspectivist mirror-games, transmutes
objects of description, even the most pungently physical
objects, into magical *objets d'art*.   When, for example,
the narrator, in a spectacular set-piece, describes all
three siblings in bed together (surely a parody of the
ménage à trois grapplings that are stock scenes of pornographic literature), he invites us to view the action as
though it were reflected in the ceiling mirror of a fancy
brothel, and then proceeds to convert the rampant eroticism into a formal contrasting and blending of colors
and movements.   Physical details are not spared — 'the
detail is all,' Van Veen had affirmed earlier about the

reality of all experience and memory — but, to cite a
strategic instance, the exposed sexual fluff of redheaded
Lucette and black-haired Ada becomes here a new-fledged
firebird and an enchanting blue raven, varicolored birds
of paradise in a poet's Wonderland.

When we move from effects of style to the larger narrative patterns of the novel, it is difficult to make full
sense of the incestuous complications without attention to
the ubiquitous use of literary allusion. In order to
talk about the allusions, something first must be said
about the setting. The principal action of 'Ada' takes
place in the late 19th and early 20th centuries of a world
alternately referred to as Antiterra and Daemonia, which
has the same geography as our world but a teasingly different though parallel history. The area we call Russia
having been conquered some centuries earlier by the Tartars,
America has been settled by Russian as well as English and
French colonists, and so Nabokov's own three native languages and literary traditions are able to flourish side
by side, as complementary parts of a single national culture. From a terrestrial viewpoint (Terra the Fair, by the
way, is a supposedly celestial place believed in mainly
by the deranged on Antiterra), historical periods as well
as cultural boundaries have been hybridized — the Daemon-
ian 19th century combines the quiet country houses of
Chekhov and Jane Austen with telephones, airplaces, sky-
scrapers; a mock-Maupassant figure is contemporaneous with
the author of a 'Lolita'-like novel masquerading (ana-
grammatically) as J.L. Borges. This device of a fictional
antiworld gives Nabokov a free hand to combine and permute
the materials of culture and history in piquant and suggestive ways, though perhaps it also sometimes tempts him
into self-indulgence, so that one begins to feel he is
playing his games of anagrams, trilingual puns, coded
hints, and conflated allusions for their own sake, not
because they have any imaginative necessity in a larger
design. (It must be admitted, though, that many of the
incidental games, especially those involving literary
figures, are so delightful in themselves that one would
hesitate to give them up. My own favorite is the treatment of T.S. Eliot, who appears as a truncated version
of his own ape-necked Sweeney, 'solemn Kithar Sween, a
banker who at sixty-five had become an *avant-garde* author;
... had produced "The Waistline," a satire in free verse
on Anglo-American feeding habits'; and who is seen, in
most poetic justice for a versifier of anti-Semitic in-
nuendoes, in the company of 'old Eliot,' a Jewish real-
estate man.)

The most important advantage, in any case, that Nabokov gains through the freedom he allows himself to shuttle across temporal and cultural boundaries is that he is able to compress into the life-space of his protagonist a parodistic review of the development of the novel. The story begins in the classic age of the novel, and, really, everything that happens occurs in purely novelistic time and novelistic space. Ardis Manor, where young Van Veen will meet Ada, is glimpsed for the first time, characteristically, in the following fashion: 'At the next turning, the romantic mansion appeared on the gentle eminence of old novels.' The narrative is frequently punctuated with such notations to remind us that everything is taking place against a background of jaded literary conventions, as the view shifts quickly, and not necessarily chronologically, from Romantic *récit* to Jane Austen, Turgenev, Dickens, Flaubert, Tolstoy, Dostoevsky, the pornographic novel, the Gothic novel, Joyce, Proust, and Nabokov beyond them. The 'plot,' in fact, is from one point of view comprised of a string of stock scenes from the traditional novel — the young man's return to the ancestral manor, the festive picnic, the formal dinner, a midnight blaze on the old estate, the distraught hero's flight at dawn from hearth and home as the result of a misunderstanding, the duel, the hero's profligacy in the great metropolis, and so forth.

Though the technique of allusion is common to all of Nabokov's novels, there is a special thematic justification for this recapitulation in parody of the history of a genre, for what Ven Veen's story represents is a reversal of the major thematic movement of the novel as a genre. The novel characteristically has concerned itself with lost illusions — the phrase, of course, was used as a title by Balzac — from the quixotic knight who finally abandons his pursuit of a Golden Age, a broken man renouncing his chivalric vision and dying: to Flaubert's Emma, spitting out her daydreams of a blue Beyond in the last hideous retches of an arsenic suicide; to Anna Karenina — the first sentence of her story is quoted, in reverse, in the first sentence of 'Ada' — ending her tortured love under the wheels of a locomotive. What 'happy endings' one finds in the classic novel are generally a matter of mere acquiescence to convention (Dickens) or sober accommodation of the protagonists to society (Jane Austen, George Eliot). 'Ada,' in direct contrast, is an attempt to return to paradise, to establish, in fact, the luminous vision of youth and love's first fulfillment as the most intensely, perdurably *real* experience we know. It bears affinities to both Molly Bloom's great lyric recall of

first flowering love at the end of 'Ulysses' and to
Proust's triumph over time through art in the last
volume of his novel, but it is a more concerted frontal
attack on Eden than either.

Two key allusions are especially helpful in understanding
what Nabokov is up to with his incestuous lovers. One
is simple, a mere negative parallel to serve as a foil;
the other is complex, being a kind of imaginative model
for the whole book and ramifying into other, related
allusions. Several passing references are made to
Chateaubriand; Ada jokingly calls Van her 'René'; and
the first half of the novel's title, 'Ada or Ardor,' looks
suspiciously like a parody of that most Romantic title,
'René ou les effets des passions.' René, like Van, is
a singular man with an artist's soul who enjoys the rare
delights of bucolic ambles with his dear sister until
the incestuous nature of her attachment to him forces
them to separate. So much for the parallels; all the
rest is pointed contrast. 'René' is a book suffused
with Romantic *mal de siècle*, and René and Amélie, unlike
the Veen siblings, are anything but 'children of Venus';
the paradisiac fulfillment of premoral desire is quite
unthinkable for René and his sister, so that the very
existence of such desire drives Amélie into a convent
and ultimately leads to martyrs' deaths for both of them.
In 'Ada', one can see from the sunlit river Ladore near
the Ardis estate a view of Bryant's Castle (Gallicized,
Château-Briand), 'remote and romantically black on its
oak-timbered hill.' The chief quality of Van Veen's
world, by contrast, is brightness and intimate closeness,
social and sexual, tactile and visual; and its oak trees,
as we shall see, are part of a landscape very different
from the dark romantic wood. René actively longs
for death, even before the revelation of his sister's
passion; he sees in it a hazy, alluring *ailleurs*, as
though the concrete objects of this world could not conceivably satisfy the needs of his own swoon of infinite
desire. Nabokov's hero and heroine, on the other hand,
delight in the concrete particulars of this world, observe and recall them with tender meticulous care, and
they both passionately love existence in this world, each
being the other's ultimate point of anchorage in it, Van's
male V or arrowhead (*ardis* in Greek) perfectly fitting
into its inverted and crossed female mirror-image, the
A of his sister-soul (ideogrammatists take note, Freudians beware).

The mirror play of Van's and Ada's initials — under-
scored at one point when Nabokov finds dramatic occasion

to print the A upside-down — suggests that the two are
perfect lovers because ultimately they are complementary
halves of one self. Indeed, Van's book is really 'written'
by the two of them, one imagination called 'Vaniada'
expressing itself in two antiphonal voices. The birth-
mark on the back of Van's right hand reappears in exactly
the corresponding spot on Ada's left hand, for both physically and psychically the lovers are really the two
halves of that androgynous pristine human zestfully described by Aristophanes in Plato's 'Symposium.' According
to rabbinic legend, Adam in the Garden before the creation
of Eve was androgynous, and it is clear that Nabokov, like
the rabbis, has conjoined the Greek and the Hebrew myths,
creating in his deliciously intertwined sister and brother
an image of prelapsarian, unfragmented man.

A major clue to Nabokov's intention in this respect is
the repeated allusion, especially in the Ardis section of
the novel, to one of the most splendidly realized experiences of paradise in English poetry, Marvell's The Garden.
Adolescent Ada tries to translate the poem into French
(in her version, an oak tree stands prominently at the
beginning of the second line); after the lovers' first
separation, the poem, most appropriately, serves as a
code-key for the letters in cipher that they exchange.
The second stanza of the poem, not quoted in the novel, begins as follows: 'Fair quiet, have I found thee here, / And
Innocence thy Sister dear! / Mistaken long, I sought you
then / In busie Companies of Men.' The lines are, of
course, applicable point for point to the novel, a kind
of adumbration of its plot, though both 'sister' and 'innocence' are given rather different meanings. Marvell's
poem is a vision of bliss beyond the raging of physical
passion; the solitary garden-dweller, however, does revel
in the pleasures of the senses, luscious fruit dropping
from the trees to delight his palate, while his mind with-
draws into the happiness of self-contemplation where it —
like the author of 'Ada'? — 'creates, transcending these, /
Far other Worlds, and other Seas.' In 'Ada's' ardisiac
setting, luscious fruit also comes falling from the branches,
when the tree-climbing young Ada slips and ends up straddling
an astonished Van from the front, thus offering him an un-
expectedly intimate first kiss, since, as we are told several times, she wears no underpants. In a moment Ada will
claim that this is the Tree of Knowledge, brought to the
Ardis estate from Eden National Park, but her slip from its
branches clearly enacts a Happy Fall, for in this garden,
as in Marvell's, no fatal sin is really possible. Marvell's
poem also gives us a comic image of a Fall with no evil consequences: 'Stumbling on Melons, as I pass, / Insnar'd with

Flow'rs, I fall on Grass.' The interlaced limbs of ardent-
ly tumbling Van and Ada are similarly assimilated to the
premoral world of vegetation, likened to tendril climbers;
and Van, rushing away from a last embrace of Ada at the
moment of their first separation, is actually described
'stumbling on melons,' an allusion which would seem to
promise that he will eventually return to his Ada-Ardis-
Eden.

It is the concluding stanza, however, of Marvell's
Garden that offers the most suggestive model for what
Nabokov seeks to achieve in 'Ada.' After the garden-
dweller's soul, whetting and combing its silver wings
among the branches, has experienced ecstasy, the poet
glances backward at the first Adam's paradise and then returns us to the 'real' world of time, but it is a time
now transfigured by art, nature ordered by 'the skilful
Gardner' in a floral sundial to measure time. The indus-
trious bee, then, no less than man, 'computes its time'
(in 17th-century pronunciation, a pun on 'thyme' and thus
a truly Nabokovian wordplay) with herbs and flowers; time
the eroder has been alchemized in this artful re-creation
of paradise into a golden translucence, delighting palate
and eye. Nabokov means to create just such an inter-
involvement of art and pleasure transcending time, or
rather capturing its elusive living 'texture,' as Van
Veen calls it, and this, finally, is the dramatic function
of the novel's unflagging emphasis on erotic experience.
The point is made clearer in the novel by still another allusion. Marvell's Garden modulates into several other
poems in the course of the narrative, but the most significant is Baudelaire's 'Invitation au voyage,' which is
burlesqued in the novel with an oak tree inserted in the
second and third line, to establish the cross-link with
Marvell. The Baudelaire poem is also a ravishing dream
of a perfect world, a world saturated with both generally
sensual and specifically erotic delight, but realized, as
such bliss can only be realized, through the beautiful
ordering of art. Against the background of the novel,
the famous opening lines of the poem become an evocation
of Ardis, Van addressing Ada: 'Mon enfant, ma soeur, /
Songe à la douceur / D.'aller là-bas vivre ensemble! / Aimer
à loisir / Aimer et mourir / Au pays qui te ressemble!'
('My child, my sister, / Think of the delight / Of going
there to live together! / To love at ease / To live and
die / In the land that resembles you!') It is noteworthy
that fragments of these lines are bandied about by Ada at
the point in the narrative when their first sexual intimacy is recollected; significantly, this is the one moment in the novel when Ada actually says to Van that they

are not two different people.

Baudelaire's poem, then, suggests what is also clear in the novel in other ways, that 'Ada' is formed on the paradox of rendering the perfect state of nature through a perfect state of art, self-conscious, allusive, and exquisitely ordered. In this respect, Nabokov also follows the model of Milton (who is burlesqued in tetrameters at one point) in the fourth book of 'Paradise Lost,' where prelapsarian Eden is described through the most finely ostentatious artifice — a natural garden full of sapphire founts, sands of gold, burnished fruit, crystal-mirror brooks, in which the preceding literary tradition of envisioned paradises is incorporated through the cunning strategy of negation ('Not that fair field / Of Enna...,' and so forth). It may be that 'Ada' pays a price as a novel for being an extended poetic vision of Eden: Van and Ada sometimes seem to be more voices and images in a lyric poem than novelistic characters; the excess of perfection they must sustain makes them less interesting individually, less humanly engaging, than many of Nabokov's previous protagonists. In compensation, the expression in 'Ada' of a lover's consummated delight in life and beauty is an achievement that has very few equals in the history of the novel. Let me offer a brief representative instance, in which the lovers' present is juxtaposed with their ardisiac past:

> Her plump, stickily glistening lips smiled.
> (When I kiss you *here*, he said, the balcony when you were eating a *tartine au miel*; so much better in French.)
> The classical beauty of clover honey, smooth, pale, translucent, freely flowing from the spoon and soaking my love's bread and butter in liquid brass. The crumb steeped in nectar.

The honeyed bread-slice here is very much a Nabokovian equivalent of Proust's *petite madeleine* and of that more erotic tidbit, the ambrosial seedcake which Molly Bloom puts from her mouth into her young lover Leopold's. Through its sweetness past and present fuse, or, to speak more precisely, they fuse through its sweetness minutely observed and recollected, then distilled into the lucid order of a poem that moves in alliterative music through a poised choreography of dactyls and trochees to the culminating metaphorical paradox of the honey as liquid brass and the final substitution of nectar for the honey, now become 'literally' food for the gods.

At several points in the novel the narrator takes pains to
inform us that Ada in Russian means 'hell.' The point, I
would assume, is that Ada and Van in their Eden are in a
state before the knowedge of good and evil, when heaven
and hell cannot be distinguished. This also suggests,
however, that there could be an ambiguous underside of
evil in the edenic fulfillment offered Van by his sister-
soul, and the suicide to which the two of them inadvert-
ently drive Lucette may indicate that a paradisiac love
can have evil consequences when it impinges on the lives
of others outside the Garden. In any case, the ultimate
sense of the novel is of all threats of evil, including
the evil of the corrosive passage of time, finally trans-
cended by the twinned power of art and love. One last
clue encodes this idea as a signature of affirmation at
the end of the novel. Moving around mysteriously in the
background of the concluding section is an unexplained
figure named Ronald Oranger. Since he marries the typist
responsible for Van's manuscript, and since he and his
wife, according to a prefatory note, are the only significant persons mentioned in the book still alive when it
is published, one may assume that his is the final responsibility for the text of 'Ada' he the presiding spirit
at the end. All we really know about him is his name, which
means 'orange tree' in French. No orange trees are explicitly mentioned in Marvell's Garden, though they are spec-
tacularly present in Bermudas, another remarkable poem by
Marvell about a garden-paradise. In any event, 'Ronald
Oranger' has an anagrammatic look, and could be rearranged
as a reversal of the book's title, 'angel nor ardor' —
which is to say, the fixative force of art, working
through the imagination of love, has extracted heaven from
hell, Eden from Ada, has established a perfected state
that originates in the carnal passions but goes quite beyond them. Fortunately, the code-games and allusions in
'Ada' are merely pointers to the peculiar nature of the
novel's imaginative richness, which does not finally depend on the clues. Few books written in our lifetime afford so much pleasure. Perhaps the parody-blurb at the
end is not so wrong in proffering the novel as a volumi-
nous bag of rare delights: Nabokov's garden abounds with
the pleasurable visions whose artful design I have tried
to sketch out here, and, as the blurb justifiably concludes, with 'much, much more.'

64.   UNSIGNED REVIEW, 'TIMES LITERARY SUPPLEMENT'

2 October 1969, 1121

Any author worth parodying will sometimes achieve self-
parody ('Sordello', 'Pericles', 'The Golden Bowl', 'The
Kreutzer Sonata', 'Across the River and into the Trees').
Mr Nabokov is no exception. 'Ada' is the most Nabokovian
novel ever, an idyll of aristocratic incest decked out with
enough word games to stock an ocean liner. To appreciate
it fully one should have perfect command of English, French
and Russian, a working knowledge of botany and entomology,
a flair for anagrams and a good deal of patience. (Well
he's not writing for cretins is he?) If it ends in delight,
it begins in hard labour. This book is clearly the author's
Waterloo: it's less clear whether he figures as Wellington
or Napoleon....
    One can recognize in 'Ada' the high point of a style,
a stance, or a distillation of pedantry. If literature was
invented for critics to practise on, 'Ada', like 'Finnegans
Wake', might crown the arch of European writing. It is,
like 'The Golden Bowl', a hard read. Perhaps for that reason, true Nabokovians should find it his masterpiece. The
peasants may grumble.

'Mary'

1970

Originally written in Russian as 'Mashenka' and published
in Berlin, 1926. Translated by Michael Glenny 'in collaboration with the author' and published in New York, 1970,
and London, 1971.

65. ANITA VAN VACTOR IN 'LISTENER'

25 February 1971, 250

...'Mary' supplies any number of prefigurations. What's
very good, and belongs to this book alone, is its picture,
realised with a fresh, loving eye, of the sadness and
awfulness of Russian émigré life in 1920s Berlin. Nabokov himself confesses to liking 'Mary' for its scenes of
his Russian youth; he feels they contain 'a headier extract of personal reality' than the much later autobiography; yet, for me, it's in 'Speak, Memory' that, refrac-
ted by distance, they achieve a kind of dazzling plenitude
in comparison with which Ganin's recollections seem willed,
rhetorical.

66. DAVID J. GORDON IN 'YALE REVIEW'

March 1971, 428-9

David J. Gordon (born 1929) teaches at Hunter College,
The City University of New York, and is the author of
'D.H. Lawrence as a Literary Critic' (1966).

Vladimir Nabokov's slight but appealing first novel,
written in Russian in 1925 and now translated with the
author's collaboration, etches Chekhovian portraits of a
group of Russian *émigrés* in a Berlin *pension* during the
1920s: among them a pathetic young spinster; two effemi-
nate dancers; an ill, touchingly obsolete poet over-
whelmed by the difficulty of getting a visa; a ridiculous husband flamboyantly awaiting the arrival of his
wife, Mary; and, chiefly, Ganin, a bored and brooding
young man who has reason to believe that Mary is none
other than the adolescent girl with whom, nine years earlier, he had shared the supremely intense experience (un-
recoverable except, for a moment, in memory) of first love.
   The book contains foreshadowings of Nabokov's later
interest in the figure of the double and in complicated
games, but the primary link is thematic: 'Mary' helps us
see that its author's central subject has always been the
power and pain of the memory of lost love. What saves
him, unlike Hemingway, from self-pity is his passionate
intellectual interest in the workings of memory, his
psychological fidelity. Ganin is not at all embarrassed
to say that Mary's image was largely fashioned before he
met her or that he cannot 'grasp' the fact that so exalted
a memory must die with his own death. He remembers scrupulously that he loved her more poignantly when he knew
he was falling out of love with her, that the farther
away she got from his actual life the more clearly he knew
that he could never forget her. And so his initial excitement at the idea of seeing Mary again — which had enabled
him to break out of a tiresome liaison, to look at the
urban scene with pristine eyes, and even to gull the rival-
husband — finally yields to the ironic knowledge that the
four glorious days in which he has revived his memory of
her image have also exhausted it. Nabokov is assuredly
a writer with a psychological bent, and his obstinate
prejudice against what the prefatory note calls 'the
Viennese delegation' probably is an oblique recognition
of the fact that the delegation's concerns overlap his own.

'Glory'

1972

Originally written in Russian as 'Podvig'; serialized in
'Sovremennye Zapiski' (Paris), 1931-2; published in volume
form in Paris, 1933. Translated by Dmitri and Vladimir
Nabokov and published in New York and London, 1972.

67. UNSIGNED REVIEW, 'TIMES LITERARY SUPPLEMENT'

24 March 1972, 325

'Glory' completes the set of Nabokov's Russian novels,
and in his foreword he openly savours the ironic possibilities of his re-living his early works in English translation. He offers a general retrospect of 'Glory' ('Podvig', 1932), adopting that affectionate and conspiratorial
air authors extend to their grandchildren rather than their
children. The contrast between the present Nabokov parading his black beasts (Freudians, critics, 'human-interest
seekers') and the past Nabokov-in-translation is an odd
one: he seems to have grown younger, more restless,
moody, playful: 'Glory' was obviously written by a more
controlled, sensitive, shy fellow than the chap who enjoys
it so much in the preface. 'Glory', after all (he hardly
disguises it), was a rather pallid and brittle affair. The
easiest metaphor for the style (and for the 'autobiographical' manner) is an old photograph, whose dimness and
blotches have become part, inseparably, of the façade, the
ruined landscape. The dull patina of the phrase-making
('a linden's mobile shade') seldom lets up, though
minarets do remind the hero of factory chimneys, so that

he does share a little of that vital propensity Nabokov's
best people have for mating the exotic with the commonplace. Indeed if Nabokov's Europe is always less exciting at first than his America, it seems to be because he
never found there the special mix of 'eerie vulgarity'
and enchantment he discovered so definitively in 'Lolita'.
It does, after that, take some coaxing to adjust to this
rather prim, faded texture.... The piling-on of pastiche
(Joyce the topmost layer here) acts out what exile means —
the endless multiplication of dislocated, if delightful,
identities.... And like Martin, 'Glory' has an ambivalent
existence on obscure frontiers, projecting an irretriev-
ably oblique sensibility.

One way of seeing this is as a prophetic inkling of
what (in his note on 'Lolita') Nabokov called 'my private
tragedy': 'I had to abandon my natural idiom, my untrammeled, rich, and infinitely docile Russian tongue
for a second-rate brand of English....' But like the
other Russian novels that have been translated rather
than (like 'King, Queen, Knave') transposed, 'Glory' seems
to imply a rather different reading of Nabokov's progress.
'Reduced' to impersonation, rather than narration, he is
immeasurably more gross and vital than his youthful
shadow. Appropriating on behalf of his later heroes the
brainless logic and coarse jargons they use and encounter,
he has, perhaps, become more coarse and logical himself.
But it's not really paradoxical to suggest that this com-
bative toughness involves an increased fineness of perception, a sharper awareness of how to protect and preserve
those 'immemorial and tender banalities' of love and hero-
ism that have always been his central concern.

68. BRIGID BROPHY IN 'LISTENER'

27 April 1972, 552-3

Brigid Brophy (born 1929) has published novels, plays and
criticism.

...From the moment the narrative's impetus turns the
migrant towards home it slackens. The Cambridge scenes,
which resemble E.M. Forster at his most 'Boy's Own Paper'

and include a fight between Martin and his best friend
which renders them even better friends, have the flat
unreality that usually comes from an author's
knowing by experience (instead of imagining) what he is
writing about.   Perhaps some ironic distance has been
lost in translation.   Certainly, the stiffness is not
eased by Americanisms that create impossibilities of
dialogue, causing, for instance, an English undergraduate
in the early Twenties to say, 'You ought to wash up,' when
(it is after that fight) he means: 'You ought to wash.'

   Probably, however, the end is diminished by the nature
of the excellence of the beginning.   Martin had to be a
third-person hero, so that he could vanish, and the preface boasts that Nabokov is not so far identified with
him as to have made him an artist.   But the Russia and
the childhood from which he is exiled are created by Nabokov's narrative, which is the work of an artist.   It's
hard for readers to inhabit Martin's need to go home when
the narrative can evoke 'home' at will.   The early chapters of 'Glory' are excitingly and mockingly beautiful,
a restoration of the reader to the childhood immediacy of
experience from which we are all exiles, a magic succession of images like (and like that visible in) the penholder that Martin leaves behind in the compartment when,
on the way home from Biarritz via Berlin, his family
changes trains at the frontier: 'the penholder with the
tiny glass lens, in which, when held up to your eye, a
mother-of-pearl and blue landscape would flash into
being'.

   Nabokov published 'Glory' in Russian in Paris in 1932.
'Exploit', he explains, is a more direct translation of its
Russian title discarded, however, lest it be read as verb
instead of noun.   Perhaps in the choice of 'Glory' there
is a sense of answering, not necessarily antagonistically,
the title of the still too little praised novel on themes
historically similar which William Gerhardie published
in 1922, that novel that exists as wholly in the spaces
between people as 'Glory' does in the sensuous essence of
objects — 'Futility'.

'Transparent Things'

1972

Written in English;   published in New York and London, 1972.

69. SIMON KARLINSKY IN 'SATURDAY REVIEW OF THE ARTS'

January 1973, 45

Simon Karlinsky (born 1924) is Professor of Slavic Languages at the University of California at Berkeley. His
books include a study of Gogol (1976), and he has edited
'The Nabokov-Wilson Letters' (1979).

Like Nabokov's other recent novels, 'Transparent Things'
contains its requisite complement of ostentatiously displayed false doors that turn out not to work and a few
hidden trapdoors that do. The fictional character of the
German novelist R. has been lent a few of Nabokov's own
more superficial traits. (He resides in Switzerland,
writes in English, and publishes his books in America).
Already several critics have sprung at the bait and
hastened to identify R. as the author's self-portrait.
This is as wide of the mark as the similarly hasty identification of Van and Ada with Nabokov and his wife that
some of our otherwise thoughtful commentators on Nabokov
had suggested after the publication of 'Ada.' Not only
is everything that really matters about R. totally unlike Nabokov, but his constant mangling of idiomatic ex-

pressions and popular sayings is rather obviously derived from the similar trait of Zina Mertz's disagreeable stepfather in 'The Gift' — surely a character who could not by any stretch of the imagination be mistaken for the author's self-portrait.

Multilingual puns and literary allusions — something that we've come to expect from Nabokov — are present in 'Transparent Things,' but in a more subdued form than in its immediate predecessors....

There are, however, aspects of 'Transparent Things' that connect this novel to Nabokov's native literary tradition in ways more substantial than puns or literary games. The two ill-matched lovers, the seductive, sullen, sensuous, basically unkind, and not very intelligent Armande and the clumsy, socially inept, but inwardly sensitive and responsive Hugh — aren't they a transposition into modern terms of Tolstoy's Helene and Pierre from 'War and Peace'? Scenes of sleepwalking, a crime committed in one's sleep, the abundance of prophetic dreams and premonitions, false presentiments of disaster and genuine prophecies not heeded, and finally the hero's clearly preordained and spectacular death by fire, all of them organized into an elegant verbal structure — this is all very close to a strain in Russian literature that can be termed Hoffmannesque. Normally, we would not expect to list Nabokov among the Russian followers of E.T.A. Hoffmann, that is, among such figures as that master magician of Russian Romantic prose Vladimir Odoevsky (to whose work Nabokov is apparently indifferent) and, in the twentieth century, the outstanding stylist Alexei Remizov (whose writings Nabokov does know and admire). There is much in 'Transparent Things' that brings to mind the themes and images of these two predecessors, and in this respect the novel is a new departure for Nabokov.

In its essence, however, 'Transparent Things' owes nothing to anyone but Nabokov. Once more he has managed to shape a formless, potentially threatening reality into a precise and transparent work of literary art while continually demonstrating for the benefit of attentive and imaginative readers the exact means employed for bringing about this transformation. In this sense all of Nabokov's novels are 'transparent things,' and their transparency is, to borrow Marina Tsvetaeva's phrase, the author's 'ultimate victory over time and gravity.' This is why one closes this little book, so full of tragic and violent events, with the final feeling of lightness and joy.

70. JONATHAN RABAN IN 'ENCOUNTER'

September 1973, 74-6

Jonathan Raban (born 1942) has taught at the Universities
of Aberystwyth and East Anglia. His books include 'The
Technique of Modern Fiction' (1968).

The deepest feeling in Nabokov's novels — often their
only feeling — is pathos; an autumnal sentimental sadness
at the loneliness and transitoriness of things. He is
the Busby Berkeley of *weltschmerz* (or *weltschmaltz*): a
great choreographer and prestidigitator whose most ambitious
and brilliant set-pieces are mounted around a single tear-
jerking tableau. The halitotic Kinbote peers miserably
through his window at the lavish party being thrown by
the Shades next door; Humbert sees his masterpiece, his
Lolita, transformed itno a suburban slut called Mrs
Richard F. Schiller. Unwrap a Nabokov novel from its
packaging of games, tricks with mirrors and tough ironical
philosophising, and one is left with an exquisite weepie.
'Lolita' began, so he has said, with the image of a luck-
less ape whose hard-luck story Nabokov chanced upon in a
newspaper. This creature, when it was equipped by its
keepers with paints and paper, was only able to draw the
bars of its cage. Nabokov himself has gone on to ever
more delicately shaded aquatints of the interior of the
prison, but at the heart of each new novel there squats
the same mangy, dishevelled ape, clutching its brush in a
hairy paw and rolling huge appealing eyes in the direction
of the RSPCA. Lately, the ape has begun to look uncannily
like Nabokov: its furrowed brow and hanging jowls, its
dyspeptic manner and heavy Russian accent, increasingly
give it the appearance of a pantomime costume, in which
the sweating novelist has thinly disguised himself.
    'Transparent Things' is a novel about the pathos of
authorship, the lonely solipsism of the fiction writer
busily peopling an illusory world. It is both the least
admirable, and the most revealing, of all Nabokov's
novels. The reader is invited to eavesdrop on the relationship between an author and his character — poor Hugh
Person, summoned out of the void and made to dance his
shallow, evanescent life through the pages of the book.
Hugh is pronounced 'you', and Person is used in its primary sense, as 'mask' or 'persona'. Nabokov nets him like

a butterfly in the first sentence, then pins him out in
a sequence of twenty-six chapterlets, muttering asides to
the reader about technical difficulties as he does so.
For even a mask drips with gobbets of its own history;
it is not a transparent thing. Transparency is a condition
of living in the present, of moving through objects and
events with a careless disregard for their natures and
histories.

> A thin veneer of immediate reality is spread over
> natural and artificial matter, and whoever wishes to
> remain in the now, with the now, on the now, should
> please not break its tension film.

In Nabokov's fiction, the only people who live comfort-
ably with this transparency, who walk effortlessly on the
water, are the girls, bright and insensate as lepidoptera.
Lolita, content with her candy and pin-ups of film stars,
was Nabokov's supreme skater on the surface tension of
life; her inconsequential, butterfly-death in childbirth
was an essential ingredient of her talent for remaining
in the now. In the new novel, there is a descendant of
hers, a bland, pretty, open-air girl called Armande, whose
passion is for skiing down Swiss mountainsides. But the
snow she slides over, hardly denting with her fibreglass
skis, is a glacial crust which keeps the world of feeling
at one remove from her feet. Like Lolita, she is heading
for a casual demise, to be throttled by Person in his
sleep.
     Novelists, and persons too, are poor skiers. Person
stumbles wheezily behind Armande, never able to keep up.
He is burdened by his age, his past, his job as publisher's
editor (he is in Switzerland to attend to the latest manuscript of R., a novel called 'Tralatitions' written in a
style of Nabokovian rococo). Unable to manage the trudge
up the mountain, he sits on the hotel terrace trying to
spot Armande's brightly coloured parka through a pair of
binoculars. But Person, like R., is only a stand-in for
Nabokov himself; as Person chases Armande in Switzerland,
Nabokov chases Person in his book. Round and round they
go, continuous as a frieze round an urn. Nabokov crops
up, anagrammatised, as a 'minor character' in 'Tralatitions' called Adam von Librikov. In 'Transparent Things'
(the parallel between the two novels is clearer if we know
that 'tralatitious' is a synonym for 'metaphoric') Nabokov is his own major character: his fictional people make
up a paper chase of transparent metaphors which lead
straight back to the groaning novelist, weighed down by a
world he has himself created.

His control over this world has a godlike arbitrariness. He knows what he chooses to know. The book is dotted with parentheses which enclose fragments of a total knowledge which would render the selections and suspenses of fiction trivial and absurd. So, when Person looks at a green carved figurine of a skier in a souvenir-shop window, Nabokov is able to remark:

> (it was 'alabasterette', imitation aragonite, carved and coloured in the Grumbel jail by a homosexual convict, rugged Armand Rave, who had strangled his boyfriend's incestuous sister.)

The only point of view from which this passage could have been written is from beyond the grave; a hypothetical position of ultimate memory to which all the gropers and stumblers in the novel (Person, R., Nabokov) are trying to aspire. Nabokov gives them what they want: he kills off R. with a disease of the liver, and immolates Person in an hotel fire. True transparency lies only on the other side, when every pun, coincidence, and historical accident can be perceived simultaneously.

But Nabokov, despite these occasional forays into the posthumous, is alive and well in a world where certainty stops at the present. 'Transparent Things' is really two novels. One is a tale told by an earthbound storyteller, judiciously guessing at what will happen next; the other is an impersonation of the sort of novel God might write on a lazy day with one eye closed. At the beginning of the twenty-fifth chapter, with Person well and truly pinned to his fate, Nabokov inquires:

> What had you expected of your pilgrimage, Person?
> A mere mirror rerun of hoary torments? Sympathy from
> an old stone? Enforced re-creation of irrecoverable
> trivia? A search for lost time in an utterly dis-
> tinct sense from Goodgrief's dreadful '*Je me souviens,
> je me souviens de la maison où je suis né*' or, indeed,
> Proust's quest? He had never experienced here (save
> once at the end of his last ascent) anything but bore-
> dom and bitterness.

The questions enshrine a list of conventional descriptions of the pleasures and duties of fiction. The novel as a form is rooted in the past: Nabokov is trying to drag it into the future, to experience the delightful melancholy of events which have not yet come about. The *temps perdus* of 'Transparent Things' have been lost to the side of and beyond the lives of the characters in the book.

But the enterprise is an indulgent one. We are left
with the lone figure of the novelist brooding over the
incompleteness of the world, imagining it from an impossible perspective so that it achieves the aesthetic perfection which it so lacks in actuality. In life, all is
boredom and bitterness; in the art of the 'miracle-worker',
shabby intractable things, like girls and publishers' editors and novelists with liver diseases, are wonderfully
transmuted into lucent transparencies.

Yet Nabokov cheats persistently. One feels none of
life's resistance in this new novel. in 'Pale Fire' and
'Lolita', there was the raw stuff of America to contend
with. To write 'Lolita', Nabokov claimed that he used to
travel around Boston on buses, collecting teenage slang.
He thrived on the vulgarity of American life, assiduous
in his observation of the motels, suburbs and freeways in
which 'Lolita' is set. Whatever else it may be, that book
is joyously steeped in the sticky liquid substance of the
United States in the 1950s; it reeks of the Howard Johnson's lunch counter and the hot stench of overheated
leatherette in a slouching, chrome-clad Buick. 'Pale
Fire', too, is marvellous on the muffled, genteel paranoia of the New England college campus. To transform
these things into the tantalising, elegant shapes they
assume in the novels was the accomplishment of a real
miracle-worker. But Nabokov now is an idle magician: he
turns water into wine out of sheer boredom.

He is irritated with his characters even before he
gives them life. They are mere cursory squiggles on the
paper, pawns in a larger game. Person is a melancholy
cipher; Armande a cut-out from an advertisement for
anoraks in a winter sports brochure. With R., Nabokov
does rather better, painting a comic self-portrait. The
novelist speaks a racy, idiomatic, foreigner's English,
in which every vernacular expression comes out slightly
wrong. 'You're jolly right son.... So long and soon
see....' But all this is done with enervated proficiency,
like a painter's telephone doodlings. And when he comes
to write of Switzerland, he crudely miniaturises the landscape, bringing it down to the pygmy-scale of the characters. The physical world which we are invited to contem-
plate in 'Transparent Things' is like a souvenir scene
made of coloured paper inside a glass sphere. Shake it,
and the snow flies up and settles in a flurry of soda-
chips. Nabokov himself shakes this paltry toy irritably,
twenty-six times.

The ideas which were once alive in his fiction are
now treated with bored petulance.

> Men have learned to live with a black burden, a huge
> aching hump: the supposition that 'reality' may be
> only a 'dream'. How much more dreadful it would be if
> the very awareness of your being aware of reality's
> dreamlike nature were also a dream, a built-in hallu-
> cination! One should bear in mind, however, that there
> is no mirage without a vanishing point, just as there
> is no lake without a closed circle of reliable land.

For all the introductory pieties about 'black burden' and
'dreadful', one feels Nabokov yawning at the notion. Perhaps he has succeeded in translating himself into that
nether world of ultimate knowledge from which everything
human looks small, silly, and woefully unaesthetic. At
any rate, 'Transparent Things' reveals a novelist who has
grown tired and irascible at his own cleverness. I can
stay dry-eyed at the pathos of such a lonely surfeit of
knowledge. Nabokov's fatal immersion in these private,
occult pursuits finally betrays — for all its cerebral
bravura — a lack of intelligence, an aridity of feeling.

71. JOYCE CAROL OATES, A PERSONAL VIEW OF NABOKOV,
'SATURDAY REVIEW OF THE ARTS'

January 1973, 36-7

Joyce Carol Oates (born 1938) is a prolific American
writer of novels, short stories and literary criticism.

The world of art offers us an astonishing galaxy of personalities — artists expressing their self-images in a
vast multiplicity of styles, some of them linked firmly
to a place and a time, the 'self' imagined as an embodiment
of a certain era, some of them quite divorced from any
earthly, temporal dimension at all. At one extreme is
that entirely American personality. Walt Whitman, whose
'Song of Myself' is hardly a song of Whitman *himself*; at
the other extreme, almost inaccessible to us, is Samuel
Beckett, whose monologue novels are an expression of a
particular self, almost selfless, pared to an existence
devoid of the 'world' as we know it. Nabokov is closer to
Beckett, of course, but his genius is far more exciting

than Beckett's because he has the ability — which is
sometimes dizzying — to reach into the world for sights,
sounds, words, hints, to use the world for his own purposes, to ransack the world of what he would, contempt-
uously, call 'ordinary,' unsubjective reality. 'Lolita'
is one of our finest American novels, a triumph of style
and vision, an unforgettable work, Nabokov's best (though
not most characteristic) work, a wedding of Swiftian
satirical vigor with the kind of minute, loving patience
that belongs to a man infatuated with the visual mysteries
of the world. Yet when Nabokov talks of the work, we are
disappointed, for there is an arrogant, contemptuous side
of his nature that tends to distract us from his genuine
accomplishments — 'Nothing is more exhilarating than
philistine vulgarity,' he says, in explaining his use of
'North American sets' for the work. And he needed his
stimulus, this 'exhilarating milieu,' or he could not have
written the novel.

Marx saw history as the process of men pursuing their
goals, in action. It is possible to see 'literature' as
the process of an infinite number of individuals pursuing
their 'images' of themselves and of their eras, each work
of art expressing the artist's nature at the time of its
execution. Yet it is necessary to realize how incredibly
different we all are, how violently differing are our
visions of reality — so that 'reality' itself must be,
in some fantastic Einsteinian paradox, an event multi-
plied endlessly, in each of our brains, an event split up
into many fragments, which are all equal. The world of
literature may be divided very loosely into those writers
who believe this, enthusiastically, recognizing divinity
everywhere — literally everywhere — like the American
Transcendentalists, like Dostoevsky, like all mystics;
into those who deny it flatly, and believe that they, as
isolated individuals, possess all that is sacred or at
least important, in themselves, and who truly do not
need any sense of communion or kinship with other people.
In fact, it is not really possible for these writers to
feel this communion, because they do not believe — not
fully — that other people exist. Nabokov has stated that
ordinary reality will begin to 'rot and stink' unless a
subjectivity is imposed upon it. This means, of course,
that ordinary human beings — not so enchanting as Lolita
or the other feminine targets of Nabokov's powerful, lust-
ful imagination — will also begin to rot and stink unless
someone comes along to give them value. Their 'value'
does not exist in themselves and certainly not in nature —
it can only be given to them, assigned to them, imagined
in them, by a confident, powerful, Magus-like personality.

Who is this godly creature? Who, reading Nabokov's most
revealing works('Speak, Memory' and 'Ada'), can doubt
that it is only Nabokov himself?

In discussing Nabokov, I must analyze my own reactions.
I believe that, as an artist, as a conscious — obses-
sively *conscious* artist — he is as exciting as any writer
who has ever lived. There are critics, such as Mary
McCarthy, who, recoiling from the tedium of 'Ada,' began
to wonder whether, perhaps, earlier works like 'Pale Fire'
were really as good as they had believed, but I think it
is unnecessary, and perhaps unfair, to put much emphasis
upon a writer's weakest books. We all want to be judged
by our highest accomplishments, and so we should extend to
others this generosity. So there are the intensely personal, obsessive, brilliant esthetic accomplishments of
Nabokov — arrangements of words on paper, exercises of
skill that bear relationship, of course, to the game of
chess. If he had written only 'Lolita,' 'Pnin,' and
'Speak, Memory,' he would be the 'Nabokov' he is today,
eccentric and brilliant. We all honor Nabokov the artist.

But my deeper and, admittedly, very personal reaction
to Nabokov is quite different. To me he is a tragic
figure, heroic in his isolation perhaps, or perhaps only
sterile, monomaniacal, deadening to retain for very long
in one's imagination. He is far more depressing than
Kafka, who believed that the 'divine' was everywhere
except in himself, but who did believe passionately that
he might gain access to it somehow, at some point in his
life. Nabokov empties the universe of everything except
Nabokov. He then assigns worth — which may seem to us
quite exaggerated, even ludicrous, as in 'Ada' — to a
few selected human beings, focusing his powerful imagination upon the happy few, lavishing contempt and ener-
getic humor upon most other people. Nabokov exhibits the
most amazing capacity for loathing that one is likely to
find in serious literature, a genius for dehumanizing
that seems to me more frightening, because it is more
intelligent, than Céline's or even than Swift's. Reeling
from the depths of Swift's unarguable hatred for much of
life, one can always rationalize that probably — perhaps —
there was a political reason for his extraordinary vigor in
attacking people who seem to us harmless or even sympathetic; and when Céline's loathing crystallized into a historical political philosophy, fascism, we could dismiss it,
or at least assign it to some temporary pathology of his
era. But of Nabokov, what excuses can we make? — that
his early years were tragic indeed, that he suffered the
loss of his father, his homeland, his entire way of life,
his 'untrammeled, rich, and infinitely docile Russian

tongue? — that, ultimately, he *is* not American, and his
scorn for the democratic ideal is something as deep in
him, as natural, as his genius for words, for chess, and
for the capturing of butterflies?

Still, assuming the immense differences between Nabokov,
as an exiled Russian, and us, as Americans, we must admit
that he is not really Russian either. He 'is' only,
supremely, himself. Therefore, it is understandable that
he should despise certain 'mediocrities' — Stendhal,
Balzac, Zola, Dostoevsky, Mann — not because they are
really mediocre but because they are not Nabokov. Dostoevsky especially arouses his contempt, for Dostoevsky
lavished love on everyone — prostitutes, drunkards,
bullies, saints, the mad, the diseased, *even* those who
might have been hilarious targets for satire — transcending any particular embodiment of 'self' to create a work
like 'The Brothers Karamazov,' in which 'self' expands to
contain the entire world and from which no one is really
excluded. With his fastidious concern for esthetic form
and the manipulation of words, Nabokov could not possibly
sympathize with or even comprehend the nature of what
Dostoevsky accomplished.

'Look at the Harlequins!'

1974

Written in English; published in New York and London, 1974.

72. RICHARD POIRIER IN 'NEW YORK TIMES BOOK REVIEW'

13 October 1974, 2, 4

Richard Poirier (born 1925) is Professor of English at Rutgers University, New Brunswick, NJ. His books include a study of Henry James.

After Joyce with his 'portrait' of Stephen, after Proust with his 'remembrance' of Marcel, there are few reasons to be surprised, and many reasons to be disappointed, by the complicated interplay between Vladimir Nabokov and the narrator of this, his 37th book. Vadim Vadimovitch is a Russian emigré writer and a mirror image or 'double' of Nabokov as man and writer; but unlike Proust or Joyce, Nabokov never uses this version of himself as a way of questioning the authenticity of his own identity. The fictional self never challenges the 'real' or authorial self. Nabokov and his works hover on the margins of the text, so to speak, as a static reality against which Vadim is to be measured. So that while the style of the novel is characteristically brilliant when it comes to erotic comedy or setting a scene or sketching in minor figures, it is deficient in another and far more important

way. It lacks the dramatic intensifications, the explora-
tory feeling that in Joyce and Proust — and in our own
time very often in Mailer — is a consequence of their
wonderfully vital, vulnerable, intimidated (and not simply
intimidating) relationship to fictional copies of themselves.

Vadim is allowed to do nothing that will surprise
Nabokov, to test nothing that Nabokov hasn't already
tested. For all his famous confidence in the power of
fiction to create reality, even while conceding the arbitrariness of the methods for doing so, Nabokov is here,
with an arrogance nearly charming in its absoluteness,
loath to surrender much if any of *his* constituted self,
as our greatest master of prose, to a mere fictional
aspirant.

The puzzles and teasers in the book are fun to figure
out when they are broadly parodistic, and altogether less
so (though in these instances the vanity of discovery
might pass for fun) when they require a detailed knowledge
of the whole of Nabokov's *oeuvre* and the byways of his
literary career. In either case the puzzles are without
the resonance of personal drama that continues to move
us in Proust or Joyce after all the exegesis is finished
and that was also powerfully at work in 'Lolita' and 'Pale
Fire'....

Behind the often delightful invitation to play of mind
there lurks a persistent didacticism. In correcting any
mistaken ideas we may have about fiction and reality,
Nabokov means to demonstrate that if fiction is not Reality,
then neither is so-called 'reality' outside of fiction.
Reality, as he is fond of saying, always belongs in quotation marks. The ground thereby claimed by Nabokov's own
fictional enterprise is, to say the very least, exorbitant
— and he chooses to govern it all by himself.

As we've seen in the past ten years, any number of
little Nabokovs will be ready to make such an investment
in a book of this kind that they end up admiring it as their
own handiwork, their own 'invention.' To some extent this
is always and quite properly the case. But the kind of
exegetical efforts we are invited to make here need to be
distinguished from those we are willing to make while
reading Melville or Joyce or Pynchon. At their many puzzling moments those writers direct the attention of the
reader not principally to their own literary texts and
lives but to the life and texts of the existent world,
with all its inheritances, in which they live and
write. Theirs seems to me an altogether more exciting
and important venture than Nabokov's, even if he has sometimes been called — and sometimes deserves to be called —
our greatest living writer.

He stands on the periphery of the great tradition of
American literature since Hawthorne and Melville, and of
20th-century literature since Joyce, in that he is,
despite his terror of solipsism, its most awesome practitioner. He is not sufficiently vulnerable to — and his
style is only infrequently enriched by — the power of
the social and literary institutions by which man continues
to invent himself.

In his splendid disdain for the power of most other
fictions, except for some exclusively literary ones (as
note his notorious contempt for Freud), Nabokov has at
last proposed in this novel that he himself exists as an
institution and that he is not only a product of artistic
invention but, taken all together, the exemplification of
it. It is therefore interesting to wonder, even while
acknowledging the genius displayed in 'Lolita' and 'Pale
Fire,' whether Nabokov's great admiration for Joyce would
at this point be reciprocated by a writer who left us such
decisive parodies and implicit critiques of Walter Pater.
Pater, in his disposition if not in the range of his mind
or energy, seems to me the most direct antecedent to the
Nabokov who wrote this book.

73. MARTIN AMIS IN 'NEW STATESMAN'

25 April 1975, 555-6

Martin Amis (born 1949), English novelist and journalist.

There are, very broadly, three types of Nabokov novel:
the satires, which are *tours de force* of ingenious caricature ('Pale Fire', 'Bend Sinister', 'Invitation to a
Beheading'); the black farces, which are gloating treat-
ments of murder, obsession and perverse love ('Despair',
'Lolita', 'Laughter in the Dark'); and the histories,
which are oblique recreations of individual lives ('Pnin',
'Ada', 'The Real Life of Sebastian Knight'). The new
novel is fundamentally a history — it calls itself the
'memoir' of one Vadim Vadimovich — but it serves also as
a kind of Nabokov anthology, a recapitulation of his
standard situations and themes, a scrapbook of his habi-
tual voices and moods. Nabokov being Nabokov, the for-

mula would seem to be unimprovable; and yet 'Look at
the Harlequins!' is a forlorn and ragged book.

A shrewdly observed life, Nabokov suggested in his
'Eugene Onegin' Commentary, can often disclose an artistically satisfying pattern. Well, Vadim's life, as here
described, has about as much shape as most lives have —
i.e., not much. Reinhabiting the Nabokovian locales (pre-
revolutionary Russia, Twenties Cambridge, émigré Paris,
American academe), Vadim's autobiography is loosely strung
out on his 'three or four successive marriages'....

Just as 'Ada' (1969) contained a portrait of the larval
Vladimir and 'Transparent Things' (1972) contained a cameo
of the old Nabokov, 'Look at the Harlequins!' is an appreciative review of the novelist's middle years. Typically,
Nabokov both invites and dares the reader to see the book
as tricksy autobiography: his own life and works are
pseudonymously saluted throughout (Vadim's brother-in-
law calls him 'MacNab'; his 'The Red Top Hat' is Nabokov's
'Invitation to a Beheading'), and you're evidently meant
to have a good time assembling these clues — always bearing in mind, of course, Nabokov's stylish warning in 'Speak,
Memory':

> I confess I do not believe in time. I like to fold my
> magic carpet, after use, in such a way as to super-
> impose one part of the pattern upon another. Let visi-
> tors trip.

Thus we have the twin delights of consenting to Nabokov's self-indulgence and hearing him chuckle about what
dunces he has made of us for doing so.

And this is all right. You don't read Nabokov for
reassurance — or for any of the 'human interest' perks,
he derided so expertly in 'Strong Opinions'. There is
only one incentive to turn his pages: to get more of his
sentences. The really unnerving deficiency of 'Look at
the Harlequins!' is the crudity of much of its prose.
One expects some convolution and strain in Nabokov, but
one doesn't reckon on coarse reiteration ('what shall never
be ferreted out by a matter-of-fact, father-of-muck,
mucking biograffitist'), charmless familiarity ('something
to do with a roll of coins, capitalistic metaphor, eh,
Marxy?') and the dud Georgianisms he himself chastised in
'Speak, Memory' ('I must have hung for a little while
longer ... before ending supine on the intangible soil').
In the book's 250-odd pages I found only four passages
that were genuinely haunting and beautiful; in an earlier
Nabokov it would be hard to find as many that were not.

Such a falling-off has a peculiar pathos in a writer
whom we have come to think of as our greatest stylist —
and by 'style' I mean more than mere surface fizz: after
all, you can write only as well as you can think.   The
variety, force and richness of Nabokov's perceptions have
not even the palest rival in modern fiction.   To read him
in full flight is to experience stimulation that is at
once intellectual, imaginative and aesthetic, the nearest
thing to pure sensual pleasure that prose can offer.   Confronted with such gifts of expression, it's in some way a
relief that Nabokov can neither characterise, pace nor
construct.   The lesson of 'Look at the Harlequins!' is one
we have been getting ready to learn all along: if the
prose isn't alive, nothing else is.

74.   UNSIGNED OBITUARY, 'THE TIMES'

5 July 1977, 16

...the principal recurring theme of his fiction ... is the
theme of the man who, alienated from his environment,
achieves satisfaction, indeed delight, in single-minded
exploration of a demanding bent or talent, be it for art,
chess, sexual adventure of the plotting of a murder.   The
Nabokov hero's escape into this private world has been
seen as a metaphor for his originator's own escape from
the pain of exile into the hermit-mandarin existence of the
dedicated artist.   Be that as it may, it was the portrayal
of these obsessions and delights, in frameworks of comic
sadness and in language which at its best had a flexibility
and luminosity rarely found in prose narrative, that gave
Nabokov's novels their special flavour.

75.   MARTIN AMIS IN 'NEW STATESMAN'

8 July 1977, 55-6

Don't you think', John Updike nervously asked himself, in
the course of a grudging review of 'Ada' (1969), 'that

your plebeian cavils were anticipated and scornfully dis-
missed in advance by this towering, snorting wizard?' The
wariness is characteristic — and entirely understandable.
Few writers have cared less about being 'accessible' than
Vladimir Nabokov. Indeed, many readers suspect that his
oeuvre is specifically designed to repulse, perplex and
humble their own cautious efforts to participate in it....
'I pride myself', he told reporters in 1962,

> on being a person with no public appeal. I have never
> been drunk in my life. I never use schoolboy words of
> four letters. I have never worked in an office or in
> a coal mine. I have never belonged to any club or
> group. No creed or school has had any influence on
> me whatsoever.

Does this blend of austerity and arrogance (never more
brazen than in his comically lordly prefaces and interviews) explain why many readers find him resistible? His
stature is by now unshakeable, but a few plebeian cavils
still linger. There are critics (Updike is among them)
who believe that the unswerving robustness of Nabokov's
life cut him off from the sense of sickness and queasy
foreboding which 20th-century critics so prize; Nabokov,
apparently, was uninterested in 'psychology and sociology':
his fiction 'purposely undervalued its own humanistic content'. Other critics feared for Nabokov's moral hygiene —
wasn't there a bit too much brio in his empathy with the
racked paedophile of 'Lolita', the devious homo of 'Pale
Fire', the witty murderer of 'Despair'? Yet other critics
— and many lay readers — objected flatly to his hybrid
style, which they seemed to regard as a conceited elaboration, a tediously roundabout way of saying fundamentally
simple things.

Nabokov had two ways of dealing with these objections.
The first way consisted to critic-baiting (a hobby rival-
ling his love of lepidoptery). Everything Nabokov said
about his art was as crushing and deadened as the Preface
to 'Dorian Gray': 'My books have no comment to make....
Nothing bores me more than the literature of social intent.... Big, sincere ideas [in novels] amount in the end
to bloated topicalities.... I have no purpose at all when
composing my stuff except to compose it.' Nabokov gave
no help to his marooned commentators, who felt that they
had to plant their feet firmly in one discipline before
daring to lean on another: 'What makes a work of fiction safe from larvae and rust is not its social importance but its art, only its art.'

And what was that like? Nabokov's final answer was
to create a prose style equal to the unique delicacy and
richness of his perceptions, a prose that does not shirk
these socio-moral quibbles but includes and embodies
them, simply by presenting the imaginative choices as
intensely as possible. Here is a paragraph from the early
pages of 'Lolita', where the demented Humbert finds himself making nightly love to the middle-aged mother of the
child he adores. It has the callous lyricism typical of
Humbert's voice, but its lilt turns out to hold all kinds
of balances in view:

So I tom-peeped across the hedges of years, into wan
little windows. And when, by means of pitifully ar-
dent, naïvely lascivious caresses, she of the noble
nipple and massive thigh prepared me for the performance of my nightly duty, it was still a nymphet's scent
that in despair I tried to pick up, as I bayed through
the undergrowth of dark decaying forests.

Select Bibliography

APPEL, ALFRED, JR, and CHARLES NEWMAN, 'Nabokov: Criticisms, Reminiscences, Translations and Tributes' (Evanston, Ill., 1970).

DEMBO, L.S., 'Nabokov: The Man and his Work' (Madison, Wis., 1967). Includes Jackson R. Bryer and Thomas J. Bergin, Jr, Vladimir Nabokov's Critical Reputation in English: A Note and A Checklist (225-76).

FIELD, ANDREW, 'Nabokov: His Life in Art' (Boston, Mass., 1967).

FIELD, ANDREW, 'Nabokov: A Bibliography' (New York, 1973).

FIELD, ANDREW, 'Nabokov: His Life in Part' (New York, 1977).

FOSTER, LUDMILA A., Nabokov in Russian Émigré Criticism, in 'A Book of Things about Vladimir Nabokov, ed. Carl R. Proffer (Ann Arbor, Mich., 1974).

GRAYSON, JANE, 'Nabokov Translated: A Comparison of Nabokov's Russian and English Prose' (Oxford, 1977).

STEGNER, PAGE, 'Escape into Aesthetics: The Art of Vladimir Nabokov' (New York, 1966).

STRUVE, GLEB, Notes on Nabokov as a Russian Writer, 'Wisconsin Studies in Contemporary Literature' (special Nabokov number), VIII (1967), 153-64.

Index

I (b) NABOKOV: THEMES AND CHARACTERISTICS

II NEWSPAPERS AND PERIODICALS

III   AUTHORS OF CRITICAL COMMENT

IV   GENERAL INDEX

THE CRITICAL HERITAGE SERIES

GENERAL EDITOR: B. C. SOUTHAM

Volumes published and forthcoming